New Frontiers in Regional Science: Asian Perspectives

Volume 9

New Frontiers in Regional Science: Asian Perspectives

This series is a constellation of works by scholars in the field of regional science and in related disciplines specifically focusing on dynamism in Asia.

Asia is the most dynamic part of the world. Japan, Korea, Taiwan, and Singapore experienced rapid and miracle economic growth in the 1970s. Malaysia, Indonesia, and Thailand followed in the 1980s. China, India, and Vietnam are now rising countries in Asia and are even leading the world economy. Due to their rapid economic development and growth, Asian countries continue to face a variety of urgent issues including regional and institutional unbalanced growth, environmental problems, poverty amidst prosperity, an ageing society, the collapse of the bubble economy, and deflation, among others.

Asian countries are diversified as they have their own cultural, historical, and geographical as well as political conditions. Due to this fact, scholars specializing in regional science as an inter- and multidiscipline have taken leading roles in providing mitigating policy proposals based on robust interdisciplinary analysis of multifaceted regional issues and subjects in Asia. This series not only will present unique research results from Asia that are unfamiliar in other parts of the world because of language barriers, but also will publish advanced research results from those regions that have focused on regional and urban issues in Asia from different perspectives.

The series aims to expand the frontiers of regional science through diffusion of intrinsically developed and advanced modern regional science methodologies in Asia and other areas of the world. Readers will be inspired to realize that regional and urban issues in the world are so vast that their established methodologies still have space for development and refinement, and to understand the importance of the interdisciplinary and multidisciplinary approach that is inherent in regional science for analyzing and resolving urgent regional and urban issues in Asia.

Topics under consideration in this series include the theory of social cost and benefit analysis and criteria of public investments, socioeconomic vulnerability against disasters, food security and policy, agro-food systems in China, industrial clustering in Asia, comprehensive management of water environment and resources in a river basin, the international trade bloc and food security, migration and labor market in Asia, land policy and local property tax, information and communication technology planning, consumer "shop-around" movements, and regeneration of downtowns, among others.

More information about this series at http://www.springer.com/series/13039

Soushi Suzuki • Peter Nijkamp

Regional Performance Measurement and Improvement

New Developments and Applications of Data Envelopment Analysis

Springer

Soushi Suzuki
Department of Life Science
and Technology
Hokkai-Gakuen University
Sapporo, Japan

Peter Nijkamp
Tinbergen Institute
Amsterdam, The Netherlands

ISSN 2199-5974 ISSN 2199-5982 (electronic)
New Frontiers in Regional Science: Asian Perspectives
ISBN 978-981-10-0241-0 ISBN 978-981-10-0242-7 (eBook)
DOI 10.1007/978-981-10-0242-7

Library of Congress Control Number: 2017933848

Printed on acid-free paper

This Springer imprint is published by Springer Nature
The registered company is Springer Nature Singapore Pte Ltd.
The registered company address is: 152 Beach Road, #21-01/04 Gateway East, Singapore 189721, Singapore

This book is dedicated to the memory of
Prof. Dr. Piet Rietveld†
Prof. Dr. Hideo Igarashi†
Ayako, Sayako, and Souta

Preface

Data Envelopment Analysis (DEA) has in the past years become a well-established method for comparative assessment studies among economic agents. The focus of DEA is normally on the efficiency performance of these agents, on the basis of quantitative input and output indicators. Despite its popularity, it has also various limitations and weaknesses, in particular, the conventional projection technique on the efficiency frontier, the lack of discrimination in performance among many efficient agents, and the like. The present book aims to address these shortcomings by extending the scope of DEA and to demonstrate the potential of new operational approaches through an extensive set of empirical and pedagogical applications to mainly Japan and Asia.

This is the first book to fully introduce the newly developed DFM (distance friction minimization) model which is one of the new efficiency improvement projection approaches in DEA. The DFM model is able to produce a most appropriate solution in efficiency improvement projections for inefficient economic agents (decision-making units or DMUs). This book aims to offer a set of fresh contributions to a quantitative assessment of the performance of policy entities in a regional, transportation, and environmental context by:

- Offering a state-of-the-art overview of current DEA models and approaches, followed by the operational design of various new types of DEA models, each of them serving to address some weaknesses in the traditional DEA approaches
- Illustrating the assessment potential of DEA – and its new variants, in particular, the DFM model and subsequent extensions – on the basis a broadly composed collection of empirical case studies, centering mainly – but not exclusively – on Japan and Asia

The focus in these studies will be on energy, environment, transportation, urban development, local public finance, and airport operations. This book is a useful source of information for readers who seek for DEA applications in regional science, operational research, political science, environmental management, and related fields. Such new model applications appear to offer a meaningful contribution to decision making and planning for an operational efficiency improvement in these fields.

Sapporo, Japan
Amsterdam, The Netherlands
December 2016

Soushi Suzuki
Peter Nijkamp

Contents

Chapter 1
Introduction

Abstract This chapter introduces the aims and scope of this book on Data Envelopment Analysis for regional development, with a view on Japan. We will discuss the necessity of regional performance measurement in the light of the Japanese socioeconomic and spatial development from the end of WW2 up to the present, while we also highlight the future challenges of a changing population in this country. We discuss the main evaluation methods for each era and highlight the significance of Data Envelopment Analysis (DEA). This approach has in the past years become a well-established method for comparative assessment studies on efficiency of economic agents. Despite its popularity, this method has also various limitations, in particular, the projection technique on the efficiency frontier, the lack of an unambiguous discrimination among many efficient agents, and the like. We, therefore, emphasize the necessity of an improved DEA, with special reference to our new DEA method, called a distance friction minimization (DFM) approach. This method does not use a value judgment of an agent or decision-making unit (DMU); in this context, a generalized distance friction function is presented to assist a DMU to attain a solution on the efficiency frontier. Based on these cornerstones, we provide finally a summary of the book.

Keywords Aims and scope • Summary of the book • Data Envelopment Analysis (DEA) • Distance friction minimization (DFM)

1.1 Regional Performance Measurement in Perspective

Regions are complex spatial economic decision units. They usually have different economic outcomes and performance levels. To address effectively such spatial disparities, regions have to improve their performance through appropriate development strategies. But the question is how to reach such an improvement in economic conditions. We will articulate this question by referring to the Japanese spatial-economic situation over the past decades. The demographic development pattern of Japan shows interesting features, as in illustrated in Fig. 1.1 and Table 1.1.

S. Suzuki, P. Nijkamp, *Regional Performance Measurement and Improvement*, New Frontiers in Regional Science: Asian Perspectives 9,
DOI 10.1007/978-981-10-0242-7_1

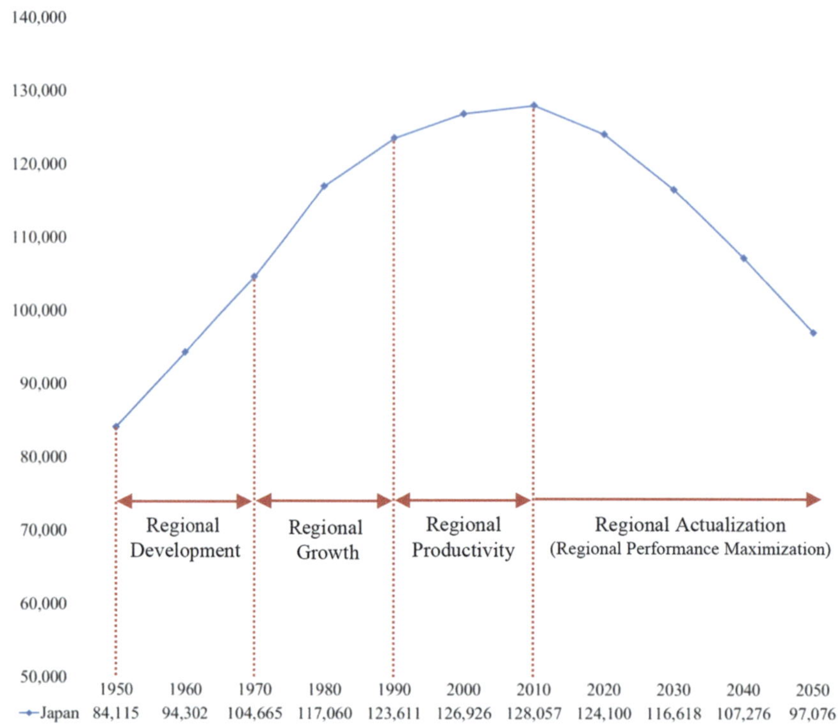

Fig. 1.1 Population change in Japan (1000 persons) (Reference: UN, World Population Prospects: The 2012 Revision)

Table 1.1 Keywords and evaluation methods for each Japanese era

Era	Keywords	Evaluation method
1950–1970	Regional development . . . compensate for deficiency	I/O model, multi-regression analysis, shift-share analysis, etc.
1970–1990	Regional growth . . .quantitative expansion	
1990–2010	Regional productivity . . .efficiency evaluation	Data Envelopment Analysis, Stochastic Frontier Analysis, etc.
2010–	Regional actualization (Regional performance maximization) . . . a new approach in which DEA and DFM may have a potential for effectiveness evaluation in the era of regional actualization	

From 1950 to 1970, Japan faced the postwar restoration era. A keyword in this era was *regional development*, to compensate for a feeble economic situation. The period 1970 to 1990 was a high-speed growth era in Japan. The keyword in this era was *regional growth*. The intensity of population influx was too high for the old type of city and region, and the social amenities were insufficient yet. The higher priority placed on a quantitative expansion in the regional growth era led to the need for an appropriate evaluation of these developments.

Various evaluation methods were designed in this era: input/output (I/O) models, regression analysis, shift-share analysis, etc.

I/O models are a quantitative economic technique that analyzes interdependencies between different industries and regional economies. Based on these features, the I/O model can analyze ripple effects on regional economies caused by regional development projects.

Regression analysis is a statistical model for estimating the relationships between a dependent variable and independent variables. This analysis is used to understand how much the independent variables are related to the dependent variable and to estimate how much the dependent variable will be changed in response to a change in independent variables. Based on these features, regression analysis can predict regional growth effects as a result of development projects.

Shift-share analysis is an analytical method for mapping out the sectoral growth factors of a regional economy. A traditional shift-share analysis assumes that each regional change is decomposed into three components: a national growth effect, an industry mix effect, and a regional share effect. Based on these features, shift-share analysis can evaluate the regional features and can analyze the regional influence of development projects.

These methods have all a common characteristic: a quantitative analytical tool in regional research in case of an expanding regional economy.

From 1990 to 2010, the country faced an economic bubble burst, and a slow growth era started in Japan. The Nikkei stock average reached a peak in the year 1989 of approximately 39,000 yen. The Japanese economy has ever since been in a prolonged recession period known as the "lost 10 years." With 1989 as the economic peak, the Japanese economy has in the meantime even been in the "lost 20 years" until 2010. It changed from an era directed toward growth and expansion to a new direction for balanced contraction. Against this background, the need for an adjusted strategic viewpoint based on "productivity" and "efficiency" arose. The social environment in Japan has also changed from the previous growth period to a period of maturation, an aging society with a declining birth rate, and a slow-growth economy. A societal sense of new values and an adjusted lifestyle emerged, which put more emphasis on "quality of life" and "sustainability." The keyword in this era was *regional productivity*.

From 2010 onward, Japan is facing an acceleration of a declining birth rate and an aging population; the decline in the productive-age population occurs in combination with a protracted recession and a low-growth economy. As a result of the previous factors, Japan is now facing huge deficits in state finances and a structural inefficiency, a decline in city performance, and an inefficient operation of public enterprises, especially regarding public transportation and airport operations. This calls urgently for improvement through effective policy strategies. As the one misfortune followed the other one, Japan faces now the problem of the Tohoku earthquake disaster and an emission of radiation at the time of the nuclear accident, while the subsequent problems of the environment and energy put the country in deep trouble.

In these circumstances, a shift is needed in the subsequent era of societal development. This new society is not based on a quantitative expansion and high growth; it should be more a *performance maximization society*. This society would imply that each actor, ranging from households, companies, or organizations to the public sector, or region and country as a whole, maximizes his/her ability and effort to contribute to a progress of society. The country needs, therefore, a performance measurement system for each actor to consider its improvement. The keyword in this new era will be *regional actualization*. In our view, the main evaluation methods for this era are to be based on data envelopment analyses (DEA). This will be further outlined in Sect. 1.2.

1.2 The Need for Data Envelopment Analysis

Japan – and many other Asian countries – shows a high spatial and demographic dynamics. We will briefly describe here the Asian countries based on the population changes, included in Fig. 1.2 and Table.1.2.

From Fig. 1.2 and Table. 1.2, we can easily see that Japan has already changed into a depopulating society. Korea, Thailand, and China will also become depopulating societies in the period 2020–2040, and other countries will sooner or later also show a downward trend in the rate of population growth.

Quantitative expansion will be the demise in the near future in Asia. All Asian countries will largely go through the same experiences as Japan. Consequently, these Asian countries will also need to make a shift to a "performance maximization society." In this sense, Japan is at the forefront of a new development in Asia.

It is clear that there are many similar issues that deserve a solid analytical treatment. This holds, for instance, for land use planning, transportation, urbanization, infrastructure, energy supply, and environmental management.

The evaluation of new trends among agents, countries, or public actors – or, in general, decision-making units (DMUs) – calls for transparent and tailor-made quantitative assessment tools. One of the novel prominent and promising assessment methods is Data Envelopment Analysis (DEA).

The original DEA model was developed by Charnes et al. (1978) (CCR model hereafter), and it was developed to assess the relative efficiency of decision-making units (DMUs) by constructing a piecewise linear production frontier and then projecting each firm onto the frontier. The frontier gives the maximum output that can be achieved given an input set (or, alternatively, the minimum input necessary to achieve an output target). A DMU that is located on the frontier is efficient, while a DMU that is not on the frontier has room for improvement and is thus inefficient. An inefficient DMU can become efficient by reducing its inputs (or increasing its outputs). DEA makes it possible to get an idea on the quantitative improvement potential for each DMU. It is a method for quantitative analysis of

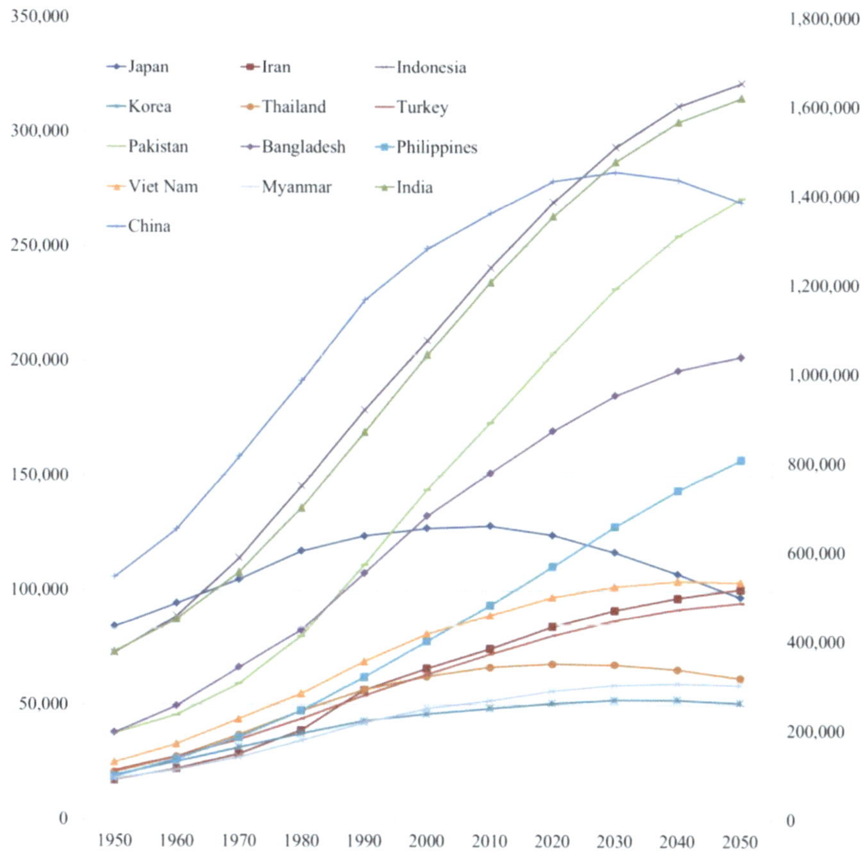

Fig. 1.2 Population change in Asia (1000 persons) (Reference: UN, World Population Prospects: The 2012 Revision)

relative performance based on the specific features of each DMU. Clearly, DEA may become a very appropriate method for a performance measurement of DMUs in the challenging scenario of a "performance maximization society." But its scope is clearly much broader that the abovementioned concerns on Japan.

1.3 Why Do We Need an Improved DEA?

In the standard DEA method, a comparative efficiency assessment of DMUs is achieved by a uniform reduction in all inputs, i.e., a proportional linear projection. In principle, however, there are an infinite number of improvements that can be made to reach the efficiency frontier, and hence there are many solutions for a DMU to enhance its efficiency. The existence of an infinite number of solutions to reach

Table 1.2 Population change in Asia (1000 persons)

Year	1950	1960	1970	1980	1990	2000
Japan	84,115	94,302	104,665	117,060	123,611	126,926
Iran	17,119	21,958	28,607	38,890	56,362	65,911
India	376,325	449,595	555,200	698,966	868,891	1,042,262
Indonesia	72,592	88,693	114,067	145,494	178,633	208,939
Korea	19,211	25,074	31,437	37,451	42,972	45,977
Thailand	20,607	27,362	36,879	47,369	56,583	62,343
China	543,776	650,680	814,378	984,016	1,165,429	1,280,429
Turkey	21,238	27,553	34,772	43,906	53,995	63,174
Pakistan	37,542	45,541	59,204	79,984	111,091	143,832
Bangladesh	37,895	49,537	66,309	82,498	107,386	132,383
Philippines	18,580	26,272	35,805	47,398	61,949	77,652
Viet Nam	24,949	32,912	43,783	54,897	68,910	80,888
Myanmar	17,527	21,486	27,166	34,475	42,123	48,453
Year	**2010**	**2020**	**2030**	**2040**	**2050**	
Japan	128,057	124,100	116,618	107,276	97,076	
Iran	74,462	84,149	91,336	96,772	100,598	
India	1,205,625	1,353,305	1,476,378	1,565,509	1,620,051	
Indonesia	240,676	269,413	293,482	311,334	321,377	
Korea	48,454	50,769	52,190	52,270	51,034	
Thailand	66,402	67,858	67,554	65,520	61,740	
China	1,359,821	1,432,868	1,453,297	1,435,499	1,384,977	
Turkey	72,138	80,309	86,825	91,778	94,606	
Pakistan	173,149	203,351	231,744	254,769	271,082	
Bangladesh	151,125	169,566	185,064	195,861	201,948	
Philippines	93,444	110,404	127,797	143,516	157,118	
Viet Nam	89,047	97,057	101,830	104,155	103,697	
Myanmar	51,931	56,125	58,698	59,410	58,645	

Reference: UN, World Population Prospects: The 2012 Revision

the efficient frontier has led to a stream of literature on the integration of DEA and multiple objective linear programming (MOLP), which was initiated by Golany (1988). In short, this literature offers paths to efficiency, by taking into account the preferences of the decision maker (or DMU), in particular, in case of multiple inputs or outputs. In other words, the DMU's preference structure is used to find a route to efficiency. When the a priori information used by DMUs is biased or subjective, a wrong path to efficiency may be chosen. The challenge, therefore, is to develop a methodology for projecting DMUs on the efficient frontier that does not necessarily include such subjective valuations.

In this book, we introduce a new projection method, called the distance friction minimization (DFM) approach (see Suzuki et al. 2010), which does not use a value judgment of the DMU, but lets the data speak for itself. A generalized distance friction function is presented to assist a DMU to reach the frontier curve. Clearly, in the literature several criticisms have been expressed about the conventional radial projection method applied in DEA (see, e.g., Färe and Lovell 1978), but the standard practice in DEA packages has not changed.

In our approach, we will avoid the linear projection model, introduce new elements, and eliminate disadvantages caused by subjective preference information, while we will provide a new projection model based on a blend of input reduction and output rise. This new approach can evaluate the relative importance of each item with reference to the value of each input. The same holds for each output, where optimum weights of one output item provide a measure of the relative contribution of one output item to the overall value or efficiency score. These values show not only which items contribute to the performance of DMUs but also to what extent they do so. In other words, it is possible to express and quantify the distance frictions (or, alternatively, the potential increases) in improvement projections.

A cornerstone of the DFM model is that it focuses on the features of an actor and capitalizes the actor's strength; in other words, it develops the actor's strength in its improvement. In this way, the new DFM is a very appropriate method as a performance improvement model for regions under conditions of a "performance maximization society" and a "regional actualization era."

1.4 Summary of This Book

The adjusted DEA method is explained in more detail in the following chapters. This book is clearly of interest to a wide audience, given the abundance of applied DEA studies on many efficiency issues. Regional efficiency analysis and benchmarking is one of the fields in which DEA has been applied several times. Clearly, even when the data set includes regions with similar (homogeneous) characteristics (input and output vectors), the regions may be different in nature. For instance, Tokyo and Hokkaido are both attractive regions, but are quite different in size and services offered. In our analysis, we make a comparative study of several Japanese regions, by looking at their characteristics and their relative weights. In doing so, we let the data decide which are the "best" regions that determine the part of the frontier on which an inefficient region is projected (i.e., which are the peers which the inefficient region needs to follow). Using this methodology, we offer a "neutral" view to policy-makers on the path that inefficient regions can take toward efficiency.

The book is organized into: "Part A: DEA Model Foundations and Adjustments" and "Part B: Applications." Its detailed structure is as follows:

Part A: DEA Model Foundations and Adjustments

- Chapter 2 provides an overview of DEA and its improvements.
- Chapter 3 introduces the original DEA (CCR) model, the Super-Efficiency (SE) model, and its improvement projection. It also presents a note on the

relevance and application of DEA for regional performance measurement and improvement strategies.

- Chapter 4 introduces our new DFM methodology in more detail including an empirical illustration regarding airports.
- Chapter 5 introduces several extended DFM models. Extended DFM models are organized into a Target approach and an Adjustment approach. The Target approach is composed of a Goals-Achievement model, a Stepwise Improvement model, and a Target-Oriented model. The Adjustment approach is composed of an Adjusted-Improvement model and a Fixed-Factor model. This chapter also introduces a systematic matrix of extended DFM models, which assemble a combination of types of measurement models (CCR and SE) and extended DFM models.

Part B: Applications In the application part, the chapters present a specific spatial-economic application of the methodology in terms of the following contents:

- Chapter 6 provides a performance measurement of local government finance in Japan, which is a methodological combination of a goals-achievement model with the CCR model. It is illustrated empirically by using a data set of efficiency indicators for cities in Hokkaido prefecture in Japan.
- Chapter 7 provides a performance measurement of public transport operation in Japan. This application is a methodological combination of a Stepwise model with a CCR model. It is illustrated empirically by using a data set of efficiency indicators for 9 urban transportation authorities and 16 major private railway companies in Japan.
- Chapter 8 presents next a performance assessment of Asian cities. This is a methodological merger of a Stepwise Improvement model with an SE model. It is applied to a database on many achievement criteria of 35 major cities in the world.
- Chapter 9 describes an energy-environment performance assessment after the Fukushima disaster in Japan, which is methodologically a mix of a Target-Oriented model with an SE model. This approach is illustrated by using a data set of efficiency indicators for 10 regions related to each of the management zones for the 10 electrical power companies in Japan.
- As a next illustration, Chap. 10 deals with a study of a performance assessment of new energy supply in Japan. This chapter provides a methodological combination of an adjusted-improvement model with a CCR model. Its relevance is demonstrated by a data set of efficiency indicators for 3 input-cost criteria and one output performance criteria for new types of energy in Japan.
- Next, Chap. 11 provides then a performance evaluation of energy-environment-economic policy for the EU, APEC, and ASEAN (A&A) countries, which is a methodological combination of a Target-Oriented Fixed-Factor model with an SE model. This approach is illustrated by using a data set of efficiency indicators from the years 2003 to 2012 for a set of 27 EU countries and 20 A&A countries.

- Chapter 12, finally, provides a performance assessment of airport operations in Japan, where a methodological mix is developed of a Stepwise model and a Fixed-Factor model. This model is illustrated empirically by means of a data set on efficiency indicators for 25 airports in Japan.
- Finally, we provide some conclusions in Chap. 13 and also offer a manual for a DFM-Solver Appendix A at the end of this book.

We hope that this book will be instrumental and supportive in shaping the contours of the future Asian society in the "regional actualization" era.

References

Charnes, A., Cooper, W. W., & Rhodes, E. (1978). Measuring the efficiency of decision making units. *European Journal of Operational Research, 2*, 429–444.

Färe, R., & Lovell, C. A. (1978). Measuring the technical efficiency of production. *Journal of Economic Theory, Elsevier, 19*(1), 150–162.

Golany, B. (1988). An interactive MOLP procedure for the extension of DEA to effectiveness analysis. *Journal of the Operational Research Society, 39*, 725–734.

Suzuki, S., Nijkamp, P., Rietveld, P., & Pels, E. (2010). A distance friction minimization approach in data envelopment analysis: A comparative study on air port efficiency. *European Journal of Operational Research, 207*, 1104–1115.

Part I
DEA Model Foundations and Adjustments

Chapter 2
Overview of DEA and Its Improvements

Abstract The aim of this chapter is to provide a very concise overview of Data Envelopment Analysis (DEA) and its subsequent improvements. DEA proposed by Charnes et al. (Eur J Oper Res, 2:429–444, 1978) and based on the seminal article by Farrell (J Roy Stat Soc 120:253–290, 1957) aims to develop a comparative measure for production efficiency. We present first a brief history of the development of DEA. Next, we make a comparison of DEA and stochastic frontier analysis (SFA). DEA is a nonparametric and deterministic approach, whereas SFA is a parametric and stochastic approach. We also focus on the history of the development of the efficiency-improvement projection model in DEA. The existence of many possible efficiency-improvement solutions has in recent years prompted a rich literature on the methodological integration of multiple objective quadratic programming (MOQP) and DEA models. The first contribution was made by Golany (J Oper Res Soc 39:725–734, 1988), and we introduce here a concise overview of the history of the development of efficiency-improvement projection models in DEA. Based on these backgrounds, we present advantages and features of our DFM (distance friction minimization) model.

Keywords Data Envelopment Analysis (DEA) • Stochastic frontier analysis (SFA) • Multiple objective quadratic programming (MOQP) • DFM (distance friction minimization) model

Data Envelopment Analysis (DEA) has already a long history. The seminal article by Farrell (1957) aimed to develop a comparative measure for production efficiency. This work extended toward DEA, proposed by Charnes et al. (1978) who presented a quantitative measure for assessing the relative efficiency of DMUs using a frontier method that aims to determine the maximum volume of outputs, given a set of inputs. It is then possible to assess ex post the (in)efficiency of a production system using the distance to the production frontier (without any explicit assumptions on the production technology concerned). This is usually a deterministic analysis, which has a close resemblance to nonparametric linear programming.

In parallel, a stochastic frontier analysis (SFA) was proposed by Aigner et al. (1977) and Meeusen and Broeck (1977) who presented a parametric and stochastic

S. Suzuki, P. Nijkamp, *Regional Performance Measurement and Improvement*, New Frontiers in Regional Science: Asian Perspectives 9,
DOI 10.1007/978-981-10-0242-7_2

Table 2.1 Characteristics comparison of DEA and SFA

	DEA	SFA
Characteristic	Deterministic and nonparametric approach	Parametric and stochastic approach
Attraction	No restrictive assumptions about technology, no require any distribution assumption, low bias, etc.	Suit for panel data, formal statistical testing of hypotheses, construction of confidence intervals, etc.

approach. This approach assumed that the product function includes stochastic components which describe random shocks, such as climate or geographical factors.

A comparison of the characteristics of these approaches is provided in Table 2.1 (for more detail, see Hjalmarsson et al. (1996) and Bogetoft and Otto (2011)).

Over the years, DEA has become a popular method based on the abovementioned merits and has been used as an operational tool for analyzing efficiency problems in both the private and the public sector, where (in)efficiency is interpreted as the relative distance from an actual situation to the production frontier function.

DEA was fully developed by Charnes et al. (1978) and later on by Banker et al. (1984) to analyze the efficiency of a decision-making unit (DMU), as well as to determine improvements in performance on the basis of a DMU's appropriate choice of radial projection – using the ratio of the weighted sum of outputs to the weighted sum of inputs – given that these ratios are less than (or equal to) 1 for each DMU under consideration. The main goal is to determine the weights corresponding to each DMU in such a way that they lead to a maximum efficiency improvement.

DEA has ever since become a popular method often used in the literature to study the relative efficiency of DMUs through the use of comparative benchmarks. Emrouznejad and Thanassoulis (1997) identified already some 1500 applications of DEA, and a more recent overview by Seiford (2005) mentions some 2800 published articles on DEA. This large number of studies shows that comparative efficiency analysis has become an important topic in operational research, public policy, energy-environment management, and regional development (see for overview of DEA also Cooper et al. 2006).

A weak element in a standard DEA model is that all efficient DMUs get a score 1, so that there is no way to differentiate between them. This has led to focused research to further discriminate between efficient DMUs, in order to arrive at a ranking, or even a numerical rating of these efficient DMUs, without affecting the results for the non-efficiency. In particular, Andersen and Petersen (1993) developed a radial Super-Efficiency model, while later on Tone (2001, 2002) designed a *slacks-based* measure (SBM) of super efficiency in DEA. In general, a Super-Efficiency model aims to identify the relative importance of each individual efficient DMU, by designing and measuring a score for its "degree of influence," if this efficient DMU is omitted from the efficiency frontier (or production possibility set). If this elimination really matters (i.e., if the distance from this DMU to the remaining efficiency frontier is large) and, thus, the DMUs concerned has a high degree of influence and outperforms the other DMUs, it gets a high score (and is thus super efficient). Therefore, for each individual DMU, a new distance result is obtained, which leads to a new ranking or even a rating of all the original efficient DMUs.

Great interest has been shown in DEA during the last two decades, with major progress made in both methodological terms and in a range of applications (see, e.g., Cook and Seiford 2009, for an overview). A prominent contribution in DEA has been the successful integration of DEA and MOLP (multi-objective linear programming) models (see, e.g., Belton 1992; Belton and Vickers 1993; Doyle and Green 1993). Most of the research was inspired by the pioneering work of Golany (1988), who tried to find efficient solutions in order to map out the efficiency frontier in an interactive way. Later on Kornbluth (1991) was able to show the similarity between DEA problems and fractional multiple objective quadratic programming (MOQP) problems. This similarity holds for both input-oriented and output-oriented models.

Most contributions have their origin in the standard CCR model or in the Banker et al. (1984) (abbreviated hereafter as the BCC) model, which provide the foundations of DEA. All such models aim to find an appropriate projection for an efficiency improvement for each inefficient DMU, based on a radial projection in which the input volumes are reduced (or the output values are increased) by a uniform ratio.

The existence of many possible efficiency-improvement solutions has in recent years prompted a rich literature on the methodological integration of the MOLP and the DEA models. As mentioned, the first contribution was made by Golany (1988) who proposed an interactive MOLP procedure which aimed at generating a set of efficient points for a DMU. This model allows a decision maker to select the preferred set of output levels, given the input levels. Next, Thanassoulis and Dyson (1992) developed adjusted models which can be used to estimate alternative input and output levels in order to render relatively inefficient DMUs more efficient. These models are able to incorporate preferences for a potential improvement of individual input and output levels. The resulting target levels reflect the user's relative preference over alternative paths to efficiency. Joro et al. (1998) demonstrated the analytical similarity between a DEA model and a reference point model in an MOLP formulation from a mathematical viewpoint. In addition, the reference point model provides suggestions which make it possible to search freely on the efficient frontier for good solutions or for the most preferred solution based on the decision maker's preference structure. Later on, Halme et al. (1999) developed a value efficiency analysis (VEA), which included the decision maker's preference information in a DEA model. The foundation of VEA originates from the reference point model in a MOLP context. Here the decision maker identifies the most preferred solution (MPS), so that each DMU can be evaluated by means of the assumed value function based on the MPS approach. A further development of this approach was made by Korhonen and Siljamäki (2002) who dealt with several practical aspects related to the use of a VEA. In addition, Korhonen et al. (2003) developed a multiple objective approach which allows for changes in the time frame. And, finally, Lins et al. (2004) proposed two multi-objective approaches that determine the basis for the incorporation of a posteriori preference information. The first of these models is called MORO (multiple objective ratio optimization), which optimizes the ratios between the observed and the target inputs (or outputs) of a DMU. The second model is MOTO (multiple objective target optimization), which directly optimizes the target values.

An original contribution to DEA using stepwise preference information from a DMU was made by Seiford and Zhu (2003), who developed a gradual improvement model for an inefficient DMU. This "context-dependent" (CD) DEA has an important merit, as it aims to reach a stepwise improvement through successive levels toward the efficiency frontier. This approach is certainly important, if an unambiguous decision maker can be identified, e.g., in the private sector. In many cases, however, we are faced with a fuzzy decision situation where there is no clear decision authority (e.g., public welfare). In such circumstances, we have to resort to an approach that is not based on value judgments. In this regard, Angulo-Meza and Lins (2002) make the following observations:

> There are disadvantages in the methods that incorporate a priori information, concerning subjectivity:
>
> - The value judgments, or a priori information can be wrong or biased, or the ideas may not be consistent with reality.
> - There may be a lack of consensus among the experts or decision makers, and this can slow down or adversely affect the study.
>
> Indeed, one may want to preserve the DEA spirit in the sense of not including a priori information (p. 232).

Given these considerations, we propose in our study a new improvement projection model called the distance friction minimization (DFM) approach, which does not need to incorporate the value judgment of a decision maker. A generalized distance friction function will be presented to identify an appropriate movement toward the efficiency frontier surface. The direction of this efficiency improvement depends on the input/output data characteristics of the DMU. Each of these characteristics may have a different weight for the DMU. To achieve an appropriate rise in efficiency, we will take into account the most appropriate input/output weights of these characteristics. We can then define the projection functions for the minimization of the distance friction, using a Euclidean distance in weighted spaces. This model will use the elements of a multiple objective quadratic programming (MOQP) model. This approach has several advantages: there is no need to rely on the subjective preference information of a DMU; the use of the restrictive radial projection methods is not necessary, and the DFM model is able to treat simultaneously both input reduction and output increase choices. Furthermore, our DFM model can lead to a methodological integration with a radial Super-Efficiency model to mitigate the abovementioned problems. This idea will be further unfolded and applied in subsequent chapters.

References

Aigner, D., Lovell, C. A. K., & Schmidt, P. (1977). Formulation and estimation of stochastic frontier production function models. *Journal of Econometrics, 6*, 21–37.

Anderson, P., & Petersen, N. (1993). A procedure for ranking efficient units in data envelopment analysis. *Management Science, 39*, 1261–1264.

Angulo-Meza, L., & Lins, M. P. E. (2002). Review of method for increasing discrimination in Data Envelopment Analysis. *Annals of Operations Research, 116*, 225–242.

Banker, R. D., Charnes, A., & Cooper, W. W. (1984). Some models for estimating technical and scale inefficiencies in Data Envelopment Analysis. *Management Science, 30*, 1078–1092.

Belton, V. (1992). An integrating data envelopment analysis with multiple criteria decision analysis in A. In L. D. Goicoechea & S. Zionts (Eds.), *Multiple criteria decision making* (pp. 71–79). Berlin: Springer-Verlag.

Belton, V., & Vickers, S. P. (1993). Demystifying DEA – A visual interactive approach based on multiple criteria analysis. *Journal of the Operational Research Society, 44*, 883–896.

Bogetoft, P., & Otto, L. (2011). *Benchmarking with DEA, SFA, and R* (International series in operations research & management science, Vol. 157). New York: Springer Science + Business Media.

Charnes, A., Cooper, W. W., & Rhodes, E. (1978). Measuring the efficiency of decision making units. *European Journal of Operational Research, 2*, 429–444.

Cook, W. D., & Seiford, L. M. (2009). Data envelopment analysis (DEA) – Thirty years on. - *European Journal of Operational Research, 192*, 1–17.

Cooper, W. W., Seiford, L. M., & Tone, K. (2006). *Introduction to data envelopment analysis and its uses*. Boston: Springer Science + Business Media Inc.

Doyle, R. H., & Green, J. R. (1993). Data envelopment analysis and multiple criteria decision making. *Omega, 6*, 713–715.

Emrouznejad, A., and Thanassoulis, E. (1997) *An extensive bibliography of data envelopment analysis volume III, Supplement 1* (Research Papers, No. 258)

Farrell, M. J. (1957). The measurement of productive efficiency. *Journal of the Royal Statistical Society, 120*, 253–290.

Golany, B. (1988). An interactive MOLP procedure for the extension of DEA to effectiveness analysis. *Journal of the Operational Research Society, 39*, 725–734.

Halme, M., Joro, T., Korhonen, P., Salo, S., & Wallenius, J. (1999). A value efficiency approach to incorporating preference information in data envelopment analysis. *Management Science, 45* (1), 103–115.

Hjalmarsson, L., Kumbhakar, S. C., & Heshmati, A. (1996). DEA, DFA and SFA: A comparison. *Journal of Productivity Analysis, 7*(2), 303–327.

Joro, T., Korhonen, P., & Wallenius, J. (1998). Structural comparison of data envelopment analysis and multiple objective linear programming. *Management Science, 44*(7), 962–970.

Korhonen, P., & Siljamäki, A. (2002). On the use of value efficiency analysis and some further developments. *Journal of Productivity Analysis, 17*(1–2), 49–64.

Korhonen, P., Stenfors, S., & Syrjänen, M. (2003). Multiple objective approach as an alternative to radial projection in DEA. *Journal of Productivity Analysis, 20*(20), 305–321.

Kornbluth, J. S. H. (1991). Analysing policy effectiveness using cone restricted data envelopment analysis. *Journal of the Operational Research Society, 42*, 1097–1104.

Lins, M. P. E., Angulo-Meza, L., & Moreira da Silva, A. C. (2004). A multi-objective approach to determine alternative targets in data envelopment analysis. *Journal of Operational Research, 55*, 1090–1101.

Meeusen, W., & Broeck, J. (1977). Efficiency estimation from Cobb-Douglas production functions with composed error. *International Economic Review, 8*, 435–444.

Seiford, L. (2005). *A cyber-bibliography for data envelopment analysis (1978–2005). CD-ROM in introduction to data envelopment analysis and its uses.* New York: Springer Science Buisness Media.

Seiford, L. M., & Zhu, J. (2003). Context-dependent data envelopment analysis – Measuring attractiveness and progress. *Omega, 31*, 397.

Thanassoulis, E., & Dyson, R. G. (1992). Estimating preferred target input-output levels using data envelopment analysis. *European Journal of Operational Research, 56*, 80–97.

Tone, K. (2001). A slacks-based measure of efficiency on data envelopment analysis. *European Journal of Operational Research, 130*, 498–509.

Tone, K. (2002). A slacks-based measure of super-efficiency in data envelopment analysis. *European Journal of Operational Research, 143*, 32–41.

Chapter 3
Significance of DEA for Regional Performance Measurement

Abstract The aim of this chapter is to introduce essential features of data envelopment analysis (DEA) for regional performance measurement. We introduce basic rules of application to regional performance measurement from the viewpoint of economies of scale, treatment of input and output items, and the number of DMUs, inputs and outputs. Furthermore, in applications of DEA, we usually need to pay attention to the influence on efficiency scores by the number of DMUs, inputs and outputs. This requires an in-depth understanding, not only of the impact of the number of items or DMUs on efficiency scores but also of the influence of the quality of items on efficiency scores. This chapter focuses especially on the abovementioned critical issues; we present sensitivity analysis results of efficiency scores regarding the number of DMUs, input items and output items, based on a case study that uses input and output data on the critical energy-environment-economic (EEE) variables for a set of 47 prefectures in Japan.

Keywords Regional performance measurement • Sensitivity analysis • Number of DMUs • Number of input and output items • Energy-environment-economic efficiency • Prefectures in Japan

3.1 CCR Model

As mentioned before, DEA has become a popular tool in comparative assessment studies and benchmarking analysis on the efficiency of agents or DMUs.

A comprehensive list of studies on DEA can be found in Seiford (2005), while an excellent pedagogical treatment of DEA is contained in Cooper et al. (2006, 2007).

The Charnes et al. (1978) model (abbreviated hereafter as the CCR-input model) for a given DMU_j ($j = 1, \ldots, J$) to be evaluated on any trial concerned with DMU_o (where o ranges over 1, 2 ..., J) can be represented in the following fractional programming (FP_o) form:

S. Suzuki, P. Nijkamp, *Regional Performance Measurement and Improvement*, New Frontiers in Regional Science: Asian Perspectives 9,
DOI 10.1007/978-981-10-0242-7_3

$$
\begin{aligned}
&(FP_o) \quad \max_{v,u} \quad \theta = \frac{\sum_s u_s y_{so}}{\sum_m v_m x_{mo}} \\
&\text{s.t.} \quad \frac{\sum_s u_s y_{sj}}{\sum_m v_m x_{mj}} \leq 1 \quad (j = 1, \ldots, J) \\
&v_m \geq 0, \quad u_s \geq 0
\end{aligned}
\tag{3.1}
$$

where θ is a goal variable (efficiency score); x_{mj} is the volume of input m ($m = 1,\ldots, M$) for DMU $_j$ ($j = 1,\ldots,J$); y_{sj} is the volume of output s ($s = 1,\ldots,S$) of DMU $_j$; and v_m and u_s are the weights given to input m and output s, respectively.

Equation (3.1) is an input-oriented CCR model; its reciprocal (i.e., a reversal of the numerator and denominator in the objective function (3.1), with a specification as a minimization problem under an appropriate adjustment of the constraints) is usually called an output-oriented CCR model. The fractional programming Eq. (3.1) may be solved stepwise by assigning an arbitrary value to the denominator in Eq. (3.1) and then maximizing the numerator. The CCR model (3.1) can be shown to have the following equivalent linear programming (LP_o) specification for any DMU $_j$:

$$
\begin{aligned}
&(LP_o) \quad \max_{v,u} \quad \theta = \sum_s u_s y_{so} \\
&\text{s.t} \quad \sum_m v_m x_{mo} = 1 \\
&-\sum_m v_m x_{mj} + \sum_s u_s y_{sj} \leq 0 \\
&v_m \geq 0, \quad u_s \geq 0
\end{aligned}
\tag{3.2}
$$

The dual problem of Eq. (3.2), DLP_o, can be expressed by means of a real variable θ, using the following vector notation:

$$
\begin{aligned}
&(DLP_o) \quad \min_{\theta,\lambda} \quad \theta \\
&\text{s.t.} \quad \theta x_o - X\lambda \geq 0 \\
&Y\lambda \geq y_o \ \ \lambda \geq 0,
\end{aligned}
\tag{3.3}
$$

where the transposed (T) expression $\lambda = (\lambda_1, \ \ldots \ \lambda_J)^T$ is a nonnegative vector (corresponding to the presence of slacks for each DMU), X is an ($M\times$ J) input matrix, and Y is an ($S\times$ J) input matrix.

We are able to define the input excesses $s^- \in R^m$ and the output shortfalls $s^+ \in R^s$ and identify them as slack vectors as follows:

$$s^- = \theta x_o - X\lambda \tag{3.4}$$

$$s^+ = Y\lambda - y_o. \tag{3.5}$$

Then we can solve the following two-stage LP problem in a straightforward way:

[Step 1] Solve DLP$_o$. Let the optimal objective value be θ^*.
[Step 2] Given the value of θ^*, solve the following LP model using (λ, s^-, s^+) as slack variables:

$$\max_{\lambda, s^-, s^+} \quad \omega = es^- + es^+ \tag{3.6}$$

$$\text{s.t.} \quad s^- = \theta^* x_o - X\lambda \tag{3.7}$$

$$s^+ = Y\lambda - y_o \tag{3.8}$$

$$\lambda \geq 0, \quad s^- \geq 0, \quad s^+ \geq 0, \tag{3.9}$$

where ω is an objective variable and e a unit vector.

An optimal solution can then be expressed as follows:

$$\theta^* x_o = \sum_{j \in E_o} x_j \lambda_j^* + s^{-*}; \tag{3.10}$$

$$y_o = \sum_{j \in E_o} y_j \lambda_j^* - s^{+*}. \tag{3.11}$$

The improvement projection $(\hat{x}_o, \hat{y}_o)$ is now defined in Eq. (3.12) and Eq. (3.13) as:

$$\hat{x}_o = \theta^* x_o - s^{-*} \tag{3.12}$$

$$\hat{y}_o = y_o + s^{+*}. \tag{3.13}$$

These relations suggest that the efficiency of (x_o, y_o) for DMU$_o$ can be improved if the input values are reduced radially by the ratio θ^* and the input excesses s^{-*} are eliminated. Similarly, the efficiency can be improved if the output values are augmented by the output shortfall s^{+*}.

Up till now, the original DEA models presented in the literature have mainly focused on a uniform input reduction or a uniform output augmentation in the improvement projections, as shown in Fig. 3.1 (θ^*=OC′/OC). Clearly, there is, in principle, a wide variety of improvement projections on the efficient frontier line, such as projection 1 or projection 2 in Fig. 3.1. The improvement projection of the original DEA models is only one possible solution, based on a proportional linear projection. There are clearly many cases where this approach is not a realistic or useful assumption.

Besides the unsatisfactory projection method in the standard CCR model, these are another, often recognized, weakness in the conventional CCR model, viz., the

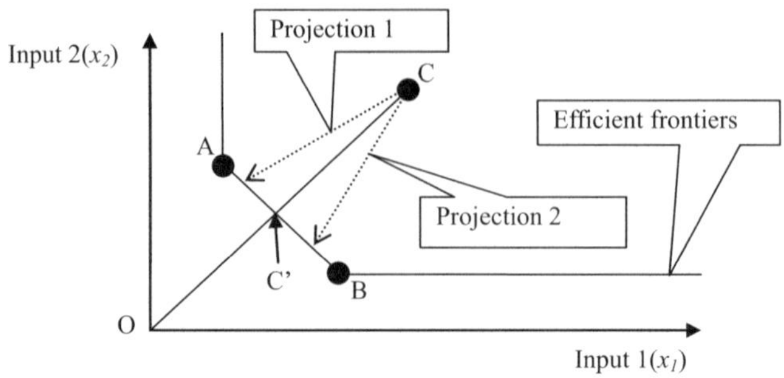

Fig. 3.1 Illustration of original DEA projection in input space

fact that all efficient DMUs receive the same score; a further discrimination between them is not possible. This will be further discussed in Sect. 3.2.

3.2 Super-Efficiency Model

In the past decades several attempts have been made to cope with the non-discriminating nature of efficient DMUs.

Anderson and Petersen (1993) have developed the Super-Efficiency model based on a radial projection (including a CCR model) to arrive at a ranking of all efficient DMUs. The efficiency scores from a Super-Efficiency model are thus obtained by eliminating the data on the DMU_o to be evaluated from the solution set. For the input model, this can then result in values, which may be regarded, according to the DMU_o, as a state of super efficiency. These values are then used to rank the DMUs, and consequently, efficient DMUs may then obtain an efficiency score above 1.000, while the score of all inefficient DMUs remains identical.

In general, a Super-Efficiency model aims to identify the relative importance of each individual efficient DMU, by designing and measuring a score for its "degree of influence," if this efficient DMU is omitted from the efficiency frontier (or production possibility set). If this elimination really matters (i.e., if the distance from this DMU to the remaining efficiency frontier is large) and thus, the DMUs concerned has a high degree of influence and outperforms the other DMUs, it gets a high score (and is thus super efficient). Therefore, for each individual DMU, a new distance result is obtained, which leads to a new ranking or even a rating of all the original efficient DMUs.

The Super-Efficiency model based on a CCR-I model can now be written as follows:

$$\min_{\theta,\lambda,S^-,S^+} \quad \theta - es^- - es^+$$

$$\text{s.t.} \quad \theta x_o = \sum_{j=1,\neq o}^{J} \lambda_j x_j + s^- \tag{3.14}$$

$$y_o = \sum_{j=1,\neq o}^{J} \lambda_j y_j - s^+$$

$$\lambda_j, s^-, s^+ \geq 0,$$

where e is a unit vector (1,...,1), representing a utility factor for all elements. This model has shown its potential in several empirical applications.

3.3 A Practical Treatment of DEA

3.3.1 Basic Rules for Application

In applications of DEA, we are often confronted with several fundamental questions on the practical side, in particular, "economies of scale," "setting of input and output items," and "number of DMUs, input and output items."

Regarding the "economies of scale," the original DEA model (3.1) is based on constant returns to scale (CRS), so that this model does not allow for the fact that a DMU may be too small or too large to operate with optimal efficiency. The adjusted variable returns to scale (VRS) model (see Banker et al. 1984) was specifically developed to consider scale effects in the analysis. But the VRS model has the disadvantage that small and large DMUs may tend to be overvalued. Therefore, we may be required to undertake a sensitivity analysis.

Regarding the issue of "setting of input and output items," input items do represent some kind of "resources," while output items do represent some kind of "production," so as to maintain a theoretical foundation. However, Ali and Seiford (1993) claimed that DEA can also be applicable in analytical scenarios when researchers are interested in ranking units where the data components cannot be strictly interpreted as inputs or outputs and where there is no evidence of an existing production function between these measures. In these cases, they advised to follow a general guideline where the classification is based according to whether it is better or not to have lower (inputs) or higher (outputs) values.

Regarding the "number of DMUs, input and output items," Dyson et al. (2001) suggested a "rule of thumb," that is, to achieve a reasonable level of discrimination, the practitioner needs a number of DMUs to be at least 2× (number of input items × number of output items). For example, in the case of four inputs and four outputs, a number of DMUs of at least 32 are needed.

In another useful contribution on DEA applications, Dyson et al. (2001) pointed out more details regarding "pitfalls and protocols in DEA."

3.3.2 Sensitivity Analysis of Efficiency Scores for Number of DMUs, Input Items, and Output Items

In applications of DEA, there is usually an uncertainty on the influence on efficiency scores by the number of DMUs, input items, and output items. Clearly, in several cases one may want to use a large number of inputs and outputs to evaluate a DMU from a broad perspective.

Answering these questions may require an understanding not only of the impact of the number of items or DMUs on efficiency scores but also of the influence of the "quality" of items for efficiency scores. This section will address the influence of the number of items and DMUs on efficiency scores for better understanding of the abovementioned issues, by using an empirical example.

To explore the above challenging questions, we present here a case study that uses the following input and output data on the energy-environment-economic (EEE) key variables for a set of 47 prefectures in Japan, as shown in Fig. 3.2. Figure 3.2 describes the inputs and outputs considered in this analysis of regional EEE efficiency in Japan.

In our analysis we will consider four inputs (I):

(I1) Electricity consumption in each prefecture (EC) (gigawatt hours/year)
(I2) Public capital stock in each prefecture (PCS) (million yen)
(I3) Private sector capital stock in each prefecture (PSCS) (million yen)
(I4) Labor in each prefecture (Lab) (employed persons)

Furthermore, two outputs (O) are incorporated:

(O1) GDP in each prefecture (GDP) (million yen/year)
(O2) Carbon emission in each prefecture (CE) (inverse number) (giga tons/year)

The more detailed explanation of the various inputs and outputs is as follows:

(I1) Electricity consumption (hereafter EC) in each prefecture (gigawatt hours/year) (2010)

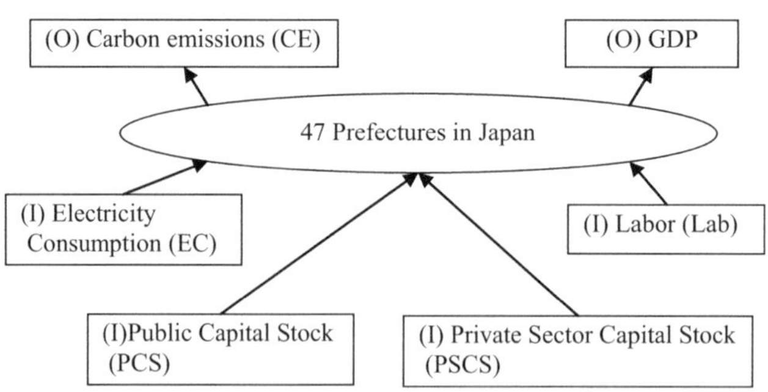

Fig. 3.2 Inputs and outputs of energy-environment-economic efficiency

This data set was obtained from statistical reports on energy consumption and the interindustry relations table. It was estimated from the basic energy consumption unit for each industry and sector. The sectors included are the industrial sector, the consumption and service sector, the consumer and residential sector, and the household car sector. We excluded the primary energy supply sector, the energy conversion sector, and the commercial traffic and cargo sector, because they supply services beyond the prefecture boundaries.

This data set also accounts for consequential (implicit) energy consumption, when one prefecture is supplied from other prefectures, in order to take into consideration "pseudo-energy saving." [Data source: "Statistical report on energy consumption for each prefecture" and "Statistics report on comprehensive strategy for energy consumption and environment (2010)," Agency for Natural Resources and Energy, Ministry of the Economy, Trade and Industry in Japan.]

(I2) Public capital stock (hereafter PCS) in each prefecture (million yen) (2010)

This data set represents the public capital stock in such sectors as transport, national conservation, health care, and education. [Data source: Economic and Fiscal model for Prefectures, Cabinet Office, Government of Japan.]

(I3) Private sector capital stock in prefecture (million yen) (2010) (hereafter PSCS)

This data set describes the private sector capital stock in such sectors as agriculture, forestry and fishery, mining, construction, manufacturing, wholesale and retail trade, finance and insurance, real estate, transportation and communication, utilities, and services. [Data source: Economic and Fiscal model for Prefectures, Cabinet Office, Government of Japan.]

(I4) Labor in each prefecture (employed persons) (2010)

This data set is based on the "National Accounts of Japan." [Data source: Economic and Fiscal model for the Prefectures, Cabinet Office, Government of Japan.]

(O1) GDP in each prefecture (million yen/year) (2010)

This data set is also based on the "National Accounts of Japan." [Data source: Economic and Fiscal model for the Prefectures, Cabinet Office, Government of Japan].

(O2) Carbon emissions (hereafter CE) in each prefecture (inverse number) (giga tons/year) (2010)

This data set is based on statistical reports on energy consumption and the interindustry relations table. It was estimated from the basic carbon emission unit for each industry and sector. The sectors included are the same as those used in electricity consumption above.

The data set even accounts for consequential (implicit) carbon emissions, when one prefecture is supplied from the other prefectures, in order to take into account "pseudo-emissions reduction." [Data source: "Statistical report on energy consumption for each prefecture" and "Statistics report on comprehensive strategy for energy consumption and environment (2010)," Agency for Natural Resources and Energy, Ministry of the Economy, Trade and Industry.]

We will now present and consider three frameworks of sensitivity analysis so as to understand the influence of varying attributes on efficiency scores.

3.3.2.1 Influence of Quality of Items for Efficiency Scores

Results of multiple optimum weights for the input (v_m) and output (u_s) items by each volume of input (x_m) and output (y_s) for the 47 prefectures based on the CCR model are given in Table 3.1. It should be noted that v_m and u_s is the set of most favorable weights of the input (v_m) and output (u_s) items for each DMU, so that we can find the relative importance of each indicator with reference to the value of each $v_m x_m$ and $u_s y_s$ for each DMU.

From Table 3.1, it can be seen that, for instance, Hokkaido obtains a $v_m x_m$ for PCS equal to 0.000, for PSCS equal to 0.972, for Lab equal to 0.028, and for EC equal to 0.000 in its inputs, while it obtains for GDP a $u_s y_s$ of 0.727 and for CE 0.125 in its output. From these results, it is noticed that Hokkaido has a relatively strong performance in PSCS and Lab; on the other hand, PCS and EC values equal zero, which means a weak performance point and no influence, if we eliminate these items from the input items for Hokkaido. From these features, we can examine the effects of the quality of items for the efficiency scores. And thus, we can count the number of weighted DMUs for each item as shown in the bottom row in Table 3.1.

It seems plausible to assume that if this impact of one item is large, then this item has a high influence on the efficiency score. Clearly, if we eliminate this item, this will lead to a large decrease or change in the efficiency score.

From Table 3.1, we infer that PCS and EC have a low influence on the efficiency score, while Lab and PSCS have a high influence on it. A large number of DMUs do not weigh for PCS (there are only 6 such DMUs in a total of 47) and EC (only 8 DMUs in a total of 47). On the contrary, the large number of DMUs related to Lab (36 DMUs in a total of 47) and PSCS (23 DMUs in a total of 47).

In this sensitivity analysis, we have only focused on input items, and we eliminated each input item from our four inputs and two outputs case. We also computed a total efficiency score of all DMUs in the case of 4I-2O and each 3I-2O to validate our hypothesis. These results are shown in Fig. 3.3.

From Fig. 3.3, we can notice that the total efficiency score of 4I-2O (38.649) was largely left unchanged from 3I (with eliminated PCS) -2O (38.573) and 3I (with eliminated EC) -2O (38.611). On the other hand, a total efficiency score of 3I (with eliminated PSCS) -2O (37.228) and 3I (with eliminated Lab) -2O (35.746) changed significantly from 4I-2O (38.649).

From these results, it is clear that our hypothesis is confirmed. From these findings, we may draw the conclusion that if an important item is eliminated, then the efficiency score will decrease significantly.

Table 3.1 Results of optimum weights of inputs and outputs for each DMU

DMU	Score	*vx* (PCS)	*vx* (PSCS)	*vx* (Lab)	*vx* (EC)	*uy* (GDP)	*uy* (CE)
Hokkaido	0.731	0	0.972	0.028	0	0.727	0.004
Aomori	0.800	0	0.967	0.033	0	0.733	0.067
Iwate	0.699	0	0.968	0.032	0	0.618	0.081
Miyagi	0.696	0	0.971	0.029	0	0.670	0.026
Akita	0.825	0	0.553	0.447	0	0.662	0.163
Yamagata	0.887	0	0.809	0	0.191	0.703	0.184
Fukushima	0.742	0	0	0.984	0.016	0.694	0.048
Ibaraki	0.739	0	0	1.000	0	0.726	0.013
Tochigi	0.764	0.043	0	0.957	0	0.708	0.055
Gunma	0.762	0	0.026	0.974	0	0.710	0.052
Saitama	0.863	0	1.000	0	0	0.858	0.005
Chiba	0.769	0	0	1.000	0	0.765	0.004
Tokyo	1.000	1.000	0	0	0	0.994	0.006
Kanagawa	0.803	0	0	1.000	0	0.800	0.003
Niigata	0.696	0	0	1.000	0	0.670	0.026
Toyama	0.872	0	0.030	0.970	0	0.721	0.150
Ishikawa	0.827	0	0.445	0.555	0	0.651	0.176
Fukui	0.993	0	0	0.981	0.019	0.712	0.281
Yamanashi	1.000	1.000	0	0	0	0	1.000
Nagano	0.752	0	0.172	0.828	0	0.708	0.044
Gifu	0.686	0	0.025	0.975	0	0.641	0.045
Shizuoka	0.738	0	0	1.000	0	0.728	0.010
Aichi	0.678	0	0	1.000	0	0.676	0.002
Mie	0.819	0	0	1.000	0	0.786	0.034
Shiga	1.000	0	0	1.000	0	0.901	0.099
Kyoto	0.868	0	0.971	0.029	0	0.831	0.037
Oosaka	0.720	0	0	1.000	0	0.717	0.003
Hyogo	0.745	0	0	1.000	0	0.741	0.005
Nara	1.000	0.363	0.637	0.000	0	0.617	0.383
Wakayama	0.811	0	0	0.985	0.015	0.694	0.116
Tottori	1.000	0	1.000	0	0	0	1.000
Shimane	0.884	0	0	0	1.000	0.386	0.498
Okayama	0.732	0	0	1.000	0	0.718	0.014
Hiroshima	0.726	0	0	1.000	0	0.718	0.008
Yamaguchi	0.787	0	0	1.000	0	0.763	0.024
Tokushima	1.000	0.067	0	0.933	0	0.483	0.517
Kagawa	0.956	1.000	0	0	0	0.359	0.597
Ehime	0.689	0	0.026	0.974	0	0.633	0.056
Kochi	1.000	0	0.798	0.202	0	0.669	0.331
Fukuoka	0.770	0	1.000	0	0	0.766	0.004
Saga	0.873	0	0	0.950	0.050	0.580	0.293
Nagasaki	0.818	0	0.814	0	0.186	0.671	0.147

(continued)

Table 3.1 (continued)

DMU	Score	*vx* (PCS)	*vx* (PSCS)	*vx* (Lab)	*vx* (EC)	*uy* (GDP)	*uy* (CE)
Kumamoto	0.767	0	0.968	0.032	0	0.707	0.059
Ooita	0.741	0	0	1.000	0	0.704	0.038
Miyazaki	0.822	0	0.968	0.032	0	0.699	0.123
Kagoshima	0.799	0	0.968	0.032	0	0.731	0.068
Okinawa	1.000	0	0.940	0	0.060	0.880	0.120
Counting of weighted DMUs		6	23	36	8	45	47

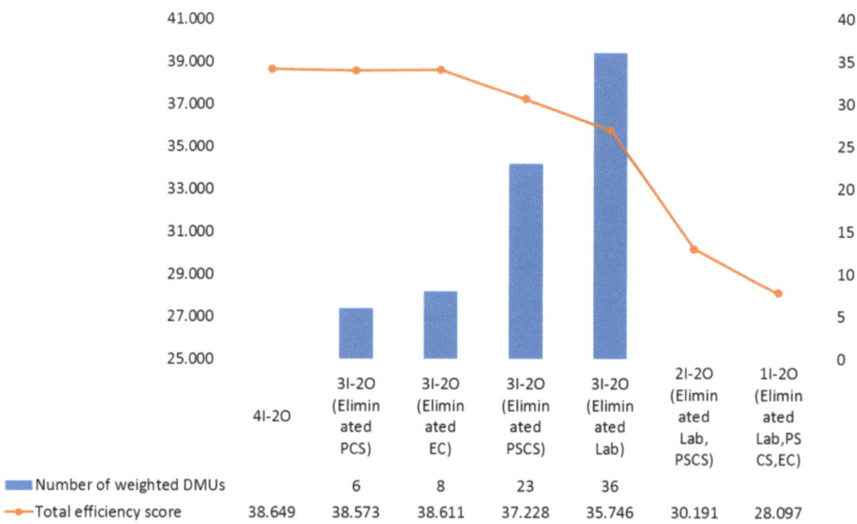

Fig. 3.3 Sensitivity analysis results of changing quality and number of items

3.3.2.2 Influence of Number of Items on Efficiency Scores

Based on above analysis, we additionally carried out a sensitivity analysis on a change in the number of items. The total efficiency scores of the combination 2I (with eliminated Lab and PSCS) -2O and the elimination 1I (with eliminated Lab, PSCS, and EC) -2O are shown in Fig. 3.3. From Fig. 3.3, it is noticed that the total efficiency score of the pair 2I-2O (30.191) and the pair 1I-2O (28.097) differs significantly from the pair 4I-2O (38.649).

From these findings, we may conclude that if the number of items is reduced, the efficiency scores may decrease significantly. In contrast, if we set many items, the efficiency scores of many DMUs will be evaluated as efficient, so that in this case it is difficult to make a judgment on the performance for each DMU. In the application, we need thus carefully select the input and output items.

3.3.2.3 Influence of Number of Efficient DMUs, Inefficient DMUs, and Quality of Efficient DMUs on Efficiency Scores

To understand the influence of the number of DMUs on efficiency scores, we need to understand the quality of DMUs, especially in terms of inefficient or efficient DMUs, and the number of reference sets of efficient DMUs.

It should be noted that efficient frontiers are composed by efficient DMUs A and B and not by an inefficient C, as shown in Fig. 3.1. From this fact, it is easily seen that if we eliminate inefficient DMUs from the DMU set, the efficiency scores for all DMUs will not change. Conversely, if we eliminate any efficient DMU, the efficiency scores will certainly change to a greater or lesser extent. To understand the quality of efficient DMUs, we need to understand the reference set from Fig. 3.1. The inefficiency of DMU C is to be evaluated by a combination of DMU A and B, because the point C′ is located on the line connecting these two points. A and B are called the reference set for C in Fig. 3.1. If one efficient DMU is the reference set for many inefficient DMUs, and if one efficient DMU is eliminated, then the efficiency score of many inefficient DMUs will be changed significantly. A number of reference sets of efficient DMUs are shown in Table 3.2. From Table 3.2, it can be seen that Tokyo (40) has a strong influence on a change in the efficiency score, while Kochi (3) has only a small influence.

Based on the abovementioned feature of DMUs, we carried out a sensitivity analysis of efficiency score for the following four cases:

Case1: All 47 DMUs
Case2: 46 DMUs, with inefficient Hokkaido eliminated
Case3: 46 DMUs, with efficient Kochi eliminated and a minimum number of reference sets
Case4: 46 DMUs, with efficient Tokyo eliminated and a maximum number of reference sets

These sensitivity analysis results are shown in Fig. 3.4. From Fig. 3.4, we notice that case1 and case 2 lead to completely the same results. We also notice that case 3 is changed a little and only influenced by the score of Yamagata and Nagasaki. Finally, case 4 is significantly influenced (with a clear increase in efficiency scores) for many inefficient DMUs, as we expected.

Table 3.2 Number of reference set for efficient DMUs

DMU	Number of references
Tokyo	40
Shiga	22
Tokushima	11
Okinawa	11
Nara	10
Yamanashi	6
Tottori	5
Kochi	3

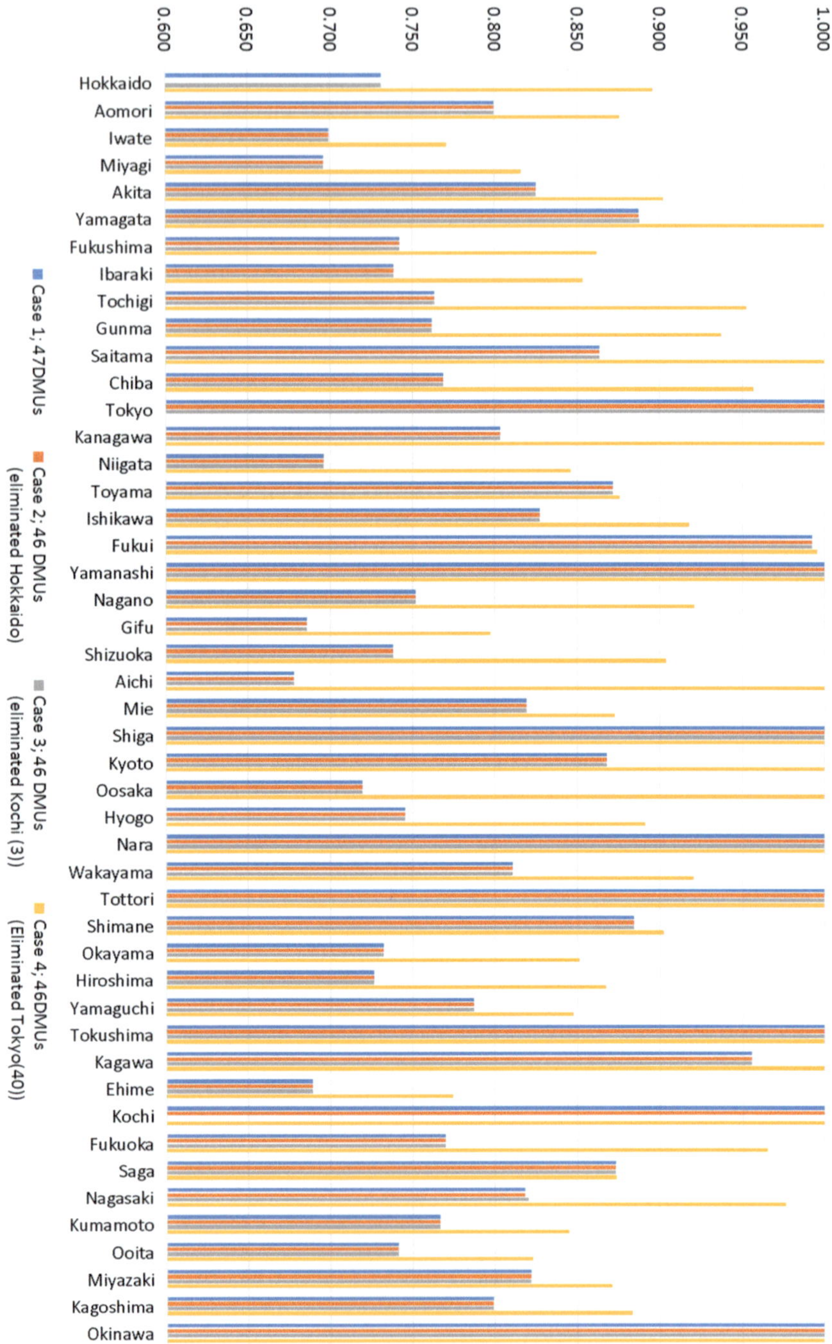

Fig. 3.4. Efficiency score results of eliminated DMUs

From these findings, we can thus trace the influence on the efficiency scores by changing the number of DMUs, including the feature of IIA (independence of irrelevant alternatives) in a DEA framework.

References

Ali, A., & Seiford, L. M. (1993). The mathematical programming approach to efficiency analysis. In H. O. Fried, C. A. K. Lovell, & S. S. Schmidt (Eds.), *The measurement of productive efficiency: Techniques and applications* (pp. 120–159). New York: Oxford University Press.

Anderson, P., & Petersen, N. (1993). A procedure for ranking efficient units in data envelopment analysis. *Management Science, 39*, 1261–1264.

Banker, R. D., Charnes, A., & Cooper, W. W. (1984). Some models for estimating technical and scale inefficiencies in data envelopment analysis. *Management Science, 30*, 1078–1092.

Charnes, A., Cooper, W. W., & Rhodes, E. (1978). Measuring the efficiency of decision making units. *European Journal of Operational Research, 2*, 429–444.

Cooper, W. W., Seiford, L. M., & Tone, K. (2006). *Introduction to data envelopment analysis and its uses*. Inc: Springer Science + Business Media.

Cooper, W. W., Seiford, L. M., & Tone, K. (2007). *Data envelopment analysis: A comprehensive text with models, applications, references and DEA-Solver software*. New York: Springer Science + Business Media.

Dyson, R. G., Allen, R., Camanho, A. S., Podinovski, V. V., Sarrico, C. S., & Shale, E. A. (2001). Pitfalls and protocols in DEA. *European Journal of Operational Research, 132*(2), 245–259.

Seiford, L. (2005). *A cyber-bibliography for data envelopment analysis (1978–2005). CD-ROM in introduction to data envelopment analysis and its uses*. New York: Springer Science Business Media.

Chapter 4
The Distance Friction Minimization (DFM) Model in DEA

Abstract The aim of this chapter is to position the newly developed distance friction minimization (DFM) model in the context of Data Envelopment Analysis (DEA). This model generates an appropriate (nonradial) efficiency-improvement projection model, for both an input reduction and an output increase. In this approach, a generalized distance function, based on a Euclidean distance metric in weighted spaces, is proposed to assist a decision making unit (DMU) to improve its performance by an appropriate movement toward the efficiency frontier surface. A suitable form of such a multidimensional projection function for efficiency improvement is given by a multiple objective quadratic programming (MOQP) model. This chapter describes the various steps involved in a systematic manner. The abovementioned DFM model is illustrated empirically by using a data set on several airports, where the aim is to offer an in-depth understanding of the advantages and features of the DFM model. In addition, the comparative analysis of these airports is able to comprise both input slacks and output slacks (or a combination of input reduction and output rise).

Keywords Distance friction minimization (DFM) model • Data envelopment analysis (DEA) • Multiple objective quadratic programming (MOQP) • Efficiency-improvement projection • Projection type

4.1 The DFM Model: Introduction

The standard DEA models, including the CCR-input model, have only focused on a uniform input reduction or a uniform output augmentation function in the improvement projections. The present chapter presents a DFM (distance friction minimization) (see also Suzuki et al. 2010) approach that offers a refreshing perspective on efficiency enhancement by employing a weighted projection function. This method can address both input reduction and output augmentation options. Our DFM model searches for the point on the efficiency frontier that is as close as possible to the DMU's inputs and outputs vector. This type of distance minimization has also been proposed in recent papers of Slavova (2006) and Beyko et al. (2005) as a related method. The DFM model developed in our study retains the advantage of the

S. Suzuki, P. Nijkamp, *Regional Performance Measurement and Improvement*, New Frontiers in Regional Science: Asian Perspectives 9,
DOI 10.1007/978-981-10-0242-7_4

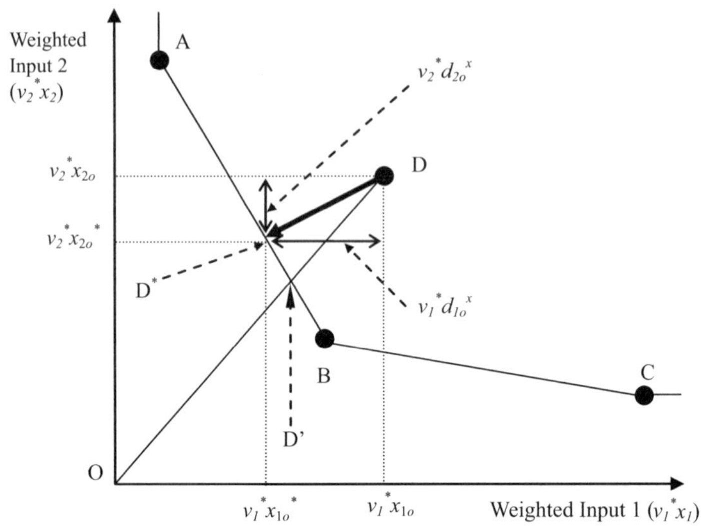

Fig. 4.1 Illustration of DFM approach (input – $v_i^* x_i$ space)

standard DEA approach that the measurement units of the different inputs and outputs need not be identical. An additional advantage is that the improvement projection in a DFM approach does not need to incorporate a priori information.

As mentioned in Chap. 3, the improvement solution in the original CCR-input model imposes the condition that the input values are reduced radially by a uniform ratio θ^* (θ^*=OD'/OD in Fig. 3.1). That is to say, the improvement solution for any arbitrary inefficient DMU_C is C′ in Fig. 3.1 (in cases where the input space is a non-weighted (i.e., normal) x-space). The general specification of a CCR model was originally based on a normal x- *or* y-space (non-weighted space) (see Fig. 3.1), in contrast to Figs. 4.1 and 4.2, which are based on weighted x- *or* y-spaces. Weighted spaces can be investigated regarding the distance frictions in improvement projections for both input and output variables in the following way (see Cooper et al. 2006).

The values of the multiplier vectors (v^*, u^*) obtained as an optimal solution for Eq. (3.1) form the basis for the optimal weights for DMU_o and reduce the subjectivity of preferences expressed by a decision maker. Clearly, these vectors are an implicit mathematical expression for an optimization process that seeks to generate the highest possible efficiency score for the DMU which is to be evaluated. However, in a fuzzy decision context without a clear decision authority, these vector values incorporate the best possible information: the relative importance of each item corresponds to $v_m^* x_{mo}$. This interpretation of weight characteristics can also be found in a standard text such as Cooper et al. (2007). A sensitivity analysis regarding the impact of input and output values would certainly be justified. If the optimal multiplier values showed unexpected fluctuations, one might resort to a

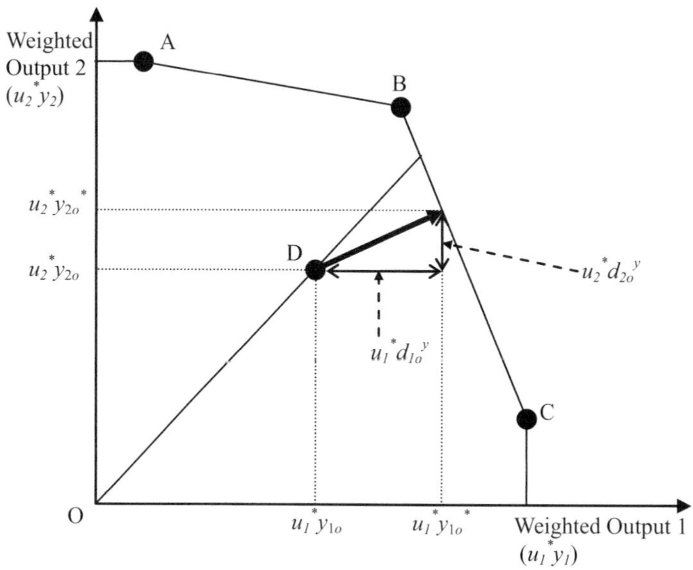

Fig. 4.2 Illustration of DFM approach (output – $u_r^* y_r$ space)

gradual improvement procedure as suggested by Seiford and Zhu (2003) or the assurance region method proposed by Thompson et al. (1996).

In general, the efficiency score can be evaluated by:

$$\theta^* = \frac{\sum_s u_s^* y_{so}}{\sum_m v_m^* x_{mo}}. \tag{4.1}$$

The denominator may arbitrarily be set equal to 1, and hence:

$$\theta^* = \sum_s u_s^* y_{so}. \tag{4.2}$$

(v^*, u^*) is the set of the most favorable weights for DMU_o, in the sense of maximizing θ^*; v_m^* is the optimal weight for the input item m, and its magnitude expresses how much in relative terms the item is contributing to efficiency; u_s^* does the same for the output item s. Furthermore, if we examine each item $v_m^* x_{mo}$ in the total input:

$$\sum_m v_m^* x_{mo} \quad (= 1). \tag{4.3}$$

We can derive the relative importance of each item with reference to the value of each $v_m^* x_{mo}$. The same holds for $u_s^* y_{so}$, where u_s^* provides a measure of the relative contribution of y_{so} to the overall value of θ^*. These values show not only which items contribute to the performance of DMU_o but also to what extent they do so. In other words, it is possible to express the distance frictions (or, alternatively, the potential increases) in improvement projections.

We will now we use the optimal weights u_s^* and v_m^* from (4.1) and then develop our efficiency-improvement projection model, DFM. A visual presentation of this new approach is given in Figs. 4.1 and 4.2.

The direction of efficiency improvement depends on the input/output data characteristics of the DMU. It is appropriate to define the projection functions for the minimization of distance friction by using a Euclidean distance in weighted spaces. A suitable form of multidimensional projection function that serves to improve efficiency is given by a multiple objective quadratic programming (MOQP) model, which aims to minimize the aggregated input reduction frictions, as well as the aggregated output augmentation frictions. Thus, the DFM approach can generate a new contribution to efficiency enhancement problems in decision analysis, by employing a weighted Euclidean projection function, while it also addresses both an input reduction and an output augmentation. DFM model has five steps which are now presented briefly.

[Step 1] Solve FP_o in Eq. (3.1). Let the optimal objective value be θ^* and the obtained optimal weights u_s^* and v_m^*.
[Step 2] Using θ^*, solve Eqs. (3.6)–(3.9) so that we obtain s^{-*} and s^{+*}. Each DMU can then be categorized by θ^*, s^{-*}, and s^{+*} as follows:

(a) In case $\theta^*=1$, $s^{-*}=s^{+*}=0$: This is the situation of an efficient DMU.
(b) In case $\theta^*=1$, $s^{-*}\neq 0$ or $s^{+*}\neq 0$: Improvement solutions are generated by formulas (3.12) and (3.13).
(c) In case $\theta^*\neq 1$, $s^{-*}\neq 0$ or $s^{+*}\neq 0$: Improvement solutions are generated by the next Steps 3, 4, and 5.

[Step 3] Introduce the distance friction functions Fr^x and Fr^y by means of Eqs. (4.4) and (4.5) which are defined by the Euclidean distance shown in Figs. 4.1 and 4.2. And solve the following MOQP, using d_{mo}^x(a reduction distance for x_{mo}) and d_{so}^y (an augmentation distance for y_{so}) as variables:

$$\min \quad Fr^x = \sqrt{\sum_m \left(v_m^* x_{mo} - v_m^* d_{mo}^x\right)^2} \tag{4.4}$$

$$\min \quad Fr^y = \sqrt{\sum_s \left(u_s^* y_{so} - u_s^* d_{so}^y\right)^2} \tag{4.5}$$

$$\text{s.t.} \quad \sum_m v_m^* \left(x_{mo} - d_{mo}^x\right) = \frac{2\theta^*}{1+\theta^*} \tag{4.6}$$

$$\sum_s u_s^* \left(y_{so} + d_{so}^y\right) = \frac{2\theta^*}{1+\theta^*}. \tag{4.7}$$

$$x_{mo} - d_{mo}^x \geq 0. \tag{4.8}$$

$$d_{mo}^x \geq 0 \tag{4.9}$$

$$d_{so}^y \geq 0, \tag{4.10}$$

where x_{mo} is the amount of input item m for an arbitrary inefficient DMU$_o$ and y_{so} is the amount of output item s for an arbitrary inefficient DMU$_o$.

The aim of function Fr^x (4.4) is to find a solution that minimizes the sum of input reduction distances which is incorporated in the improvement friction. The aim of function Fr^y (4.5) is to find a solution that minimizes the sum of output augmentation distances which is incorporated in the improvement friction.

Constraint functions (4.6) and (4.7) refer to the target values of input reduction and output augmentation. An illustration of a target value and a balanced allocation between input efforts and output efforts (total improvement room – TIR) is shown in Fig. 4.3. This simultaneous treatment of input choices and output choices is an important advantage of the DFM model, as compared with a radial projection method.

To achieve efficiency, the relative share of contributions from the input and output side is calculated as follows. The total efficiency gap (or possible improvement room) to be covered by inputs and outputs is (1 − θ*). The input and output side contribute in proportion to their initial levels 1 and θ*, implying shares θ*/(1 + θ*) and 1/(1 + θ*) to the total improvement room of (1 − θ*). Hence, the contributions from both sides equal (1 − θ*)[θ*/(1 + θ*)] and (1 − θ*)[1/(1 + θ*)].

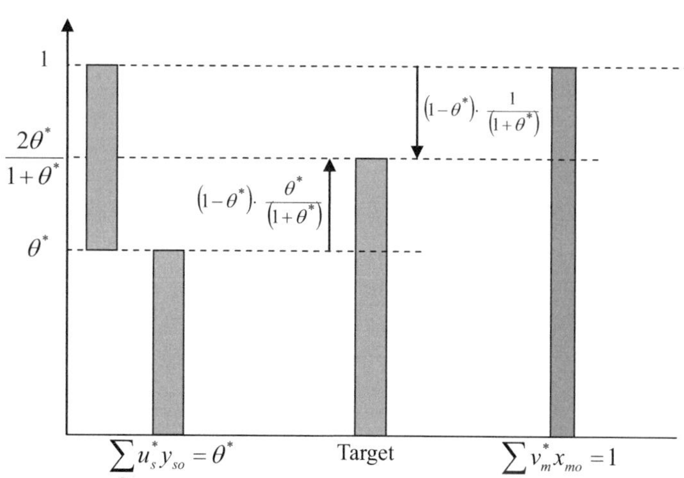

Fig. 4.3 Presentation of balanced allocation for the total improvement room (TIR = 1 − θ^*)

As a consequence, we find for the input reduction target and the output augmentation targets the following results:

- Input reduction target:

$$\sum_{m} v_m^* \left(x_{mo} - d_{mo}^x\right) = 1 - (1 - \theta^*) \times \frac{1}{(1 + \theta^*)} = \frac{2\theta^*}{1 + \theta^*}; \tag{4.11}$$

- Output augmentation target:

$$\sum_{s} u_s^* \left(y_{so} + d_{so}^y\right) = \theta^* + (1 - \theta^*) \times \frac{\theta^*}{(1 + \theta^*)} = \frac{2\theta^*}{1 + \theta^*}. \tag{4.12}$$

Constraint function (4.8) refers to a limitation of input reduction, while constraint functions (4.9) and (4.10) express simultaneously the pressure of input reduction and output augmentation. Clearly, this is a major advantage compared with the CCR-I model. It is now possible to determine each optimal distance d_{mo}^{x*} and d_{so}^{y*} by using MOQP (4.4)–(4.10).

[Step 4] The friction minimization solution for an inefficient DMU$_o$ can now be expressed by means of Eqs. (4.13) and (4.14):

$$x_{mo}^* = x_{mo} - d_{mo}^{x*}; \tag{4.13}$$

$$y_{so}^* = y_{so} + d_{so}^{y*}. \tag{4.14}$$

[Step 5] In order to ascertain the presence of slacks for input and output variables, solve Eqs. (3.3) and (3.6)–(3.9); then by using x_{mo}^*, y_{so}^*, we can obtain θ^{**}, s^{-**}, s^{+**}. In this case, we are sure that θ^{**} is calculated as 1. An optimal solution for an inefficient DMU$_o$ can be now expressed by means of Eqs. (4.15) and (4.16):

$$x_{mo}^{**} = x_{mo}^* - s^{-**}; \tag{4.15}$$

$$y_{so}^{**} = y_{so}^* + s^{+**}. \tag{4.16}$$

By means of the DFM model, we can thus determine a new efficiency-improvement solution based on the standard CCR projection. It means an increase in the options for efficiency-improvement solutions in DEA. The main advantage of the DFM model is that it yields an outcome on the efficiency frontier that is as close as possible to the DMU's input and output profile (see Fig. 4.4). As mentioned, the DFM model retains the property of the standard DEA approach that the measurement units of the different inputs and outputs need not be identical, while the improvement projection in a DFM model does not need to incorporate a priori information. The formal properties of the various DEA steps can be found inter alia in Cooper et al. (2007).

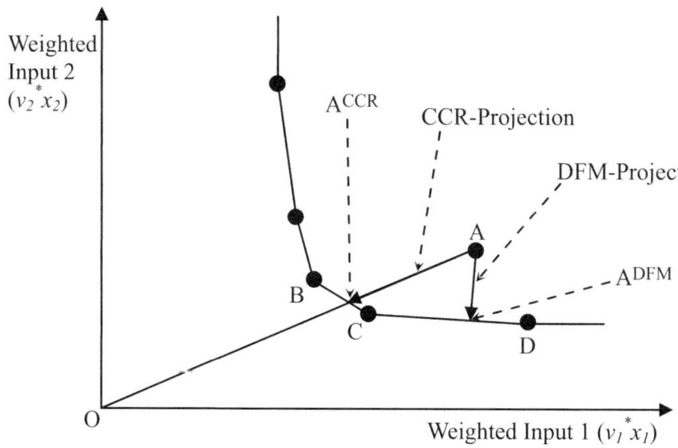

Fig. 4.4 Degree of improvement of a DFM projection and a CCR projection in weighted input space

At this stage, it may be appropriate to judge the advantages of the DFM approach in comparison with some other approaches. In particular, the additive model (Charnes et al. 1985) and the slack-based measure (hereafter SBM; Tone 2001) model are representative for the class of nonradial models, which focus only on the presence or absence of slacks in input/output space (see also as Fig. 4.5). These models generally assume an equality for each weight related to input and output items so that a characteristic feature for each input/output item for each DMU is that it does not take into account an efficiency-improvement projection. If these models need to take into account unequal weights, we need some a priori information from decision maker or policy-makers. Our DFM model is based on a radial type of model which is a completely different type of model, as this model employs optimal weights that are automatically and objectively computed by the CCR model.

The DFM model is based on both an input reduction and an output increase which is clearly a non-oriented characteristic. A non-oriented model takes into account simultaneous adjustments of outputs and inputs. A representative improvement projection model in a non-oriented space is proposed by Silva et al. (2003) and Frei and Harker (1999). These models can project the closest target onto an efficient frontier based on non-oriented models. Closest targets models can find a shortest-distance projection which is an integrated simultaneous input and output improvement, as in Fig. 4.6.

These models demonstrate a superior performance in finding an optimal improving solution in input/output space. But it may happen that one input or output item will bear almost the entire burden of improvement, for example, if input 1 requires a change of −0.5%, input 2 a change of −0.0%, and input 3 a change of −95.6%, while output 1 requires a change of +0.3% and output 2 a change of +1.2%. Clearly, the DFM model may independently produce an input improvement projection and output improvement projection as in Figs. 4.1 and 4.2. The DFM model can also

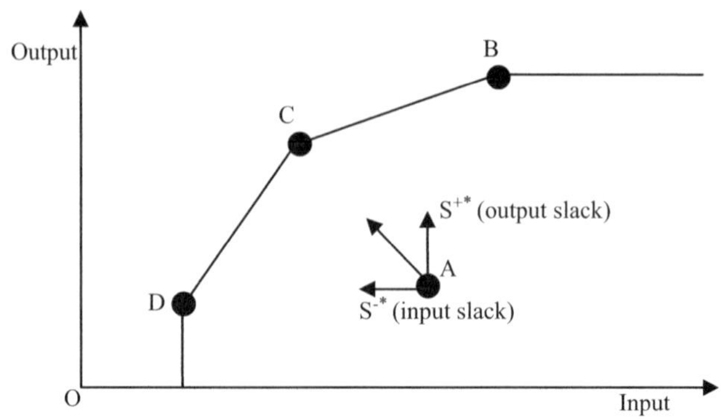

Fig. 4.5 Illustration of nonradial model in input/output space

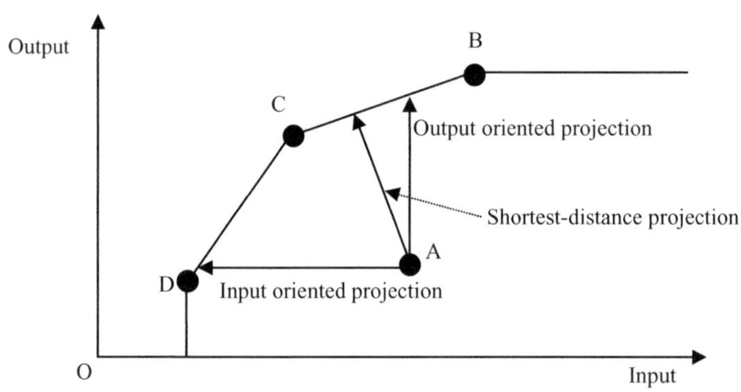

Fig. 4.6 Illustration of closest target model in input/output space

produce a projection that the balance in the distribution of shares from the input and output side ensures to achieve efficiency. The input side and the output side contribute according to their initial levels 1 and θ^*, implying shares $\theta^*/(1 + \theta^*)$ and $1/(1 + \theta^*)$ in the improvement contribution. Clearly, the contributions from both sides equal $(1 - \theta^*)[\theta^*/(1 + \theta^*)]$ and $(1 - \theta^*)[1/(1 + \theta^*)]$.

4.2 Comparison of Original Projection and DFM Projection

4.2.1 Analysis Framework

The DFM approach can, of course, be applied to many efficiency-enhancing research questions related to DEA. We shall – by way of a pedagogic experiment – apply the above DFM approach to a comparative study of airport efficiency in Europe.

The liberalization of the airline industry in Europe – and elsewhere – has not only prompted fierce competition between carriers (leading, e.g., to the rise of low-cost carriers), but also increasing competition (in terms of price and quality) between airports, which increasingly have to be run as private businesses. Each airport seeks to attract a maximum share of the available relevant market, ranging from national to global (see, e.g., Dempsey 2000; Goetz 2002; Graham 2001). This naturally calls for efficiency-enhancing strategies at all airports.

DEA has frequently been employed in the analysis of airport efficiency. For instance, Adler and Golany (2001) apply a DEA-Principal Component Analysis to hub-and-spoke airline network in the Western Europe. Fernandes and Pacheco (2002) apply the BCC model to Brazilian airports. Bazargan and Vasigh (2003) apply the CCR model to US airports, and Martín and Román (2001) and Pels et al. (2003) apply the BCC model to Spanish and European airports, respectively. Yoshida and Fujimoto (2004) analyze the efficiency of Japanese airports using both DEA and TFP methods. Although many useful insights were derived, all these studies assume that an efficiency improvement can be achieved when all input volumes are reduced by a uniform ratio. Our approach may therefore be useful to map out the efficiency-improvement potential of airports and their relative differences. Using objective criteria, the efficiency of certain airports will be compared with that of other airports with similar input/output characteristics. We will focus our attention here on 30 European airports, all operating under European regulations, and all facing European and intercontinental demand, so that the operating conditions are generally speaking similar. But some of these airports are hubs, while others are regional airports serving local markets so that there is at least one source of heterogeneity.

The steps followed in the analysis are shown in Fig. 4.7.

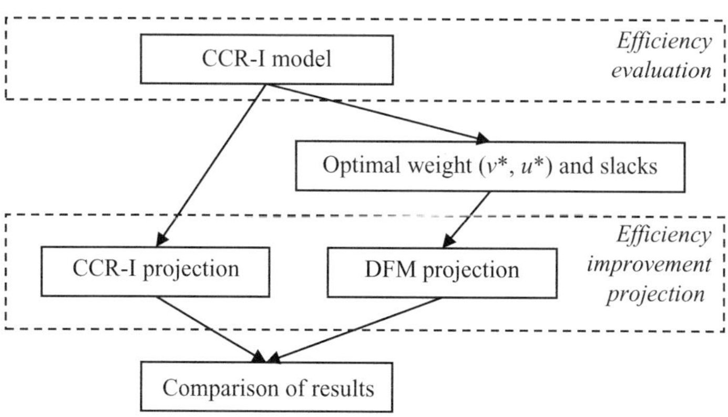

Fig. 4.7 Analysis framework of CCR-I and DFM models (Note: See Table 4.1 for an explanation of the airport abbreviations)

Next, in Sect. 4.2.2, we discuss the characteristics of the data sets pertaining to these airports. In Sect. 4.2.3, we present the efficiency evaluation results based on the CCR-input (CCR-I) model. Finally, in Sect. 4.2.4, we present the efficiency-improvement projection results based on the combined CCR-I and DFM approach and compare these with the CCR-I and DFM projections and outcomes.

4.2.2 Data Sets

In our practical example, we have used a data set on European airports originating from ABR2005 (Air Transport Research Society (2005)). Airports which had inadequate data were not taken into consideration. Ultimately, we used an extensive data set on 30 European airports (see Table 4.1), which were appropriate for an efficiency analysis based on the DFM approach.

Next, we identified a set of identical relevant input and output variables for which data were available for each airport. We have included in our application four input variables and two output variables based on ABR2005, viz., [Input 1] RN: Number of runways (2003), [Input 2] TS: Terminal space (m^2) (2003), [Input 3] GN: Number of gates (2003), [Input 4] EN: Number of employees (2003), [Output 1] PN: Number of passengers (2003), and [Output 2] AM: Aircraft Movements (2003). These data are used in our DFM approach. For the sake of comparison, we first present in Sect. 4.2.3 the results of the standard CCR-I model, followed by a presentation of the DFM model results in Sect. 4.2.4.

4.2.3 Efficiency Evaluation Based on CCR-I

The efficiency evaluation results for the selected European airports based on the CCR-I model are given in Fig. 4.8. We notice that the efficient DMUs (with a score = 1.000) – i.e., the most efficiently operating airports – are in particular: BCN, EDI, LGW, LHR, MAD, and WAW. Furthermore, there is apparently a wide variation in the efficiency performance of European airports.

4.2.4 Comparison of CCR-I Projection and DFM Projection

We have already noticed that the DFM model has four projection types depending on the existence of slacks: non-slack type, input-slack type, output-slack type, and input-/output-slack type. Efficiency-improvement projection results based on the CCR-I and the DFM model for relevant airports in Europe depend on the slack patterns presented below (see from Tables 4.2, 4.3 and 4.4).

Table 4.1 DMUs (airports in Europe)

No.	Airport (IATA)	City
1	AMS	Amsterdam
2	ARN	Stockholm
3	BCN	Barcelona
4	BHX	Birmingham
5	BRU	Brussels
6	CDG	Paris-Charles de Gaulle
7	CGN	Cologne
8	CIA	Rome-Ciampino
9	CPH	Copenhagen
10	DUS	Düsseldorf
11	EDI	Edinburgh
12	FCO	Rome-Fiumicino
13	FRA	Frankfurt
14	GVA	Geneva
15	HAM	Hamburg
16	HEL	Helsinki
17	IST	İstanbul
18	LGW	London-Gatwick
19	LHR	London-Heathrow
20	LIS	Lisbon
21	MAD	Madrid
22	MAN	Manchester
23	MUC	Munich
24	MXP	Milan-Malpensa
25	ORY	Paris-Orly
26	OSL	Oslo
27	PRG	Prague
28	VIE	Vienna
29	WAW	Warsaw
30	ZRH	Zürich

In Table 4.2, we illustrate the empirical outcomes for HAM (Hamburg) as an example of a *non-slack projection* type. This type of projection is illustrated in Fig. 4.9. It appears that the DFM projection involves both input reduction and output augmentation. Clearly, the DFM projection does not involve a uniform ratio, because this model looks for the optimal input reduction (i.e., the shortest distance to the frontier or distance friction minimization[1]). The overall efficiency level for HAM is 0.52 according to the CCR-I model, indicating that, in principle, *all* inputs

[1]The CCR-I model has a uniform reduction of inputs when slack is ignored. Dividing the values in column 3 ($\theta^* x_0$) by the values in column 2 ("data") leads to a percentage of 48 percent; this is the input reduction accounting for slack. When slack is included, the percentage in column 7 can be calculated.

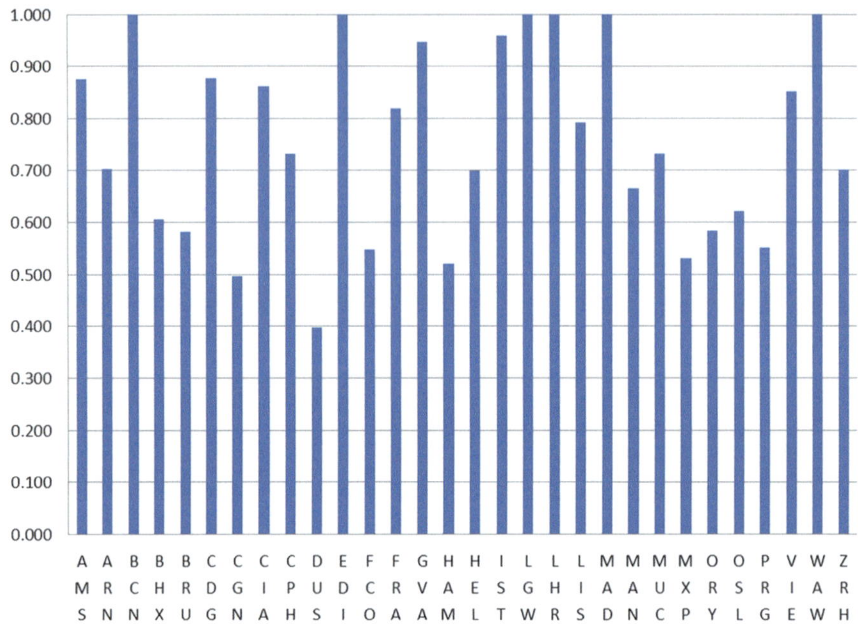

Fig. 4.8 Efficiency evaluation results of CCR-I model

could be reduced by 48%.[2] The results of the DFM model show that HAM is inefficient only in the first input (number of runways[3]). Note that the change ratios in the DFM model are smaller than those in the CCR model, as is also suggested in Fig. 4.4.

Table 4.3 shows the outcomes for CDG (Paris-Charles de Gaulle) as an illustration of the *input-slack projection* type. This type of projection is illustrated in Fig. 4.10. The uniform reductions in inputs (i.e., without slacks) are 12.3%. Again, the DFM model has no uniform reductions. The results indicate that CDG should substantially reduce terminal size and the number of employees, while a moderate reduction in the number of gates is also necessary to achieve efficiency. The number of runways should not be changed. The CCR-I model requires a uniform reduction in all inputs and the elimination of the slacks.

Next, it appears that in our case study, there is no single case of an *output-slack projection* type. If the database were to include more airports, we could expect that an example of this type might also be obtained. An illustration of this type of projection is given in Fig. 4.11.

[2] $OA^{CCR}/OA = 52\%$; $A^{CCR}A/OA = 48\%$.

[3] This, of course, ignores two aspects: runways are to a certain extent fixed assets so that a reduction of 44 percent is not possible in practice, while a certain number of runways may be required on account of, for instance, weather conditions. We use this example only to illustrate the working of the model and leave the issue of fixed factors for future work.

Table 4.2 Efficiency-improvement projection results of CCR-I and DFM (example of non-slack projection type: HAM)

DMU: HAM		CCR-I model Score(θ*)					DFM model Score(θ**)				
I/O	Data	$\theta^* x_o$	$-s^{-*}$ s^{+*}	Projection	Difference	%	d_{mo}^{x*} d_{so}^{y*}	$-s^{-**}$ s^{+**}	Projection x_{mo}^{**} y_{so}^{**}	Difference $-d_{mo}^{x*}-s^{-**}$ $d_{so}^{y*}+s^{+**}$	%
		0.520					1.000				
(I)RN	2	−1.0	0.0	1.0	−1.0	−48.0	−0.9	0.0	1.1	−0.9	−43.9
(I)TS	68,300	−32761.3	0.0	35538.7	−32761.3	−48.0	0.0	0.0	68300.0	0.0	0.0
(I)GN	50	−24.0	−5.4	20.6	−29.4	−58.7	0.0	0.0	50.0	0.0	0.0
(I)EN	777	−372.7	−57.8	346.5	−430.5	−55.4	0.0	0.0	777.0	0.0	0.0
(O)PN	9529,924		79629.1	9609553.1	79629.1	0.8	0.0	0.0	9529924.0	0.0	0.0
(O)AM	126,878		0.0	126878.0	0.0	0.0	40030.2	0.0	166908.2	40030.2	31.6

Note: See Sect. 4.2.2 for an explanation of the abbreviations for the input and output variables in column 1

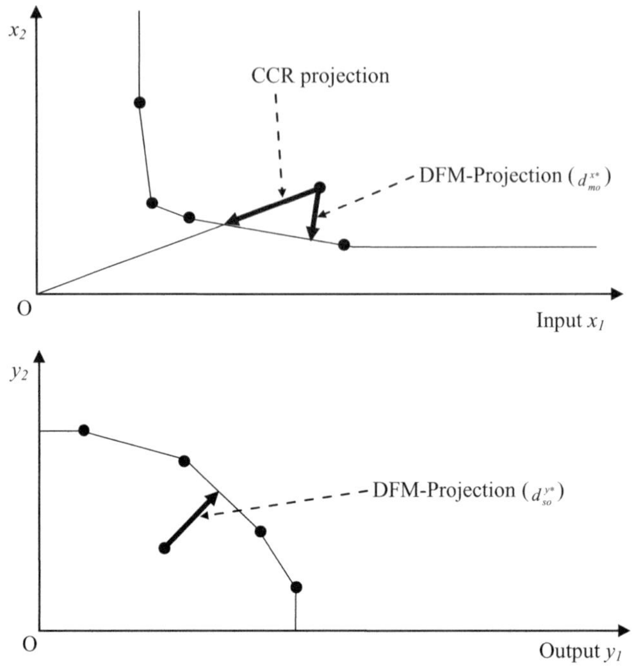

Fig. 4.9 Illustration of non-slack projection type (HAM)

Finally, FRA (Frankfurt) is presented in Table 4.4 as an example of the input-/output-slack projection type. This type of projection is illustrated in Fig. 4.12. The uniform input reduction in the CCR-I model is 18.1%, but, because of slacks, the projected reduction in inputs may exceed this percentage. Again, there is no uniform reduction in the DFM model. Frankfurt resembles CDG, in that it should substantially reduce terminal size and the number of employees, while a moderate reduction in the number of gates is also necessary to achieve efficiency. The number of runways should not be changed.

4.3 Conclusion

Our analysis has clearly demonstrated that DEA is an important strategic assessment vehicle in modern benchmark analysis. In this chapter, we have incorporated the DFM model in DEA, as an alternative to the standard CCR model. The difference concerns in particular the direction of the efficiency improvement. The DFM has three merits: It avoids the use of a linear proportional improvement, it allows both input reduction and output increase, and it is not based on subjective or a priori valuations by a DMU. Moreover, the measurement units of the various input and outputs need not be identical.

Table 4.3 Efficiency-improvement projection results of CCR-I and DFM (example of input-slack projection type: CDG)

DMU: CDG		CCR-I model					DFM model				
		Score(θ*)					Score(θ**)				
I/O	Data	$\theta^{*}x_{o}$	$-s^{-*}s^{+*}$	Projection	Difference	%	d_{mo}^{x*} d_{so}^{y*}	$-s^{-**}s^{+**}$	Projection x_{mo}^{**} y_{so}^{**}	Difference $- d_{mo}^{x*} - s^{-**} d_{so}^{y*} + s^{+**}$	%
		0.877					1.000				
(I)RN	4	−0.5	0.0	3.5	−0.5	−12.3	0.0	0.0	4.0	0.0	0.0
(I)TS	542,300	−66779.7	−266919.2	208601.1	−333698.9	−61.5	0.0	−338105.9	204194.1	−338105.9	−62.3
(I)GN	124	−15.3	0.0	108.7	−15.3	−12.3	−15.3	0.0	108.7	−15.3	−12.3
(I)EN	4071	−501.3	−1634.2	1935.5	−2135.5	−52.5	0.0	−2330.2	1740.8	−2330.2	−57.2
(O)PN	48,122,038		0.0	48122038.0	0.0	0.0	0.0	0.0	48122038.0	0.0	0.0
(O)AM	515,025		0.0	515025.0	0.0	0.0	39447.3	0.0	554472.3	39447.3	7.7

Note: See Sect. 4.2.2 for an explanation of the abbreviations for the input and output variables in column 1

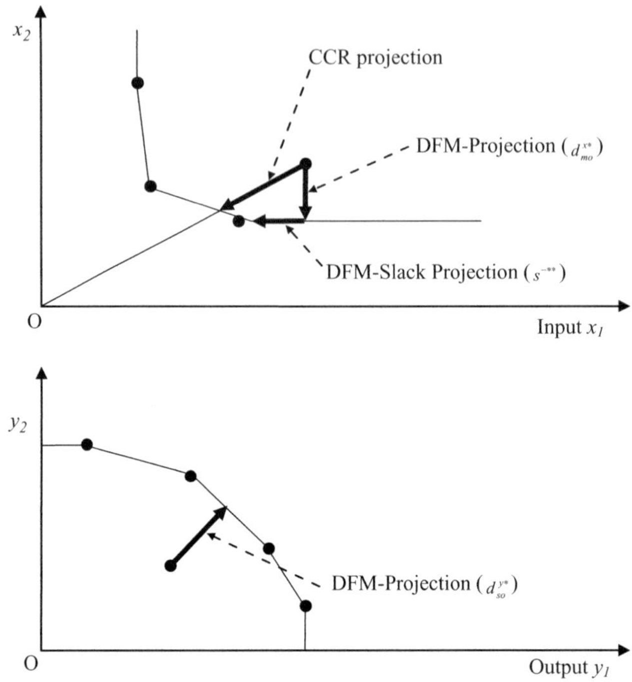

Fig. 4.10 Illustration of input-slack projection type (CDG)

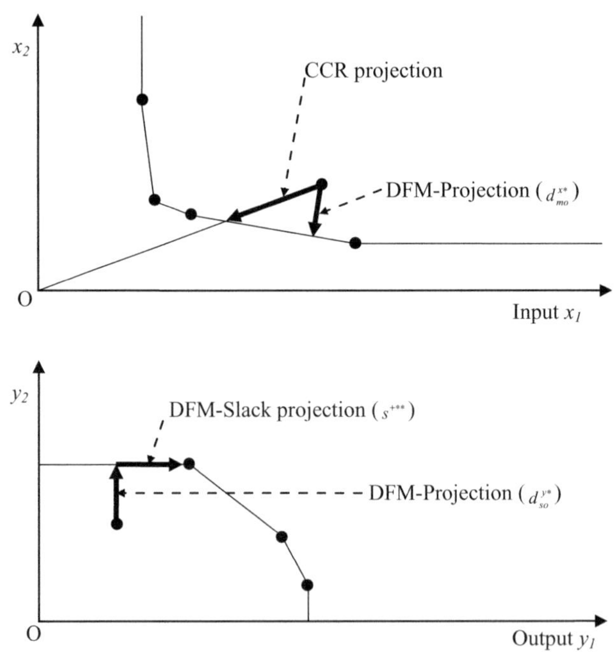

Fig. 4.11 Illustration of output-slack projection type

Table 4.4 Efficiency-improvement projection results of CCR-I and DFM (example of input/output slack projection type: FRA)

DMU: FRA		CCR-I model					DFM model				
		Score(θ*)					Score(θ**)				
I/O	Data	$\theta^{*} x_{o}$	$-s^{-*} s^{+*}$	Projection	Difference	%	d_{mo}^{x*} d_{so}^{y*}	$-s^{-**} s^{+**}$	Projection x_{mo}^{**} y_{so}^{**}	Difference $- d_{mo}^{x*} - s^{-**} d_{so}^{y*} + s^{+**}$	%
		0.819					1.000				
(I)RN	3	−0.5	0.0	2.5	−0.5	−18.1	0.0	0.0	3.0	0.0	0.0
(I)TS	800,000	−145077.1	−407409.3	247513.6	−552486.4	−69.1	0.0	−555680.9	244319.1	−555680.9	−69.5
(I)GN	147	−26.7	0.0	120.3	−26.7	−18.1	−25.9	0.0	121.1	−25.9	−17.6
(I)EN	13,006	−2358.6	−7883.8	2763.6	−10242.4	−78.8	0.0	−10661.5	2344.5	−10661.5	−82.0
(O)PN	48,359,320		2391059.1	50750379.1	2391059.1	4.9	0.0	2559627.7	50918947.7	2559627.7	5.3
(O)AM	458,865		0.0	458865.0	0.0	0.0	45755.5	0.0	504620.5	45755.5	10.0

Note: See Sect. 4.2.2 for an explanation of the abbreviations for the input and output variables in column 1

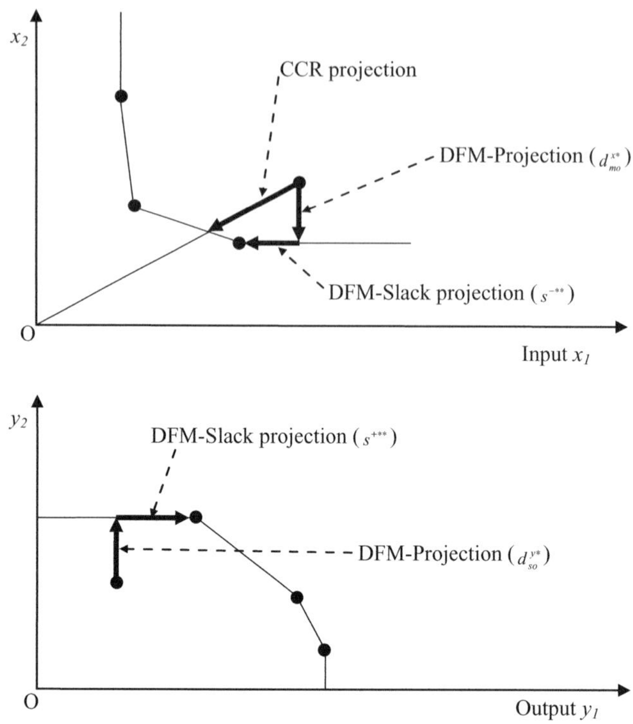

Fig. 4.12 Illustration of input/output-slack projection type (FRA)

We have applied this method as a tool for a comparative study on the efficiency of 30 airports in Europe. The results turn out to be promising. The DFM model looks for the shortest distance to the frontier and indicates which inputs should be reduced. In all three examples (HAM, CDG, and FRA), some inputs should be changed to achieve efficiency, while other inputs could be left unaltered. This is a more realistic approach than the standard CCR model, which indicates that all inputs should be reduced by the same percentage, as well as the elimination of slacks. The implication of this finding is that inefficient DMUs are not necessarily confronted with peers that have an entirely different configuration. Instead, certain DMUs are compared with other DMUs that have a similar configuration, where the criteria for comparison are determined by the data itself, by minimizing the distance to the frontier. However, in determining the price caps and expected efficiency improvements, the regulator needs the inputs in the policy-making process to be as precise as possible. The DFM model has the advantage that efficiency is determined by minimizing the distance to the frontier, in particular, by using a balanced and neutral guideline to compare a DMU with other DMUs of a similar configuration.

There is still a considerable methodological agenda ahead of us. DFM models need to be extended to suit more realistic circumstances. The DFM model is able to calculate either an optimal input reduction value or an output increase value in order to reach an efficiency score of 1.000, even though in reality this might be hard to achieve for low-efficiency DMUs. Therefore, we need propose a method that is categorized as a "target approach." On the other side, in many cases, input or output factors may not be flexible or adjustable due to the indivisible nature or inertia in the input or output factor. Usually, the original DEA model and DFM model do not allow for such a noncontrollable or fixed factor. Therefore, we need to design a class of methods categorized as "Adjustment approach" that takes this into consideration. This book will describe these extended DFM models in the next chapter.

References

Adler, N., & Golany, B. (2001). Evaluation of deregulated airline networks using data envelopment analysis combined with principal component analysis with an application to Western Europe. *European Journal of Operational Research, 132*(2), 260–273.

Air Transport Research Society. (2005). *Airport benchmarking report 2005*, Paradentologie 2.

Banker, R. D., Charnes, A., & Cooper, W. W. (1984). Some models for estimating technical and scale inefficiencies in data envelopment analysis. *Management Science, 30*, 1078 1092.

Bazargan, M., & Vasigh, B. (2003). Size versus efficiency: A case study of US commercial airports. *Journal of Air Transport Management, 9*(3), 187–193.

Beyko, I. W., Bodachivsjka, L. J. , & Korobko, T. W. (2005). *The problems of multicriteria estimations with incomplete data with the use of the aggregated Slavova criteria in problems of stochastic and discrete optimization* (pp. 111–112). International Ukrainian- Polish Workshop, Kaniv.

Charnes, A., Cooper, W. W., & Rhodes, E. (1978). Measuring the efficiency of decision making units. *European Journal of Operational Research, 2*, 429–444.

Charnes, A., Cooper, W. W., Golany, B., Seiford, L. M., & Stutz, J. (1985). Foundation of data envelopment analysis for Pareto-Kopmans efficient empirical production functions. *Journal of Econometrics, 30*, 91–107.

Cooper, W. W., Seiford, L. M., & Tone, K. (2006). *Introduction to data envelopment analysis and its uses*. Berlin: Springer-Verlag.

Cooper, W. W., Seiford, L. M., & Tone, K. (2007). *Data envelopment analysis, a comprehensive text with models, applications, references and DEA-Solver software*. Berlin: Springer-Verlag.

Dempsey, P. (2000). *Airport planning and development handbook*. New York: McGraw-Hill.

Dyson, R. G., & Thanassoulis, E. (1988). Reducing weight flexibility in data envelopment analysis. *Journal of the Operational Research Society, 39*(6), 563–576.

Fernandes, E., & Pacheco, R. R. (2002). Efficient use of airport capacity. *Transportation Research Part A: Policy and Practice, 36*(3), 225–238.

Frei, F. X., & Harker, P. T. (1999). Projections on to efficient frontiers: Theoretical and computational extensions to DEA. *Journal of Productivity Analysis, 11*(3), 275–300.

Goetz, A. (2002). Deregulation, competition and antitrust implications on the US airline industry. *Journal of Transport Geography, 12*, 1–18.

Graham, B. (2001). *Managing airports*. Oxford: Butterworth Heinemann.

Martín, J. C., & Román, C. (2001). An application of DEA to measure the efficiency of Spanish airports prior to privatization. *Journal of Air Transport Management, 7*(3), 149–157.

Pels, E., Nijkamp, P., & Rietveld, P. (2003). Inefficiencies and scale economies of European airport operations. *Transportation Research Part E: Logistics and Transportation Review, 39*(5), 341–361.

Seiford, L. M., & Zhu, J. (2003). Context-dependent data envelopment analysis – Measuring attractiveness and progress. *Omega, 31*, 397.

Silva, M., Castro, P., & Thanassoulis, E. (2003). Finding closest targets in non-oriented DEA models: The case of convex and non-convex technologies. *Journal of Productivity Analysis, 19*, 251–269.

Slavova T. (2006) The SOW-index for benchmark of European Stock-Exchanges. In *Proceedings of the international scientific methodological conference*: *Modern problems of the mathematical modeling, the forecasting and the optimization* (pp. 70–76). Kiev: Kamjanecj – Podiljsjk.

Suzuki, S., Nijkamp, P., Rietveld, P., & Pels, E. (2010). A distance friction min-imization approach in data envelopment analysis: A comparative study on air-port efficiency. *European Journal of Operational Research, 207*, 1104–1115.

Thompson, R. G., Dharmapala, P. S., Gatewood, E. J., Macy, S., & Thrall, R. M. (1996). DEA/assurance region SBDC efficiency and unique projections. *Operations Research, 44*(4), 533–542.

Tone, K. (2001). A Slack-based measure of efficiency in data envelopment analysis. *European Journal of Operational Research, 130*, 604–613.

Yoshida, Y., & Fujimoto, H. (2004). Japanese-airport benchmarking with the DEA and endogenous-weight TFP methods: Testing the criticism of overinvestment in Japanese regional airports. *Transportation Research Part E: Logistics and Transportation Review, 40*(6), 533–546.

Chapter 5
Extended DFM Models in DEA

Abstract This chapter aims to present a newly developed and extended distance friction minimization (DFM) model in the context of Data Envelopment Analysis (DEA), in order to comply with plausible and real-world circumstances. The DFM model is generally able to calculate either an optimal input reduction value or an output increase value in order to reach an efficiency score of 1.000, even though in reality this might be hard to achieve for low-efficiency DMUs. Most DEA models and also the DFM model have intrinsic limitations or weaknesses. Therefore, we need a method that allows for the presence of reference points that remain below the efficiency frontier. In this chapter we propose successively a Goals-Achievement model, a Stepwise Improvement model, and a Target-Oriented model based on the DFM framework. These models are categorized as "Target approaches." On the other side, in many cases, input or output factors may not be directly flexible or adjustable due to the indivisible nature or inertia in some input or output factors. Usually, the original DEA model and the DFM model do not allow for such a non-controllable or a fixed input factor. Therefore, we need a method that may take into account a flexible or adjustable factor in a DFM model. In this chapter, we propose an Adjusted-Improvement model and a Fixed-Factor model based on the DFM framework. These models are categorized as "Adjustment approaches."

Keywords Extended DFM model • Goals-Achievement model • Stepwise Improvement model • Target-Oriented model • Adjusted-Improvement model • Fixed-Factor model

5.1 Matrix of Extended DFM Model

As mentioned in Chap. 4, the DFM model may need drastic adjustments and extensions in order to comply with more realistic or practical circumstances.

The DFM model is able to calculate either an optimal input reduction value or an output increase value in order to reach an efficiency score of 1.000, even though in reality this might be difficult to achieve for low-efficiency DMUs. Clearly, most DEA models and DFM models have some intrinsic limitations or weaknesses. A major weak element is that in reality many DMUs are not able to reach a full efficiency, as the costs involved might be prohibitive. Therefore, a less efficient

S. Suzuki, P. Nijkamp, *Regional Performance Measurement and Improvement*, New Frontiers in Regional Science: Asian Perspectives 9,
DOI 10.1007/978-981-10-0242-7_5

solution might be accepted. Consequently, we need to develop a method that allows reference points that remain below the efficiency frontier. On the other hand, DMUs who are close to (or exactly on) the efficient frontier might search for an appropriate reference point for a further improvement of their efficiency. And therefore, we will introduce now successively a Goals-Achievement model, a Stepwise model, and a Target-Oriented model based on the DFM framework. These models are categorized as "Target approaches."

Another idea is that in many cases the input or output factors may not be flexible or adjustable due to the indivisible nature or inertia in the input or output factors. Usually, the original DEA model and the DFM model do not allow for such a non-controllable or a fixed input factor. Therefore, we need to propose now a method that allows for flexible or adjustable factors in the DFM model. In this chapter we propose an Adjusted-Improvement model and introduce a Fixed-Factor model based on the DFM framework. These models are categorized as "Adjustment approaches."

This book will comprise various combinations of basic efficiency measurement models (the CCR model and the Super-Efficiency model) and extended DFM models (Target approach and Adjustment approach), while it also includes a combination of the Target approach and the Adjustment approach, called a "matrix of extended DFM models," as shown in Table 5.1.

We will now describe the extended DFM model after the next subsection, while its empirical applications will be illustrated in Part. B.

5.2 Target Approach

5.2.1 Goals-Achievement Model

Any efficiency-improvement projection model which includes the standard CCR projection supplemented with the DFM projection is always directed toward achieving "full efficiency." This strict condition may not always be easy to achieve in reality, for instance, due to transaction costs. Therefore, in this subsection we will introduce a gradual and goal-oriented efficiency-improvement projection model, which aims to integrate a Goals-Achievement (GA) model (see Nijkamp and Suzuki 2009) in the framework of a DFM model.

The GA model deploys a Goal Improvement Rate (GIR) of the total efficiency gap $(1-\theta^*)$ in the DFM model. The value of the GIR ranges from 0 to 1. For example, if GIR is specified to be 0.1, then the GA model can compute an input reduction value and an output increase value in order to achieve an efficiency-improvement that is equivalent to 10% of the total efficiency gap $(1-\theta^*)$. This model will use the constraint functions (5.1) and (5.2) instead of constraint functions (4.6) and (4.7) in the DFM model. Thus, we have the following model specification for the Goals-Achievement Values (GAVs):

Table 5.1 Matrix of extended DFM model

	[Target approach] Goals-Achievement model Stepwise Improvement model Target-Oriented model	*[Adjustment approach]* Adjusted-Improvement model Fixed-Factor model
[CCR]	CCR with Goals-Achievement (Chapter 6, local government finance in Japan)	CCR with Adjusted-Improvement model (Chapter 10, eight type new energy in Japan)
	CCR with Stepwise Improvement model (Chapter 7, public transport operation in Japan)	
[Super-Efficiency: SE]	SE with Stepwise Improvement model (Chapter 8, performance of Asian cities)	SE with Fixed-Factor model (Chapter 11, energy-environment-economic efficiency for EU, APEC, and ASEAN countries)
	SE with Target-Oriented model (Chapter 9, energy-environment performance after Fukushima problem in Japan)	
[Target approach] Goals-Achievement model Stepwise Improvement model Target-Oriented model		Stepwise Improvement model with Fixed-Factor model (Chapter 12, airport operations in Japan)

$$GAV^x = \sum_m v_m^* \left(x_{mo} - d_{mo}^x\right)$$
$$= 1 - \frac{(1-\theta^*)}{(1+\theta^*)} + \frac{(1-\theta^*)(1-GIR)}{(1+\theta^*)} = \frac{2\theta^* + (1-\theta^*)(1-GIR)}{1+\theta^*}; \tag{5.1}$$

$$GAV^y = \sum_s u_s^* \left(y_{so} + d_{so}^y\right)$$
$$= \theta^* + \frac{(1-\theta^*)\theta^*}{(1+\theta^*)} - \frac{(1-\theta^*)(1-GIR)\theta^*}{(1+\theta^*)} = \frac{2\theta^* - (1-\theta^*)(1-GIR)\theta^*}{1+\theta^*}. \tag{5.2}$$

A visual presentation of constraint functions (5.1) and (5.2) is given in Fig. 5.1, which will now be clarified concisely.

First, the GA model has arbitrarily specified a GIR of the total efficiency gap equal to $(1-\theta^*)$. Next, the GAV^x and the GAV^y, which are fairly allocated between input efforts and output efforts, are computed in Fig. 5.1 by using constraint

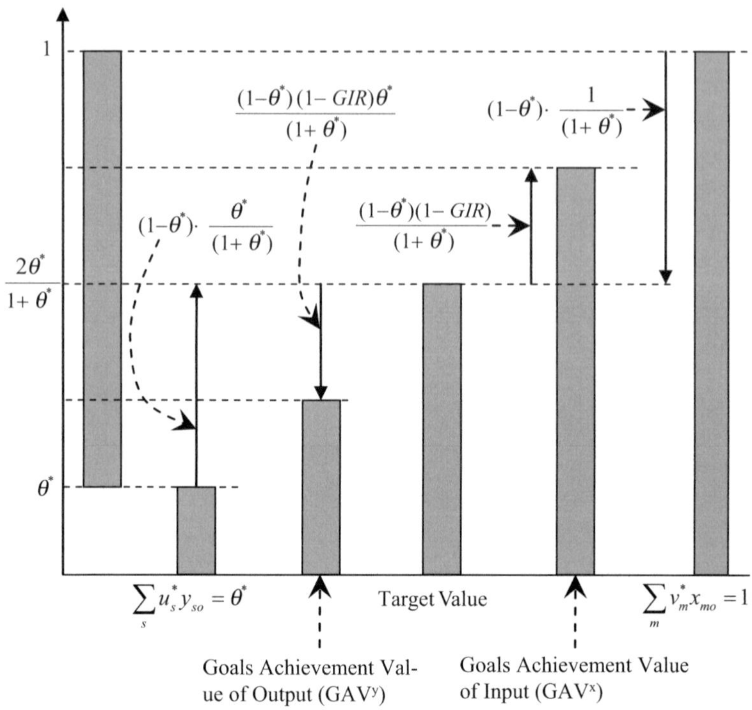

Fig. 5.1 Presentation of a GA model

functions (5.1) and (5.2). Finally, we compute an input reduction value and an output increase value in order to achieve a GAV^x and a GAV^y by using our CCR-DFM model. If the GIR = 1.0, then constraint functions (5.1) and (5.2) completely accord with constraint functions (4.6) and (4.7). In other words, the case of GIR = 1.0 represents a full improvement in the total efficiency gap $(1 - \theta^*)$. Alternatively, a case of GIR = 0.0 indicates a negligible improvement in the total efficiency gap $(1 - \theta^*)$.

5.2.2 *Stepwise Improvement Model*

The Context-Dependent (CD, hereafter; see Seiford and Zhu 2003) model can obtain efficient frontiers in different levels and can yield a level-by-level improvement projection. The CD model is formulated below.

Let $J^l = \{DMU_j, j = 1, \cdots, J\}$ be the set of all J DMUs. We interactively define $J^{l+1} = J^l - E^l$, where $E^l = \{DMU_k \in J^l | \theta^*(l, k)\} = 1$, and $\theta^*(l, k)$is the optimal value by using Eq. (3.1).

When $l = 1$, it becomes the original CCR model, and the DMUs in set E1 define the first-level efficient frontier. When $l = 2$, it gives the second-level efficient frontier after the exclusion of the first-level efficient DMUs and so on. In this manner, we identify several levels of efficient frontiers. We call El the *l*th-level efficient frontier. The following algorithm accomplishes the identification of these efficient frontiers.

Step 1: Set $l = 1$. Evaluate the entire set of DMUs, J1. We then obtain the first-level efficient DMUs for set E1 (the first-level efficient frontier).
Step 2: Exclude the efficient DMUs from future DEA runs. $J^{l+1} = J^l - E^l$ (if $J^{l+1} = \varphi$, then stop).
Step 3: Evaluate the new subset of "inefficient" DMUs. We then obtain a new set of efficient DMUs E^{l+1}(the new efficient frontier).
Step 4: Let $l = l + 1$. Go to Step 2.
Stopping rule: $J^{l+1} = \varphi$, the algorithm is terminated.

A visual presentation of the CD model is given in Fig. 5.2.

We will not try to merge the merits of the DFM and the CD approach. To that end, we will introduce a Stepwise Improvement model that is integrated with DFM and CD model (see Suzuki and Nijkamp 2011).

Any efficiency-improvement projection model which includes the standard CCR projection supplemented with the DFM projection is always directed toward achieving "full efficiency." This strict condition may not always be easy to achieve in reality. Therefore, in this section we will develop a new efficiency-improvement projection model, which aims to integrate with CD model and DFM approach, coined the "Stepwise Improvement" model. It can yield a stepwise efficiency-improvement projection that depends on *l*-level efficient frontiers (*l*-level DFM projection), as shown in Fig. 5.3.

For example, a second-level DFM projection for DMU10 (D10) aims to position DMU10 on a second-level efficient frontier. And a first-level DFM projection is just equal to DFM projection (4.4)–(4.10). We notice here that the second-level DFM projection is easier to achieve than a first-level DFM projection. A Stepwise Improvement model can yield a more practical and realistic efficiency-improvement projection than CCR projection or DFM projection.

The advantage of the Stepwise Improvement model is also that it yields an outcome on a *l*-level efficient frontier that is as close as possible to the DMU's input and output profile, which means that the Stepwise Improvement projection can compute more effective solutions than the CD projection model (see Fig. 5.3).

5.2.3 Target-Oriented Model

The DFM model is able to calculate an optimal input reduction value and an output increase value in order to reach an efficiency score of 1.000, even though in reality this might be hard to achieve for low-efficiency DMUs. Therefore we consider a method that allows reference points that remain below the efficiency frontier. On

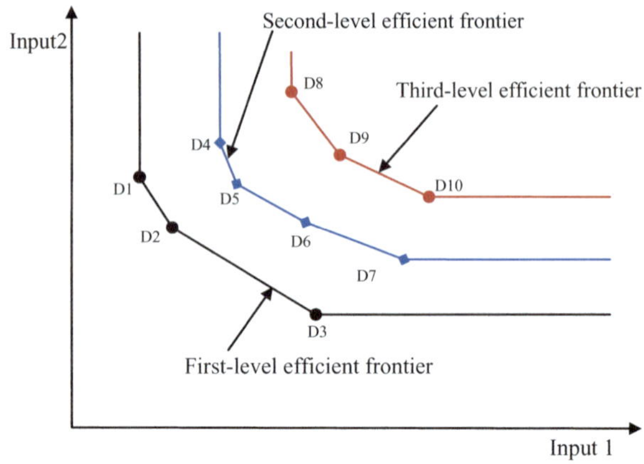

Fig. 5.2 Illustration of the CD model

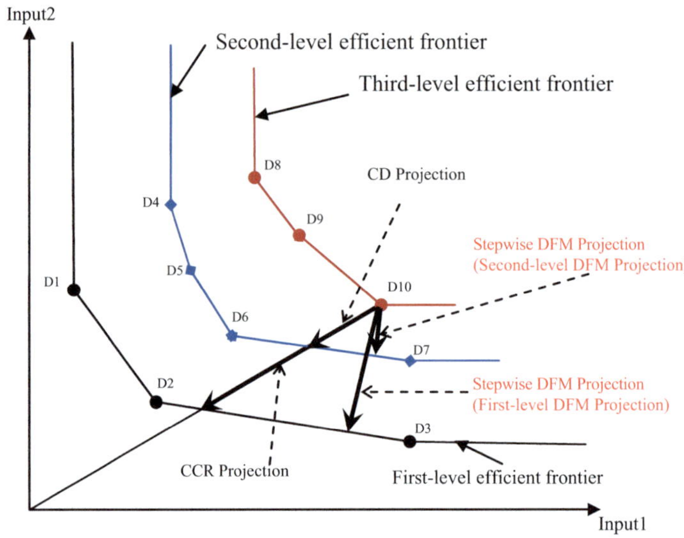

Fig. 5.3 Illustration of the CD model

the other hand, DMUs that are close to (or exactly on) the efficient frontier might search for a reference point for a further improvement of their efficiency.

This subsection introduces a Target-Oriented (TO) approach (see Suzuki et al. 2015) in the framework of the DFM model based on the Super-Efficiency model (Andersen and Petersen (1993); see Sect. 5.3.2), which is based on the CCR-I model. The TO approach comprises the following steps:

Step 1. Target Efficiency Score (TES) for DMU_o (hereafter TES_0) is set arbitrarily by the decision maker or policy-maker. Improvement projections are categorized in three types depending on the score of the TES as follows:

$\theta^* < \text{TES}_0 < 1.000$: Non-Attainment DFM projection (it does not reach the efficiency frontier). This makes sense for DMUs that are far below the efficiency frontier.

$\text{TES}_0 = 1.000$: Normal DFM projection (it just reaches the efficiency frontier).

$\text{TES}_0 > 1.000$: Super-Efficient DFM projection (it is beyond the efficiency frontier). This makes sense for DMUs that are already on the efficiency frontier.

Step 2. Solve $TES_0 = \frac{\theta^* + MP_0(1-\theta^*)\times\frac{\theta^*}{(1+\theta^*)}}{1 - MP_0(1-\theta^*)\times\frac{1}{(1+\theta^*)}}$

Then, we get MP_0, which is a Magnification Parameter as a function of TES_0.

Step 3. Solve the TO-DFM model using Eqs. (5.3), (5.4), (5.5), (5.6), (5.7), (5.8), (5.9), and (5.10); then an optimal input reduction value and output increase value to reach a TES_0 can be calculated.

$$\min \quad Fr^x = \sqrt{\sum_m \left(v_m^* x_{mo} - v_m^* d_{mo}^x\right)^2} \tag{5.3}$$

$$\min \quad Fr^y = \sqrt{\sum_s \left(u_s^* y_{so} - u_s^* d_{so}^y\right)^2} \tag{5.4}$$

$$\text{s.t.} \quad TES_0 = \frac{\sum_s u_s^* \left(y_{so} + d_{so}^y\right)}{\sum_m v_m^* \left(x_{mo} - d_{mo}^x\right)} \tag{5.5}$$

$$\sum_m v_m^* \left(x_{mo} - d_{mo}^x\right) = 1 - MP_0(1-\theta^*) \times \frac{1}{(1+\theta^*)} \tag{5.6}$$

$$\sum_s u_s^* \left(y_{so} + d_{so}^y\right) = \theta^* + MP_0(1-\theta^*) \times \frac{\theta^*}{(1+\theta^*)} \tag{5.7}$$

$$x_{mo} - d_{mo}^x \geq 0 \tag{5.8}$$

$$d_{mo}^x \geq 0 \tag{5.9}$$

$$d_{so}^y \geq 0, \tag{5.10}$$

An illustration of the TO-DFM model is given in Fig. 5.4.

From Fig. 5.4, we notice that a type of $\text{TES}_0 = 1.000$ is just equal to the normal DFM model using formulas (4.4)–(4.10). We also notice that the Non-Attainment DFM projection ($\theta^* < \text{TES}_0 < 1$) does not reach the efficiency frontier; thus, this is one of the improvement goal projections to reach a TES_0 lower than 1.000.

Additionally, a Super-Efficient DFM projection ($\text{TES}_0 > 1.000$) offers an above 1.000 improvement plan, which is relevant in particular for DMUs that are already close to the efficiency frontier.

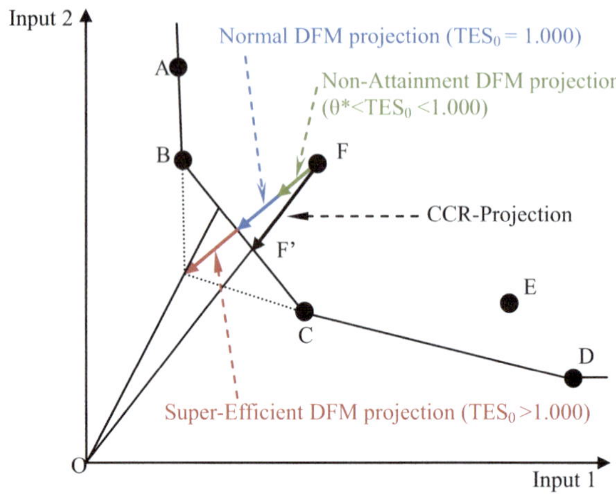

Fig. 5.4 Illustration of the Target-Oriented-DFM model for DMU F (input space)

5.3 Adjustment Approach

5.3.1 Adjusted-Improvement Model

The TO-DFM model calculates an optimal input reduction value and an output increase value in order to reach a TES, but in reality these values may represent an infeasible case, for example, a Networking Rate may be required of more than 100% in the improvement projection, but then it exceeds a physical limit.

Therefore, in this subsection we propose an Adjusted-Improvement (AI) approach based on the TO-DFM model. The AI approach specifies adjustment in input/output items based on the absence or presence of a DMU's improvement limit. This approach can compute an input reduction value and an output increase value in order to achieve a TES that maintains an improvement limit condition. The Adjusted-Improvement approach comprises the following steps:

Step 1. Target Efficiency Score (TES) for $\mathrm{DMU}_{\text{o-AI (Adjusted-Improvement)}}$ (hereafter $\mathrm{TES}_{0\text{-AI}}$) is set independently by the decision maker or policy-maker.

Step 2. Input and output items are to be resolved to unadjusted (UA) and adjusted (A) items as Eqs. (5.11) and (5.12).

Input:

$$\sum_{m \in UA} v_m^* \left(x_{mo} - d_{mo}^x\right) + \sum_{m \in A} v_m^* \left(x_{mo} - d_{mo-\text{deficiency}}^x - d_{mo-\text{limit}}^x\right) \tag{5.11}$$

Output:

$$\sum_{s \in UA} u_s^* \left(y_{so} + d_{so}^y\right) + \sum_{s \in A} u_s^* \left(y_{so} + d_{so-\text{deficiency}}^y + d_{so-\text{limit}}^y\right) \tag{5.12}$$

where UA represents unadjusted items, and A adjusted items, while $d_{mo-\text{deficiency}}^x$ is an improvement deficiency value for the adjustment input item m for any arbitrary

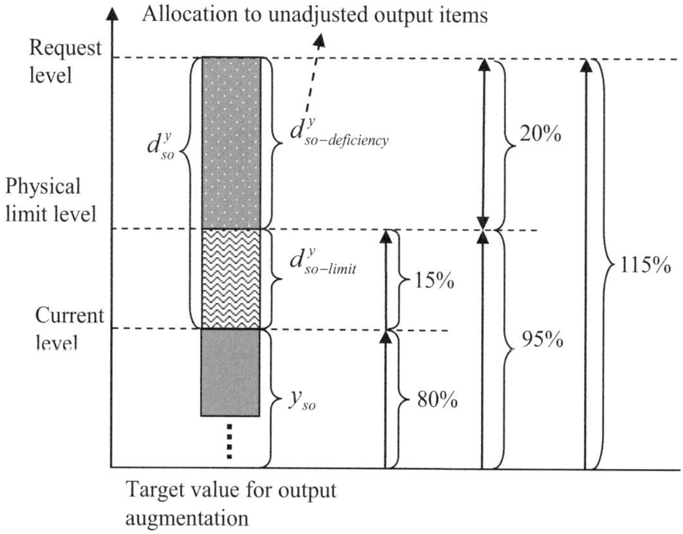

Fig. 5.5 Illustration of improvement limit condition (ex. output)

inefficient $DMU_{o\text{-}AI}$, $d^x_{mo-\text{limit}}$ is an improvement limit value for an adjustment of input item m for any arbitrary inefficient $DMU_{o\text{-}AI}$, $d^y_{so-\text{deficiency}}$ is an improvement deficiency value for adjustment output item s for any arbitrary inefficient $DMU_{o\text{-}AI}$, and $d^y_{so-\text{limit}}$ is an improvement limit value for an adjustment output item s for any arbitrary inefficient $DMU_{o\text{-}AI.}$

The meaning of Eqs. (5.11) and (5.12) is incorporated in the improvement limit condition. Now we take output (Eq. (5.12)) as an example to explain this concept, as presented in Fig. 5.5. The current volumes of the adjusted output item s of an inefficient DMU_o have a level of y_{so}, while the necessary level of output improvement projection by a normal TO-DFM projection is $d^y{}_{so}$. If we assume that the item has a physical limit level lower than y_{so} + $d^y{}_{so\text{-limit}}$, then the improvement level becomes insufficient as $d^y{}_{so\text{-deficiency}}$, and then this deficiency value allocates to unadjusted output items. To explain this situation, we assume now in Fig. 5.5 that the current level of Networking Rate of some inefficient new type energy (DMU) is 80%, and that the normal TO-DFM projection indicates 115%, but that it exceeds a physical limit of 95%. Then, we set the improvement level of the Networking Rate of this DMU equal to 95% (i.e., $d^y{}_{so\text{-limit}}$ equals 15%), and a value of 20% is allocated to unadjusted output items.

Step 3. Solve

$$TES_{0-AI} = \frac{\theta^* + \sum_{s \in A} u_s^* \cdot d_{so-\mathrm{limit}}^y + MP_{0-AI}\left[\left\{\left(1 - \sum_{m \in A} v_m^* \cdot d_{mo-\mathrm{limit}}^x\right) - \left(\theta^* + \sum_{s \in A} u_s^* \cdot d_{so-\mathrm{limit}}^y\right)\right\} \cdot \frac{\left(\sum_{s \in UA} u_s^* \cdot y_{so}\right)}{\left\{\left(\sum_{m \in UA} v_m^* \cdot x_{mo}\right) + \left(\sum_{s \in UA} u_s^* \cdot y_{so}\right)\right\}}\right]}{1 - \sum_{m \in R} v_m^* \cdot d_{mo-\mathrm{limit}}^x - MP_{0-AI}\left[\left\{\left(1 - \sum_{m \in A} v_m^* \cdot d_{mo-\mathrm{limit}}^x\right) - \left(\theta^* + \sum_{s \in A} u_s^* \cdot d_{so-\mathrm{limit}}^y\right)\right\} \cdot \frac{\left(\sum_{m \in UA} v_m^* \cdot x_{mo}\right)}{\left\{\left(\sum_{m \in UA} v_m^* \cdot x_{mo}\right) + \left(\sum_{s \in UA} u_s^* \cdot y_{so}\right)\right\}}\right]} \tag{5.13}$$

Then, we get $MP_{o\text{-}AI}$, which is a Magnification Parameter of $TES_{0\ \text{-}AI}$.

Step 4. If we solve the AI-TO-DFM model using formulas (5.14), (5.15), (5.16), (5.17), (5.18), (5.19), (5.20), (5.21), (5.22), and (5.23), then an optimal input reduction value and output increase value maintaining an adjusted-improvement condition to reach a $TES_{0\text{-}AI}$ can be calculated.

$$\min \quad Fr^x = \sqrt{\sum_{m \in UA} \left(v_m^* \cdot x_{mo} - v_m^* \cdot d_{mo}^x\right)^2 + \sum_{m \in A} \left(v_m^* \cdot x_{mo} - v_m^* \cdot d_{mo-\mathrm{limit}}^x\right)^2} \tag{5.14}$$

$$\min \; Fr^y = \sqrt{\sum_{s \in UA} \left(u_s^* \cdot y_{so} - u_s^* \cdot d_{so}^y\right)^2 + \sum_{s \in A} \left(u_s^* \cdot y_{so} - u_s^* \cdot d_{so-\mathrm{limit}}^y\right)^2} \tag{5.15}$$

$$\text{s.t.} \quad TES_{0-AI} = \frac{\sum_{s \in UA} u_s^* \left(y_{so} + d_{so}^y\right) + \sum_{s \in A} u_s^* \left(y_{so} + d_{so-\mathrm{limit}}^y\right)}{\sum_{m \in UA} v_m^* \left(x_{mo} - d_{mo}^x\right) + \sum_{m \in A} v_m^* \left(x_{mo} - d_{mo-\mathrm{limit}}^x\right)} \tag{5.16}$$

$$\begin{aligned} &\sum_{m \in UA} v_m^* \left(x_{mo} - d_{mo}^x\right) + \sum_{m \in A} v_m^* \left(x_{mo} - d_{mo-\mathrm{limit}}^x\right) \\ &\quad = 1 - \sum_{m \in A} v_m^* \cdot d_{mo-\mathrm{limit}}^x \\ &\quad - MP_{0-AI}\left[\left\{\left(1 - \sum_{m \in A} v_m^* \cdot d_{mo-\mathrm{limit}}^x\right) - \left(\theta^* + \sum_{s \in A} u_s^* \cdot d_{so-\mathrm{limit}}^y\right)\right\} \cdot \frac{\left(\sum_{m \in UA} v_m^* \cdot x_{mo}\right)}{\left\{\left(\sum_{m \in UA} v_m^* \cdot x_{mo}\right) + \left(\sum_{s \in UA} u_s^* \cdot y_{so}\right)\right\}}\right] \end{aligned} \tag{5.17}$$

$$\sum_{s\in UA} u_s^*\left(y_{so}+d_{so}^y\right)+\sum_{s\in A} u_s^*\left(y_{so}+d_{so-\text{limit}}^y\right)$$
$$=\theta^*+\sum_{s\in A} u_s^*\cdot d_{so-\text{limit}}^y$$
$$+MP_{0-AI}\left[\left\{\left(1-\sum_{m\in A} v_m^*\cdot d_{mo-\text{limit}}^x\right)-\left(\theta^*+\sum_{s\in A} u_s^*\cdot d_{so-\text{limit}}^y\right)\right\}\cdot\frac{\left(\sum_{s\in UA} u_s^*\cdot y_{so}\right)}{\left\{\left(\sum_{m\in UA} v_m^*\cdot x_{mo}\right)+\left(\sum_{s\in UA} u_s^*\cdot y_{so}\right)\right\}}\right] \tag{5.18}$$

$$x_{mo}-d_{mo}^x\geq 0 \tag{5.19}$$

$$d_{mo}^x\geq 0 \tag{5.20}$$

$$d_{so}^y\geq 0 \tag{5.21}$$

$$d_{mo\in A}^x=d_{mo-\text{limit}}^x \tag{5.22}$$

$$d_{so\in A}^y=d_{so-\text{limit}}^y \tag{5.23}$$

The meaning of functions (5.14) and (5.15) is to consider only the distance friction of UA inputs and UA outputs items, and $d^x{}_{mo\text{-limit}}$ and $d^y{}_{so\text{-limit}}$. The constraint functions (5.17) and (5.18) are target values for an input reduction and an output augmentation with a balanced allocation depending on all total input/output scores. The adjusted input and output situation is presented in Fig. 5.6. The constraint functions (5.22) and (5.23) refer to a limitation of adjusted input reduction and adjusted output augmentation.

5.3.2 Fixed-Factor Model

The Fixed-Factor model addresses the presence of indivisibilities in inputs or outputs of a DMU.

For example, airport efficiency management is usually confronted with variable inputs (like labor force) and fixed inputs (like runway capacity). In the short run, the runway capacity cannot be extended, and this limitation has to be incorporated in DEA. We introduce a version of the DFM model that takes into account the presence of such fixed factors (see Suzuki et al. 2011). The efficiency-improvement projection, which incorporates a fixed factor (FF) in a DFM model, is presented in (5.24), (5.25), (5.26), (5.27), (5.28), (5.29), and (5.30).

$$\min \quad Fr^x=\sqrt{\sum_{m\in D}\left(v_m^* x_{mo}-v_m^* d_{mo}^x\right)^2} \tag{5.24}$$

$$\min \quad Fr^y=\sqrt{\sum_{s\in D}\left(u_s^* y_{so}-u_s^* d_{so}^y\right)^2} \tag{5.25}$$

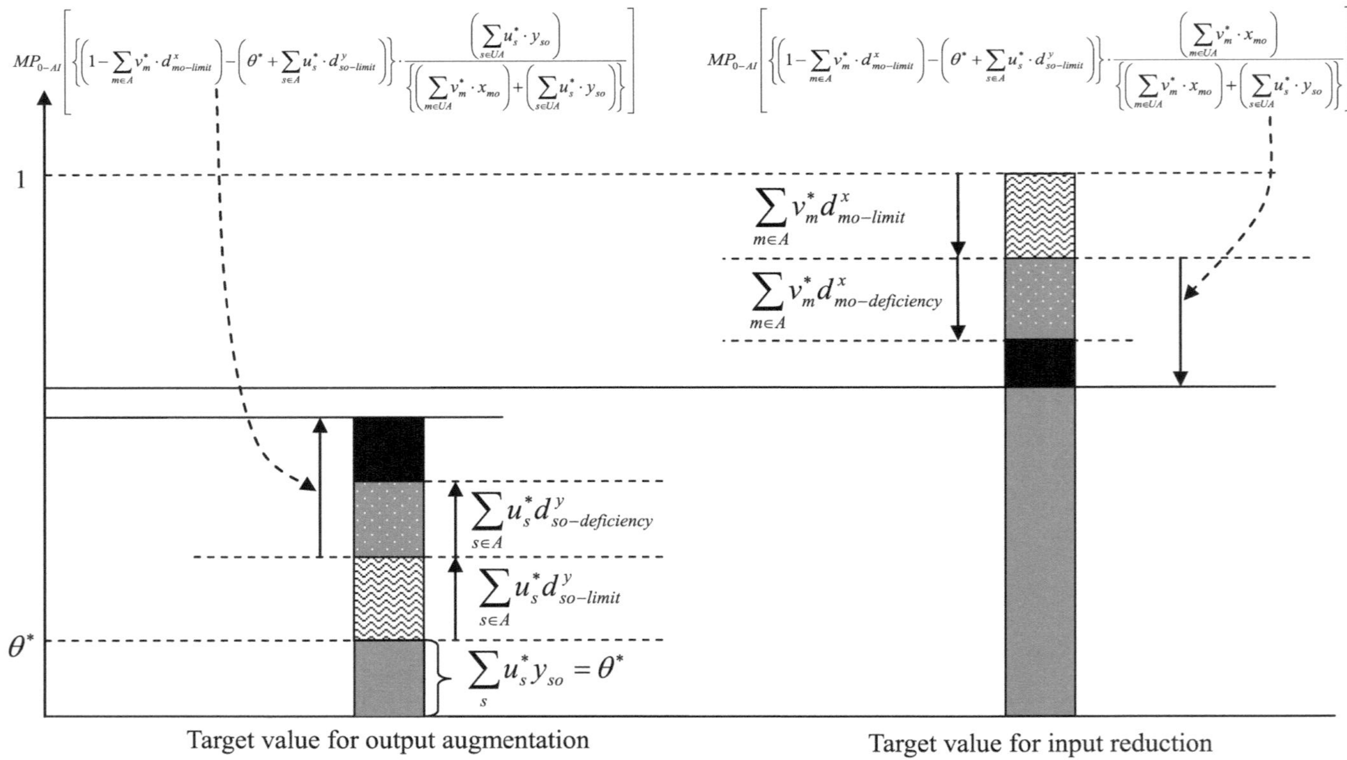

Fig. 5.6 Illustration of target values for input reduction and output augmentation with a balanced allocation

$$\text{s.t.} \quad \begin{aligned} & \sum_{m \in D} v_m^* \left(x_{mo} - d_{mo}^x\right) + \sum_{m \in ND} v_m^* x_{mo} \\ & = 1 - \frac{(1-\theta^*)\left(1 - \sum_{m \in ND} v_m^* x_{mo}\right)}{\left(1 - \sum_{m \in ND} v_m^* x_{mo}\right) + \left(\theta^* - \sum_{s \in ND} u_s^* y_{so}\right)} \end{aligned} \tag{5.26}$$

$$\begin{aligned} & \sum_{s \in D} u_s^* \left(y_{so} + d_{so}^y\right) + \sum_{s \in ND} u_s^* y_{so} \\ & = \theta^* + \frac{(1-\theta^*)\left(\theta^* - \sum_{s \in ND} u_s^* y_{so}\right)}{\left(1 - \sum_{m \in ND} v_m^* x_{mo}\right) + \left(\theta^* - \sum_{s \in ND} u_s^* y_{so}\right)} \end{aligned} \tag{5.27}$$

$$x_{mo} - d_{mo}^x > 0 \tag{5.28}$$

$$d_{mo}^x \geq 0 \tag{5.29}$$

$$d_{so}^y \geq 0, \tag{5.30}$$

where the symbols $m \in D$ and $s \in D$refer to the set of "discretionary" inputs and outputs and the symbols $m \in ND$ and $s \in ND$refer to the set of "non-discretionary" inputs and outputs.

The meaning of functions (5.24) and (5.25) is to consider only the distance friction of discretionary inputs and outputs. The constraint functions (5.26) and (5.27) are incorporated in the non-discretionary factors for the efficiency gap. The target values for input reduction and output augmentation with a balanced allocation depend all on total input/output scores and fixed-factor situations as presented in Fig. 5.7. The calculated result of (5.26) will then coincide with the calculated result of (5.27).

Finally, the optimal solution for an inefficient DMU_o can now be expressed by means of (5.31), (5.32), (5.33), and (5.34):

$$x_{mo}^{**} = x_{mo} - d_{mo}^{x*} - s^{-**}, \quad m \in D \tag{5.31}$$

$$y_{so}^{**} = y_{so} + d_{so}^{y*} + s^{+**} \quad s \in D \tag{5.32}$$

$$x_{mo}^{**} = x_{mo} \quad m \in ND \tag{5.33}$$

$$y_{so}^{**} = y_{so} \quad s \in ND \tag{5.34}$$

The slacks s^{-**}, $m \in ND$ and s^{+**}, and $s \in ND$ are not incorporated in (5.33) and (5.34), because these factors are "fixed" or "non-discretionary" inputs and

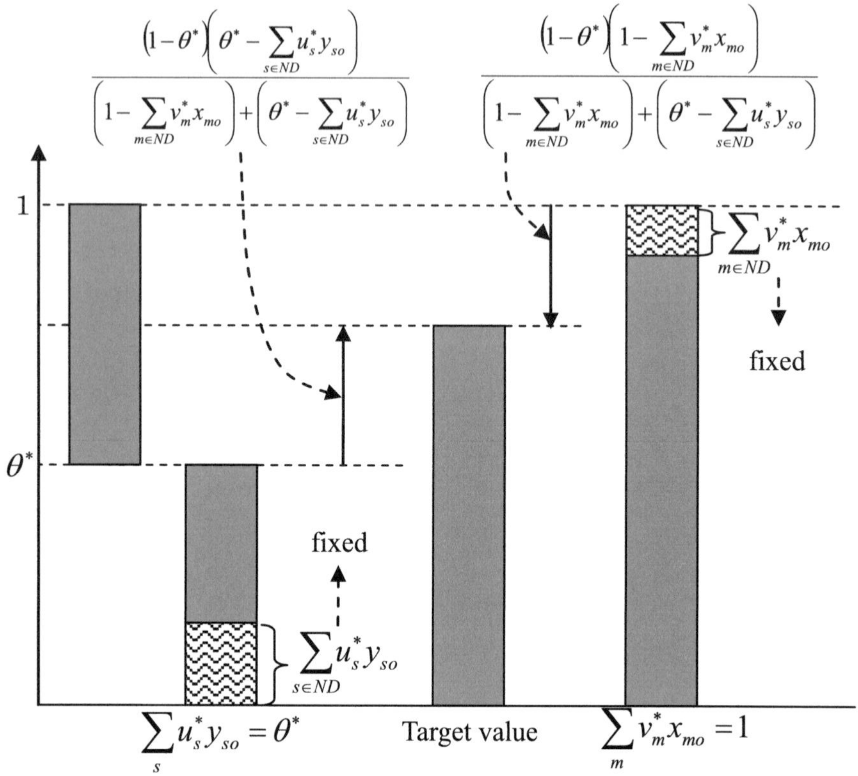

Fig. 5.7 Distribution of total efficiency gap

outputs, in a way similar to the Banker and Morey (1986) model. This approach will hereafter be described as the DFM-FF approach.

5.4 SE Model with Fixed-Factor Model

In this subsection, we introduce a version of the TO-DFM model that takes into account the presence of fixed factors (see Suzuki and Nijkamp 2016). A fixed factor is an input factor that cannot be flexibly adjusted in the short run. The efficiency-improvement projection, which incorporates a fixed factor (FF) in a TO-DFM model, is presented in the following way.

The TO-DFM-FF approach adopted here comprises the following steps:

Step 1. The Target Efficiency Score (TES) for DMU_o with a fixed factor (hereafter TES_0^{FF}) is set arbitrarily by the decision maker or policy-maker. Improvement projections are categorized in three types, depending on the score of the TES, in the same way as with the TO-DFM model.

Step 2. Solve

$$\mathrm{TES}_o^{FF} = \frac{\theta^* + \dfrac{\mathrm{MP}_o^{FF}(1-\theta^*)\left(\theta^* - \sum\limits_{s\in ND} u_s^* y_{so}\right).}{\left(1-\sum\limits_{m\in ND} v_m^* x_{mo}\right)+\left(\theta^* - \sum\limits_{s\in ND} u_s^* y_{so}\right)}}{1 - \dfrac{\mathrm{MP}_o^{FF}(1-\theta^*)\left(1-\sum\limits_{m\in ND} v_m^* x_{mo}\right)}{\left(1-\sum\limits_{m\in ND} v_m^* x_{mo}\right)+\left(\theta^* - \sum\limits_{s\in ND} u_s^* y_{so}\right)}} \tag{5.35}$$

We then get $\mathrm{MP_o}^{\mathrm{FF}}$, which is a Magnification Parameter of $\mathrm{TES_o}^{\mathrm{FF}}$. $\mathrm{MP_o}^{\mathrm{FF}}$ assumes an intermediate role by adjusting the input reduction target and the output increase target in formulas (5.39) and (5.40) in order to ensure an alignment of the $\mathrm{TES_0}^{\mathrm{FF}}$ and a DFM projection score for $\mathrm{DMU_o}$.

$$\min Fr^x = \sqrt{\sum_{m\in D}\left(v_m^* x_{mo} - v_m^* d_{mo}^x\right)^2}; \tag{5.36}$$

$$\min Fr^y = \sqrt{\sum_{s\in D}\left(u_s^* y_{so} - u_s^* d_{so}^y\right)^2}; \tag{5.37}$$

$$\text{s.t.}\quad \mathrm{TES}_o^{FF} = \frac{\sum\limits_{s\in D} u_s^*\left(y_{so}+d_{so}^y\right) + \sum\limits_{s\in ND} u_s^* y_{so}}{\sum\limits_{m\in D} v_m^*\left(x_{mo}-d_{mo}^x\right) + \sum\limits_{m\in ND} v_m^* x_{mo}}; \tag{5.38}$$

$$\sum_{m\in D} v_m^*\left(x_{mo}-d_{mo}^x\right) + \sum_{m\in ND} v_m^* x_{mo} = 1 - \frac{\mathrm{MP}_o^{FF}(1-\theta^*)\left(1-\sum\limits_{m\in ND} v_m^* x_{mo}\right)}{\left(1-\sum\limits_{m\in ND} v_m^* x_{mo}\right)+\left(\theta^* - \sum\limits_{s\in ND} u_s^* y_{so}\right)}; \tag{5.39}$$

$$\sum_{s\in D} u_s^*\left(y_{so}-d_{so}^y\right) + \sum_{s\in ND} u_s^* y_{so} = \theta^* + \frac{\mathrm{MP}_o^{FF}(1-\theta^*)\left(\theta^* - \sum\limits_{s\in ND} u_s^* y_{so}\right)}{\left(1-\sum\limits_{m\in ND} v_m^* x_{mo}\right)+\left(\theta^* - \sum\limits_{s\in ND} u_s^* y_{so}\right)}; \tag{5.40}$$

$$x_{mo} - d_{mo}^x > 0; \tag{5.41}$$

$$d_{mo}^x \geq 0; \tag{5.42}$$

$$d_{so}^y \geq 0, \tag{5.43}$$

where the symbols$m\in D$ and $s\in D$ refer to the set of "discretionary" inputs and outputs and the symbols $m\in ND$ and $s\in ND$ refer to the set of "non-discretionary" inputs and outputs. The meaning of functions (5.36) and (5.37) is to consider only the distance friction of discretionary inputs and outputs. The constraint functions (5.39) and (5.40) are incorporated in the non-discretionary factors for the efficiency gap. The target values for input reduction and output augmentation with a balanced allocation depend on all total input/output scores and fixed-factor situations, as presented in Fig.5.8 in the case of $\text{TES}_0{}^{\text{FF}} = 1.000$ (i.e., $\text{MP}_\text{o}{}^{\text{FF}} = 1.000$). The calculated result of (5.39) will then coincide with the calculated result of (5.40). Finally, the optimal solution for an inefficient DMU_o can now be expressed by means of (5.44), (5.45), (5.46), and (5.47):

$$x_{mo}^{**} = x_{mo} - d_{mo}^{x*} - s^{-**}, m \in D; \tag{5.44}$$

$$y_{so}^{**} = y_{so} + d_{so}^{y*} + s^{+**}, s \in D; \tag{5.45}$$

$$x_{mo}^{**} = x_{mo}, m \in ND; \tag{5.46}$$

$$y_{so}^{**} = y_{so}, s \in ND. \tag{5.47}$$

The slacks s^{-**}, $m \in ND$and s^{+**}, and $s \in ND$ are not incorporated in (5.46) and (5.47), because these factors are “fixed” or “non-discretionary” inputs and outputs, in a way similar to the Banker and Morey (1986) model. This approach will hereafter be described as the TO-DFM-FF approach.

5.5 Stepwise Improvement-DFM-FF Model

Several DEA models used in our subsequent applications form a blend of the DFM-FF model and the CD model. Hence, we introduce here a Stepwise Improvement-DFM-FF model that is integrated with a DFM-FF and a CD model (see Suzuki and Nijkamp 2014). Any efficiency-improvement projection model which includes the standard CCR projection supplemented with the DFM projection is always directed toward achieving “full efficiency.” This strict condition may not always be easy to achieve in reality. Therefore, it is necessary to introduce a new efficiency-improvement projection model, which aims to integrate the CD model and the DFM-FF approach to produce the “Stepwise Improvement Distance Friction Minimization Fixed Factor” (hereafter Stepwise Improvement-DFM-FF) model. It can yield a stepwise efficiency-improvement projection incorporating a set of fixed input and output factors that depends on l-level efficient frontiers (l-level DFM projection), as shown in Fig. 5.9.

For example, a second-level DFM-FF projection for DMU10 (D10) aims to position DMU10 on a second-level efficient frontier. And a first-level DFM-FF projection is just equal to a DFM-FF projection (5.24), (5.25), (5.26), (5.27), (5.28), (5.29), and (5.30). Here, we observe that the second-level DFM-FF projection is easier to achieve than a first-level DFM-FF projection. A Stepwise Improvement-DFM-FF model can yield a more practical and realistic efficiency-improvement projection than a CCR projection or a DFM-FF projection.

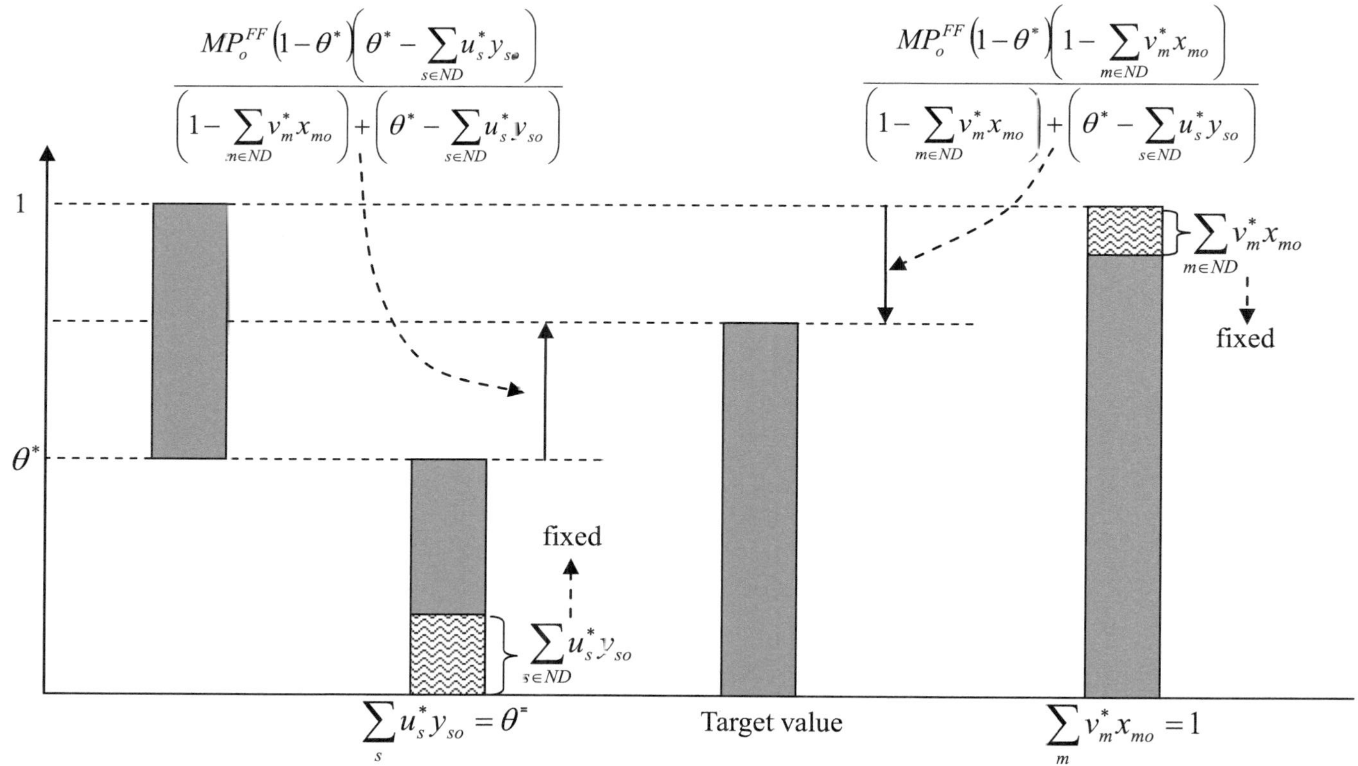

Fig. 5.8 Distribution of the total efficiency gap (in the case of $TES_0^{FF} = 1.000$ ($MP_o^{FF} = 1.000$))

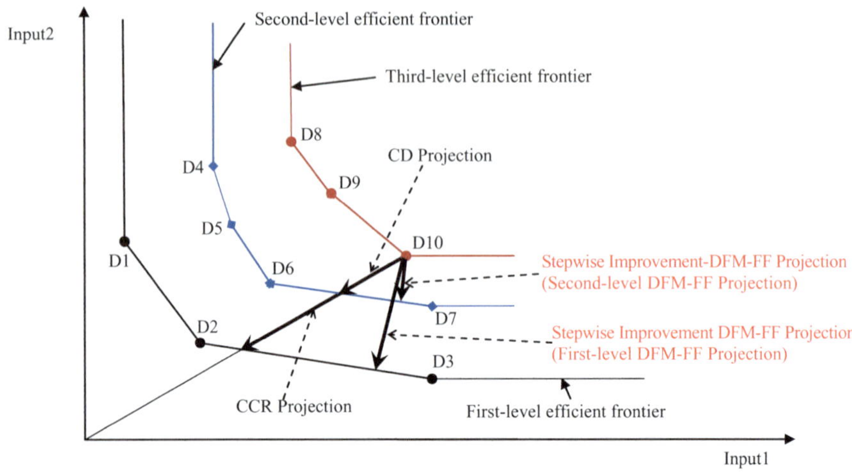

Fig. 5.9 Illustration of the Stepwise Improvement-DFM-FF model

The advantage of the Stepwise Improvement-DFM-FF model is also that it yields an outcome on an *l*-level efficient frontier that is as close as possible to the DMU's input and output profile (see Fig. 5.9). In the remaining part of this book, we will discuss new element, various empirical applications, and case studies.

References

Andersen, P., & Petersen, N. (1993). A procedure for ranking efficient units in data envelopment analysis. *Management Science, 39*, 1261–1264.

Banker, R. D., & Morey, R. C. (1986). Efficiency analysis for exogenously fixed inputs and outputs. *Operations Research, 34*(4), 513–521.

Nijkamp, P., & Suzuki, S. (2009). A generalized goals-achievement model in data envelopment analysis: An application to efficiency improvement in local government finance in Japan. *Spatial Economic Analysis, 4*(3), 249–274.

Seiford, L. M., & Zhu, J. (2003). Context-dependent data envelopment analysis -measuring attractiveness and progress. *Omega, 31*, 397.

Suzuki, S., & Nijkamp, P. (2011). A stepwise-projection data envelopment analysis for public transport operations in Japan. *Letters in Spatial and Resource Sciences, 4*(2), 139–156.

Suzuki, S., & Nijkamp, P. (2014). A stepwise efficiency improvement DEA model for airport management with a fixed runway capacity, Karlsruhe papers in economic policy research. *Volucella, 34*, 233–254.

Suzuki, S., & Nijkamp, P. (2016). An evaluation of energy-environment-economic efficiency for EU APEC and ASEAN countries: Design of a target-oriented DFM model with fixed factors in data envelopment analysis. *Energy Policy, 88*, 100–112.

Suzuki, S., Nijkamp, P., & Rietveld, P. (2011). Regional efficiency improvement by means of data envelopment analysis through Euclidean distance minimization including fixed input factors: An application to tourist regions in Italy. *Papers in Regional Science, 90*(1), 67–89.

Suzuki, S., Nijkamp, P., & Rietveld, P. (2015). A target-oriented data envelopment analysis for energy-environment efficiency improvement in Japan. *Energy Efficiency, 8*(3), 433–446.

Part II
Applications

Chapter 6
Performance Measurement of Local Government Finance in Japan: Combination of Goals-Achievement Model with a CCR Model

Abstract The aim of this chapter is to apply an extended DEA model – emerging from a blend of a distance friction minimization (DFM) and a Goals-Achievement (GA) approach on the basis of the Charnes-Cooper-Rhodes (CCR) method – in order to generate a more satisfactory efficiency-improvement projection model in conventional DEA. Another novelty of our approach is the introduction of prior goals set by a DMU by using a GA approach. The GA model specifies a goal value for efficiency improvement in a DFM model. The GA model can compute the input reduction value or the output increase value in order to achieve a prespecified goal value for the efficiency improvement in an optimal way. Next, using the integrated DFM-GA model, we are able to develop an operational efficiency-improvement projection that provides a clear, quantitative orientation for the actions of a DMU. The abovementioned DFM-GA model is illustrated empirically by using a data set of efficiency indicators for cities in Hokkaido prefecture in Japan, where the aim is to increase the efficiency of local government finance mechanisms in these cities, based on various input and output performance characteristics. In summary, this chapter presents a practical policy instrument that may have great added value for the decision making and planning tasks of both public and private actors.

Keywords Distance friction minimization • Goals-Achievement model • Data Envelopment Analysis (DEA) • Efficiency-improvement projection • Local government finance

6.1 Introduction

In recent years, the public sector has been under increasing pressure to increase its efficiency, through innovative strategies (see, e.g., Windrum and Koch 2008). To this end, it is necessary to use reliable and operational methods that can be used for benchmark and performance analysis. Data Envelopment Analysis (DEA) has become an established approach in the analysis of efficiency problems in both the public and the private sector. Worthington and Dollery (2000) have attempted to provide a concise overview of 27 empirical analyses of efficiency measurement in

S. Suzuki, P. Nijkamp, *Regional Performance Measurement and Improvement*, New Frontiers in Regional Science: Asian Perspectives 9,
DOI 10.1007/978-981-10-0242-7_6

local governments using DEA and similar methodologies, and these analyses were targeted on UK local authorities; Illinois, Minnesota, Ohio, and Wisconsin municipalities; Chinese cities; Swedish local social insurance offices; Californian municipalities; New Zealand territorial local authorities; etc. Similar applications were offered elsewhere by Borger and Kerstens (1996) that analyzed the efficiency of local governments in Belgium using DEA and three parametric frontiers (one deterministic and two stochastic). Finally, Afonso and Fernandes (2006) measured local government spending efficiency of Portuguese local governments in 2001 based on DEA. The large number of applied studies shows that efficiency analysis is an important but also intriguing topic.

We propose here a distance friction minimization (DFM) model in a DEA model that is based on a generalized distance friction function and serves to assist a DMU in improving its performance by an appropriate movement toward the efficiency frontier surface. This DFM approach aims to generate a new contribution to efficiency enhancement strategies by deploying a weighted projection function, and at the same time it may address both an input reduction and an output increase as a strategy of a DMU. A general efficiency-improvement projection model in combination with our DFM model is able to calculate either an input reduction value or an output increase value to reach an efficient score 1.000, although in reality this may be hard to achieve.

We introduce next an adjusted DEA model – emerging from a blend of a distance friction minimization (DFM) and a Goals-Achievement (GA) approach on the basis of the Charnes-Cooper-Rhodes (CCR) method – in order to generate a more appropriate efficiency-improvement projection model in conventional DEA, in Sect. 5.2.1 (see also Nijkamp and Suzuki 2009). The GA model specifies a Goal Improvement Rate (GIR) of the total efficiency gap in the framework of a DFM model. The GA model can compute an input reduction value or an output increase value in order to achieve a prior goal value for the efficiency improvement in an optimal way.

The abovementioned CCR-DFM-GA model will be empirically illustrated by using a data set of cities in Hokkaido prefecture in Japan, where the aim is to increase the efficiency of local government finance, based on various input and output performance characteristics of these cities. The relevance of our approach can be illustrated by referring to recent public financial deficits in Yubari city in Hokkaido prefecture, which was close to financial bankruptcy in March 2007. In particular, the White Paper on local public finance (Ministry of Internal Affairs and Communications 2007) has clearly illustrated that the issue of the public financial deficits of cities and prefectures is an urgent concern in Japan. This chapter thus aims to propose a policy instrument that may have great added value for the decision making and planning tasks of public finance actors.

Table 6.1 DMUs (Hokkaido prefecture's cities)

Group 1 (More than 50,000 population)			*Group 2 (Less than 50,000 population)*		
No.	*DMU*	*Population*	*No.*	*DMU*	*Population*
1	Asahikawa	355,004	1	Hokuto	48,056
2	Hakodate	294,264	2	Takikawa	45,562
3	Kushiro	190,478	3	Abashiri	42,045
4	Tomakomai	172,758	4	Wakkanai	41,592
5	Obihiro	170,580	5	Date	37,066
6	Otaru	142,161	6	Nayoro	31,628
7	Kitami	129,365	7	Nemuro	31,202
8	Ebetsu	125,601	8	Bibai	29,083
9	Muroran	98,372	9	Rumoi	26,826
10	Iwamizawa	93,677	10	Monbetsu	26,632
11	Chitose	91,437	11	Fukagawa	25,838
12	Eniwa	67,614	12	Furano	25,076
13	Kitahiroshima	60,677	13	Shibetsu	23,411
14	Ishikari	60,104	14	Sunagawa	20,068
15	Noboribetsu	53,135	15	Ashibetsu	18,899
	Sapporo	1,880,863	16	Akabira	14,401
			17	Yubari	13,001
			18	Mikasa	11,927
			19	Utashinai	5221

6.2 Analysis Framework and Database of Local Government Finance Efficiency in Hokkaido, Japan

In our empirical work, we use input and output data for a set of 34 cities (the capital Sapporo city – population 1,880,863 – was eliminated from our list of DMUs in order to avoid the extreme biased effects caused by scale differences) in Hokkaido prefecture in Japan. The cities (DMUs) used in our analysis are listed in Table 6.1. These cities were categorized, on the basis of their population size, into two groups: those with populations of more than 50,000 and those with populations of less than 50,000, in order to avoid biased effects caused by scale differences in government finance.

For our DEA, we use the following inputs and outputs:

Input:

(a) Number of municipal employees (in 2005)
(b) Expenditures by local government (in million yen) (with elimination of employment costs) (in 2005)
(c) Amount of outstanding city bonds (in million yen) (in 2005)

Output:

(d) Tax revenues by local government (in million yen) (in 2005)
(e) Public service level (in 2005)

Data on "(a) Number of municipal employees" were obtained from "The local authority regular data base 2005, Ministry of Internal Affairs and Communications, Japan." Data on "(b) Expenditures by local government" and "(c) Amount of outstanding city bonds," and "(d) Tax revenues by local government," were obtained from "The Municipality Accounting Card 2005, Ministry of Internal Affairs and Communications, Japan." Data on "(e) Public service level" were calculated by a standardized score method using six types of data, viz., "Number of elementary and junior high schools," "Number of community centres and libraries," "Road extensions (municipality road)," "Number of urban parks," "Number of care facilities for the elderly," and "Number of day-care centres for children," which were obtained from "Statistical observations of SHI, KU, MACHE, MURA 2005, Ministry of Internal Affairs and Communications, Japan."

In our application, we first applied the standard CCR model, and then the results of this analysis were used to determine the CCR-DFM and CCR-DFM-GA projections. The steps followed in our analysis are shown in Fig. 6.1.

In Sect. 6.3, we present the efficiency evaluation results based on the CCR model. Next, in Sect. 6.4, we present the optimum weights of input and output variables based on the CCR model. In Sect. 6.5, we present the efficiency-improvement projection results based on the CCR-DFM model and compare these with the CCR projections and outcomes. Finally, in Sect. 6.6, we present the efficiency-improvement projection results based on the CCR-DFM-GA model.

6.3 Performance Evaluation Based on CCR-I Model

The efficiency evaluation results for the 15 larger cities (more than 50,000 population) and the smaller 19 cities (less than 50,000 population) based on the CCR model are given in Figs. 6.2 and 6.3.

From Fig. 6.2, it can be seen that Tomakomai city, Obihiro city, Chitose city, Kitahiroshima city, and Ishikari city are efficiently operating cities. It should be noted that Tomakomai city and Ishikari city have a large-scale industrial area and a harbor, while Chitose city has the New Chitose International Airport. Obihiro city produces a high agricultural output, and well-known confectionary companies are also based in the city. And finally, Kitahiroshima city has many industrial complexes and printing factories.

On the other hand, Iwamizawa city has a low efficiency (i.e., an efficiency score around 50%) in terms of government finance. It is also clear that this city has in the past flourished on the basis of its coal production and its railway links, but most coal mines in Hokkaido were closed down after 1970s.

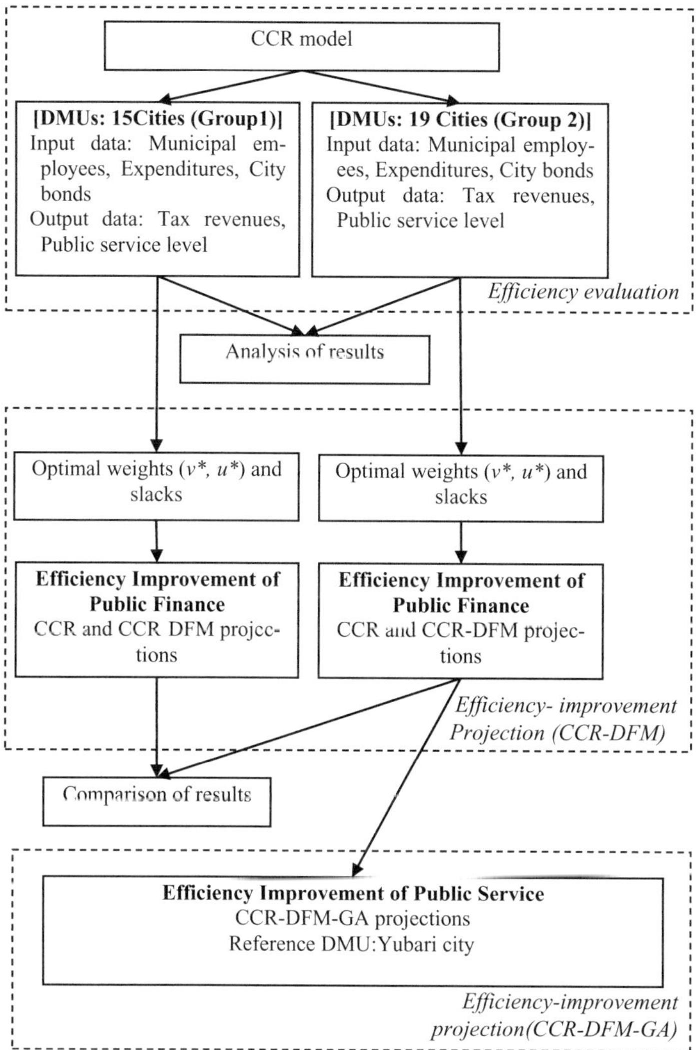

Fig. 6.1 Analysis framework

From Fig. 6.3, it can be seen that Hokuto city, Furano city, and Utashinai city are efficient. It is noteworthy that Hokuto city has promoted mergers of cities, towns, and villages, in order to improve the efficiency of the city administration. Furthermore, this city has a large-scale factory which is a subsidiary of a cement company in Japan. On the other hand, Yubari city and Bibai city are low-efficiency cities in terms of government finance. It is also noteworthy that these cities have flourished as former coal mining areas, but now they have been deprived from their main industry.

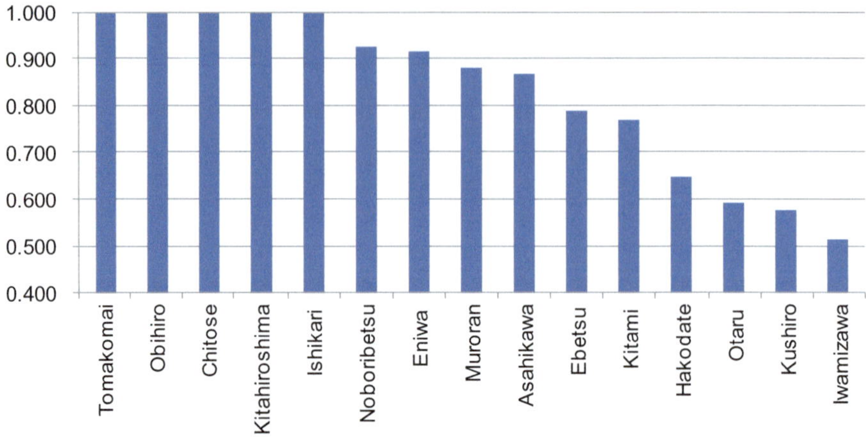

Fig. 6.2 Efficiency score based on the CCR model (15 larger cities: more than 50,000 population)

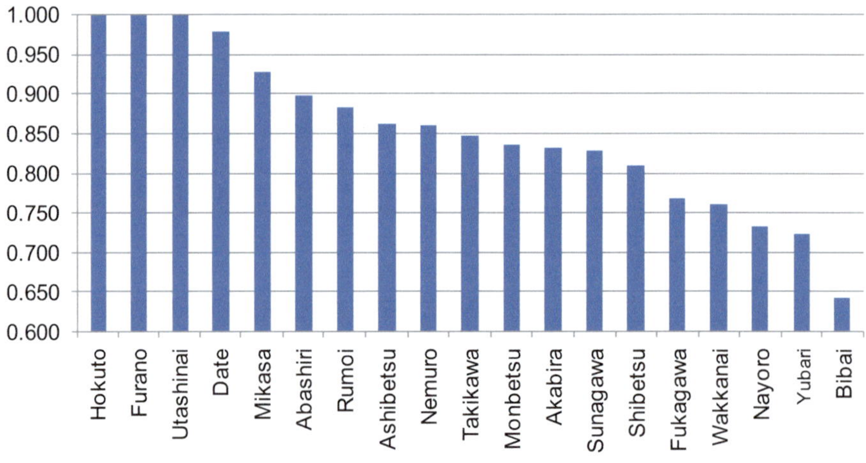

Fig. 6.3 Efficiency score based on CCR model (19 smaller cities: less than 50,000 population)

6.4 Optimum Weights of Input and Output Items

The optimum weights of the input and output variables for the 15 larger cities (more than 50,000 population) and the smaller19 cities (less than 50,000 population) based on the CCR model are given in Figs. 6.4, 6.5 and Figs. 6.6, 6.7, respectively.

It should be noted that (v^*, u^*) is the set of most favorable weights for each DMU, so that we can find the relative importance of each indicator with reference to the value of each $v_m^* \, x_{mo}$ and $u_s^* \, y_{so}$ for each DMU. From these results, it can be seen that, for instance, Eniwa city obtains a weight for municipal employees equal to 0.442 and for city bonds equal to 0.558 in its inputs, while it obtains for tax

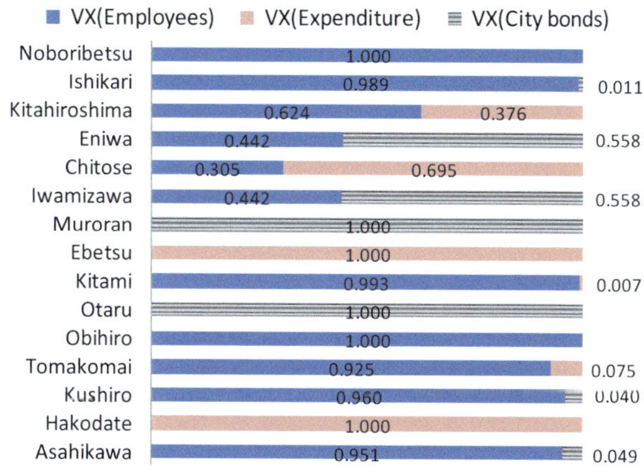

Fig. 6.4 Input optimum weights (15 larger cities)

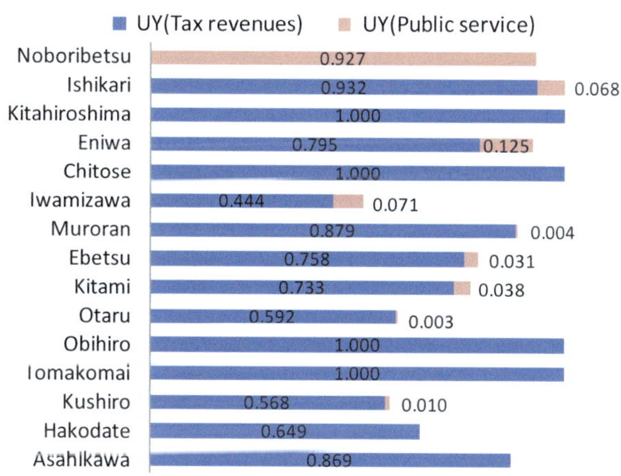

Fig. 6.5 Output optimum weights (15 larger cities)

revenues a weight of 0.795 and for public service levels 0.125 in its output. These results offer meaningful insights for policies on efficiency improvement of local government finance.

6.5 Performance Improvement Projection Based on CCR and CCR-DFM Model

The efficiency-improvement projection results based on the CCR and CCR-DFM model for inefficient cities (only non-slack type) are presented in Fig. 6.8.

In Fig. 6.8, it appears that the ratios of change in the CCR-DFM projection are smaller than those in the CCR projection, as was expected. In Fig. 6.8, this particularly applies to Kushiro, Kitami, Iwamizawa, Eniwa, and Bibai, which are non-slack type cities (i.e., s^{-**} and s^{+**} are zero). The CCR-DFM projection

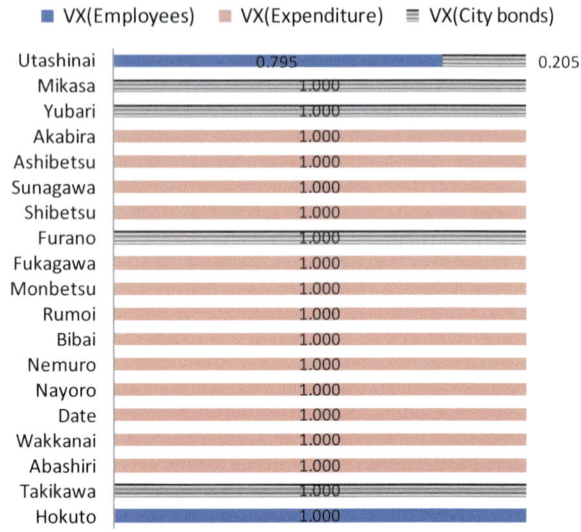

Fig. 6.6 Input optimum weights (19 smaller cities)

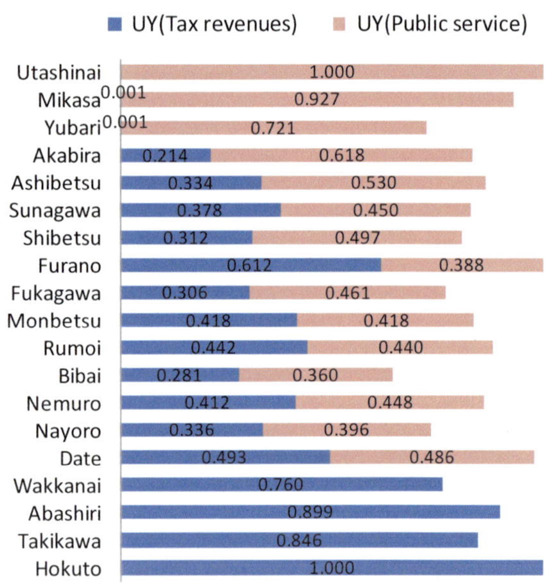

Fig. 6.7 Output optimum weights (19 smaller cities)

involves both input reduction and output increase, and, clearly, the CCR-DFM projection does not involve a uniform ratio because this model looks for the optimal input reduction (i.e., the shortest distance to the frontier or distance friction minimization). For instance, the CCR projection shows that Eniwa should reduce the urban employees and city bonds by 8.1% and its expenditures by 25.7% in order to become efficient. On the other hand, CCR-DFM results show that a reduction in city bonds of 7.5% and an increase in the tax revenues of 4.9% are required to

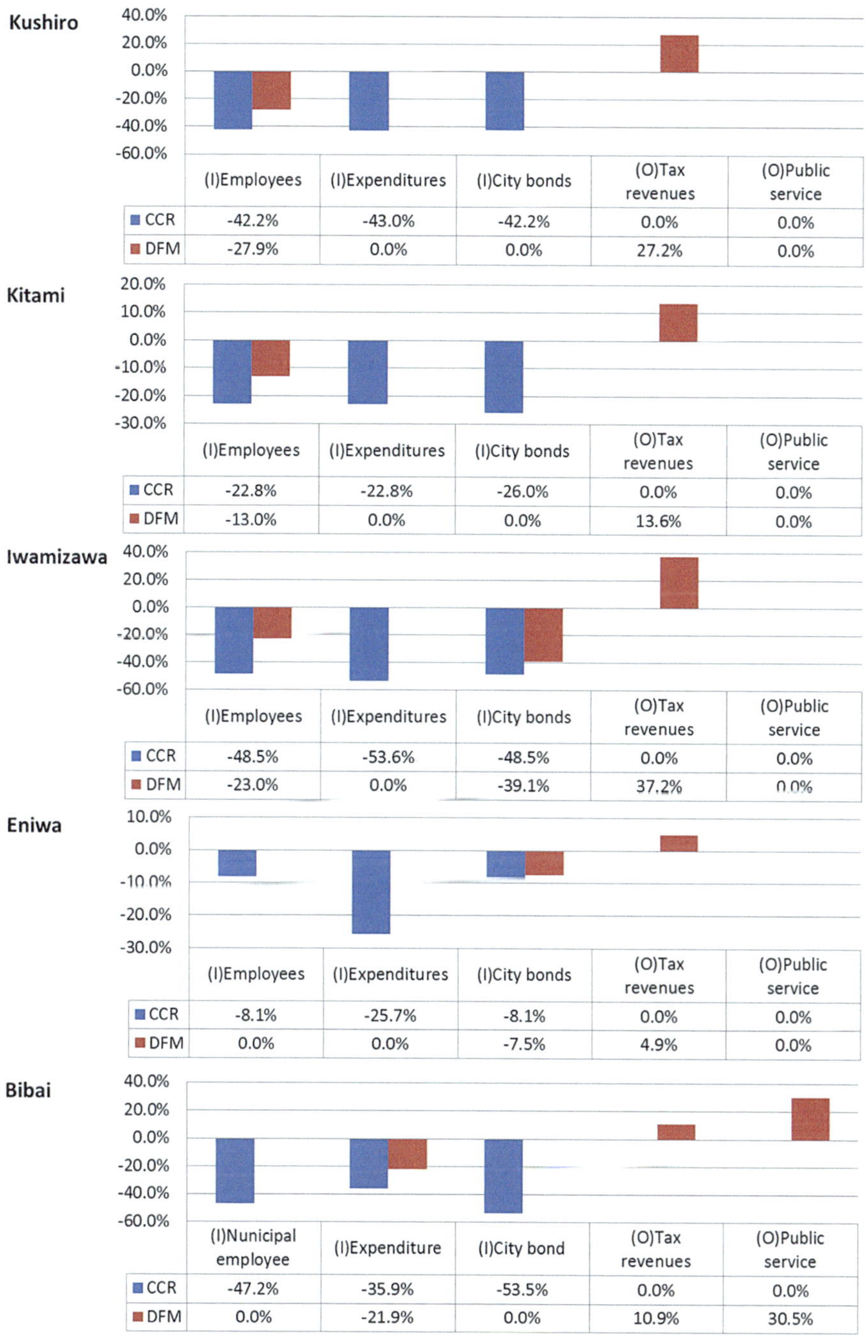

Kushiro

	(I)Employees	(I)Expenditures	(I)City bonds	(O)Tax revenues	(O)Public service
CCR	-42.2%	-43.0%	-42.2%	0.0%	0.0%
DFM	-27.9%	0.0%	0.0%	27.2%	0.0%

Kitami

	(I)Employees	(I)Expenditures	(I)City bonds	(O)Tax revenues	(O)Public service
CCR	-22.8%	-22.8%	-26.0%	0.0%	0.0%
DFM	-13.0%	0.0%	0.0%	13.6%	0.0%

Iwamizawa

	(I)Employees	(I)Expenditures	(I)City bonds	(O)Tax revenues	(O)Public service
CCR	-48.5%	-53.6%	-48.5%	0.0%	0.0%
DFM	-23.0%	0.0%	-39.1%	37.2%	0.0%

Eniwa

	(I)Employees	(I)Expenditures	(I)City bonds	(O)Tax revenues	(O)Public service
CCR	-8.1%	-25.7%	-8.1%	0.0%	0.0%
DFM	0.0%	0.0%	-7.5%	4.9%	0.0%

Bibai

	(I)Nunicipal employee	(I)Expenditure	(I)City bond	(O)Tax revenues	(O)Public service
CCR	-47.2%	-35.9%	-53.5%	0.0%	0.0%
DFM	0.0%	-21.9%	0.0%	10.9%	30.5%

Fig. 6.8 Efficiency-improvement projection results of the CCR and the CCR-DFM model (more than 50,000 population cities)

become efficient. Apart from the practicality of such a solution, the models show clearly that a different and a perhaps more efficient solution is available than the standard CCR projection to reach the efficiency frontier.

6.6 Performance Improvement Projection Based on Goals-Achievement DFM Model

We will now provide a comprehensive picture of the results of our integrated CCR-DFM-GA model and use Yubari city as a reference (target) city. It should be noted that Yubari city was in a state of financial crisis in March 2007. Now, however, this city has a local government that is responsible for a financial reconstruction, and hence it has put local public finance on the road to recovery. But the city does not have resources to achieve a full efficiency improvement, as shown in Table 6.2.

In this subsection, we will use as an inefficient reference city (DMU) Yubari city and present a stepwise efficiency-improvement projection result based on the CCR-DFM-GA model so as to assess its consequences for various relevant policy variables. We assume that the GIR uses steps from 0.0 to 1.0 at intervals of 0.1. Next, the efficiency scores and the input reduction values and the output increase values based on the CCR-DFM-GA model are calculated in Tables 6.3 and 6.9. This table shows the extent to which the city under consideration is able to improve its current financial-economic performance, given the a priori fixed goal improvement ambition. The results follow a rather smooth pattern; a jump only occurs at the extreme margin of GIR = 1, especially if one considers the difference between weak efficiency (WE) and full efficiency (FE) as a result of the introduction of slacks.

The findings from Table 6.3 and Fig. 6.9 illustrate, for instance, that if the city wishes to implement an efficiency-improvement plan with a GIR amounting to 0.5 (i.e., 50% of the total efficiency gap), only a reduction in the city bonds of 8.1% and an increase in public services of 8.1% are required, while then the efficiency score improves from 0.722 to 0.849. However, if a financial plan with a GIR of 1.0 under weak efficiency conditions (i.e., 100% of the total efficiency gap, $\theta^* = 1$) is to be implemented, a reduction in the bonds of 16.2% and an increase in public services of 16.2% are required, and then the efficiency score improves from 0.722 to 1.000. It should be noted that the results of a plan with a GIR of 1.0 under full efficiency conditions (i.e., $\theta^* = 1$, and all slacks are zero) are in agreement with the results of our CCR-DFM model in Table 6.2. Yubari city in Japan is clearly to be treated as an input-slack type of city (i.e., s^{-**} is not zero). If a new plan with a GIR of 1.0 (with full efficiency) is to be implemented in this case, it would have to incorporate both a slack of employees (−108.4) and a slack of expenditures (−2590.6).

These results offer a meaningful contribution to decision support and planning for the efficiency improvement of local government finance. And this generalized DEA model may thus become a policy instrument that may have great added value for decision making and planning of both public and private actors.

Table 6.2 Efficiency-improvement projection results of the CCR and the CCR-DFM model (Yubari city)

DMU: Yubari		CCR-I model Score(θ*)			DFM model Score(θ**)				
							Projection	Difference	%
					d_{mo}^{x*}	$-s^{-**}$	x_{mo}^{**}	$-d_{mo}^{x*} - s^{-**}$	
I/O	Data	Projection	Difference	%	d_{so}^{y*}	s^{+**}	y_{so}^{**}	$d_{so}^{y*} + s^{+**}$	
		0.722			1.000				
(I) Municipal employee	406	259.1	−146.9	−36.2	0.0	−108.4	297.6	−108.4	−26.7
(I) Expenditure	10183.9	6775.0	−3408.9	−33.5	0.0	−2590.6	7593.3	−2590.6	−25.4
(I) City bond	14873.9	10737.6	−4136.3	−27.8	−2402.2	0.0	12471.7	−2402.2	−16.2
(O) Tax revenues	946.7	946.7	0.0	0.0	0.0	0.0	946.7	0.0	0.0
(O) Public service	45	45.0	0.0	0.0	7.3	0.0	52.3	7.3	16.2

Table 6.3 Efficiency-improvement projection results based on the CCR-DFM-GA model (Yubari city)

GIR	Score	s^{-**} *(employees)*	s^{-**} *(expenditures)*	d_x *(city bonds)*	d_y *(public services)*	Employees (%)	Expenditures (%)	City bonds (%)	Public services (%)
0.0	0.722	0	0.0	0.0	0.0	0.0	0.0	0.0	0.0
0.1	0.746	0	0.0	−240.2	0.7	0.0	0.0	−1.6	1.6
0.2	0.770	0	0.0	−480.4	1.5	0.0	0.0	−3.2	3.2
0.3	0.795	0	0.0	−720.7	2.2	0.0	0.0	−4.8	4.8
0.4	0.822	0	0.0	−960.9	2.9	0.0	0.0	−6.5	6.5
0.5	0.849	0	0.0	−1201.1	3.6	0.0	0.0	−8.1	8.1
0.6	0.877	0	0.0	−1441.3	4.4	0.0	0.0	−9.7	9.7
0.7	0.906	0	0.0	−1681.5	5.1	0.0	0.0	−11.3	11.3
0.8	0.936	0	0.0	−1921.7	5.8	0.0	0.0	−12.9	12.9
0.9	0.967	0	0.0	−2162.0	6.5	0.0	0.0	−14.5	14.5
1.0(WE)	1.000	0	0.0	−2402.2	7.3	0.0	0.0	−16.2	16.2
1.0(FE)	1.000	−108.438	−2590.643	−2402.2	7.3	−26.7	−25.4	−16.2	16.2

Legend: *WE* weak efficiency, *FE* full efficiency

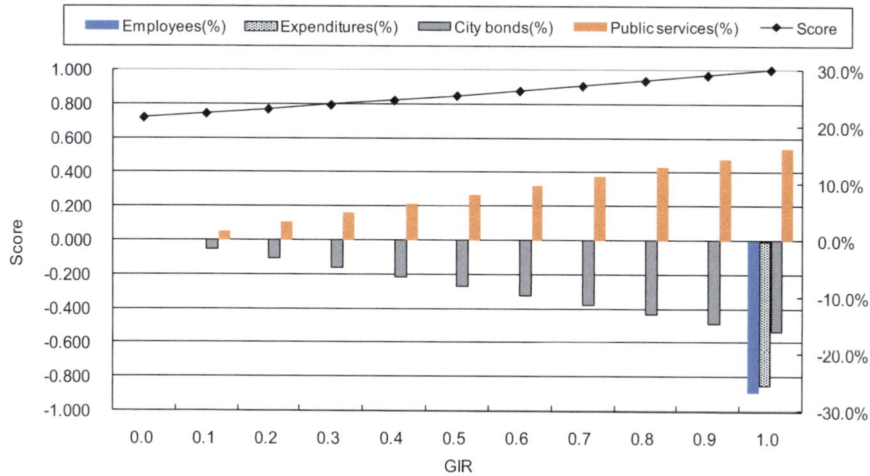

Fig. 6.9 Efficiency-improvement projection results based on the CCR-DFM-GA model (Yubari city)

6.7 Conclusion

Nonparametric models of the DEA type have proven to be very useful tools for improving the efficiency of corporate organizations on the basis of various relevant strategic input and output variables. In this chapter we have presented a new methodology for finance authorities in an inefficient city to reach the efficiency frontier and to achieve the prior goal set by a DMU. This new methodology does not require a uniform reduction of all inputs, as in the standard model. Instead, the new method minimizes the distance friction for each input and output separately. As a result, the reductions in inputs and increases in outputs necessary to reach the efficiency frontier are smaller than in the standard model. This offers more flexibility for management of an organization. In addition, the introduction of a Goals-Achievement method allows DMUs to include various levels of ambition regarding the ultimate performance in their strategic judgment. In conclusion, our CCR-DFM-GA model is able to present a more realistic efficiency-improvement plan and may thus provide a meaningful contribution to decision making and planning for efficiency improvement of relevant agents.

References

Afonso, A., & Fernandes, S. (2006). Measuring local government spending efficiency: Evidence for the Lisbon region. *Regional Studies, 40*(1), 39–53.

Borger, B., & Kerstens, K. (1996). Cost efficiency of Belgian local governments: A comparative analysis of FDH, DEA, and econometric approaches. *Regional Science and Urban Economics, 26*(2), 145–170.

Ministry of Internal Affairs and Communications, White Paper on local Public Finance. 2007. National Printing Center, 2007.
Nijkamp, P., & Suzuki, S. (2009). A generalized goals-achievement model in data envelopment analysis: An application to efficiency improvement in local government finance in Japan. *Spatial Economic Analysis, 4*(3), 249–274.
Windrum, P., & Koch, P. (Eds.). (2008). *Innovation in public sector services*. Cheltenham: Edward Elgar.
Worthington, A., & Dollery, B.. (2000). *Efficiency measurement in the local public sector: Econometric and mathematical programming Frontier techniques* (School of Economics and Finance Discussion Papers and Working Papers series from School of Economics and Finance, Queensland University of Technology, No. 78).

Chapter 7
Performance Measurement of Public Transport Operation in Japan: Combination of Stepwise Improvement Model with CCR Model

Abstract Tightening public expenditure budgets prompts the need for a careful analysis of the performance of public bodies in terms of an efficient execution of their tasks. A standard tool to judge the efficiency of such organizations is data envelopment analysis (DEA). In the past years, much progress has been made to extend this approach into various directions. Examples are the distance friction minimization (DFM) model and the context-dependent (CD) model. The DFM model is based on a generalized distance friction function and serves to improve the performance of a decision making unit (DMU) by identifying the most appropriate movement toward the efficiency frontier surface. Likewise, the CD model yields efficient frontiers in different levels, while it is based on a level-by-level improvement projection. The present chapter will offer an integrated DEA tool – emerging from a blend of the DFM and CD model – in order to design a balanced stepwise efficiency-improvement projection model for a conventional DEA. The abovementioned stepwise-projection model is illustrated on the basis of an application to the efficiency analysis of public transport operations in Japan.

Keywords Data envelopment analysis (DEA) • Distance friction minimization • Context-dependent • Stepwise projection • Public transport operations

7.1 Introduction

With tightening budgets and increasingly critical reviews of public expenditure, there is a need for a careful analysis of the performance of public bodies in terms of an efficient execution of their tasks. These questions show up everywhere in the public domain, for instance, in the provision of medical facilities, the operation of postal services, or the supply of public transport. Data envelopment analysis (DEA) has become an established approach in the analysis of efficiency problems in both the public and the private sector. The need for a critical efficiency judgment of public agencies may also stem from exogenous circumstances; for example, the rapid aging process in Japan calls for a careful analysis of the performance of public transport facilities.

S. Suzuki, P. Nijkamp, *Regional Performance Measurement and Improvement*, New Frontiers in Regional Science: Asian Perspectives 9,
DOI 10.1007/978-981-10-0242-7_7

In this framework, various empirical studies have been undertaken. Kerstens (1996) evaluated the performance of a sample of French urban transit companies using a data envelopment analysis (DEA) and a Free Disposal Hull (FDH) model. Pina and Torres (2001) compared the efficiency of public and private sectors in the provision of urban transportation services in Spain based on DEA. Karlaftis (2004) evaluated the efficiency and effectiveness of 256 US urban transit systems over a 5-year period using DEA. Piacenza (2006) investigated the way subsidization mechanisms affect the cost-efficiency of public transit systems based on DEA and applied this on a 7-year panel of 44 Italian transit companies. And Hirschhausena and Cullmannc (2010) presented a nonparametric comparative efficiency analysis of 179 communal public transport bus companies in Germany (1990–2004) based on DEA. This large number of studies shows that efficiency analysis is an increasingly popular tool in the public sector.

We propose here a distance friction minimization (DFM) model in a DEA model that is based on a generalized distance friction function and serves to assist a DMU in improving its performance by an appropriate movement toward the efficiency frontier surface. This DFM approach aims to generate a new contribution to efficiency enhancement strategies by deploying a weighted projection function, and at the same time it may address both input reduction and output increase as a strategy of a DMU. A general efficiency-improvement projection model including a DFM model is able to calculate either an optimal input reduction value or an output increase value to reach a full efficiency score of 1, even though in reality this may be hard to achieve. For example, it may be nearly impossible for one single regional city public transport system (e.g., Kyoto transportation authorities) to completely attain a maximum efficiency with one metropolitan private transport company (e.g., Tokyo Metro). It is therefore meaningful to develop a more practical and feasible efficiency-improvement projection model, especially based on the DFM model.

It is noteworthy that Seiford and Zhu (2003) have developed a gradual improvement model for an inefficient DMU. This "context-dependent (CD)" DEA has an important merit, as it aims to reach a stepwise improvement through successive levels toward the efficiency frontier.

We introduce now an adjusted DEA model – emerging from a blend of the DFM and CD model – namely, a Stepwise Improvement model, in Sect. 5.2.2 (see also Suzuki and Nijkamp (2011)). This model can provide a stepwise efficiency-improvement projection to provide more practical and feasible solutions for realistic circumstances and requirements in an efficiency-improvement projection. The abovementioned stepwise-projection model is applied to a performance analysis in the context of an efficiency-improvement plan for public transport operations in Japan.

Table 7.1 A listing of DMUs

No	Major private railway companies	No	Urban transportation authorities
1	Tobu	1	Sapporo
2	Seibu	2	Sendai
3	Keisei	3	Tokyo
4	Keio	4	Yokohama
5	Odakyu	5	Nagoya
6	Tokyu	6	Kyoto
7	Keikyu	7	Osaka
8	Sotetsu	8	Kobe
9	Meitetsu	9	Fukuoka
10	Kintetsu		
11	Nankai		
12	Keihan		
13	Hankyu		
14	Hanshin		
15	Nishitetsu		
16	Tokyo Metro		

7.2 Analysis Framework and Database of Public Transport Efficiency Management in Japan

The Stepwise Improvement model offers many opportunities for a critical comparative judgment of the performance of corporate organizations in both the public and private sector. As an empirical illustration, we will offer here a benchmark analysis of the efficiency achievements of Japanese public transport companies. In our empirical work, we use input and output data for a set of nine urban transportation authorities and 16 major private railway companies in Japan. The DMUs used in our analysis are listed in Table 7.1.

In this chapter, we use the following inputs and outputs:

Input:

(I) Operating cost (in 2007)

(I) Railway business property (in 2007)

Output:

(O) Operating revenues (in 2007)

All data were obtained from the "Railway annual statement 2007."

In our application, we first applied the standard CCR model, while next the results were used to determine the CCR and DFM projections. Additionally, we applied the CD model, and then the results were used to determine the CD and Stepwise Improvement projections. Finally, these various results were mutually compared. The steps followed in our analysis are shown in Fig. 7.1.

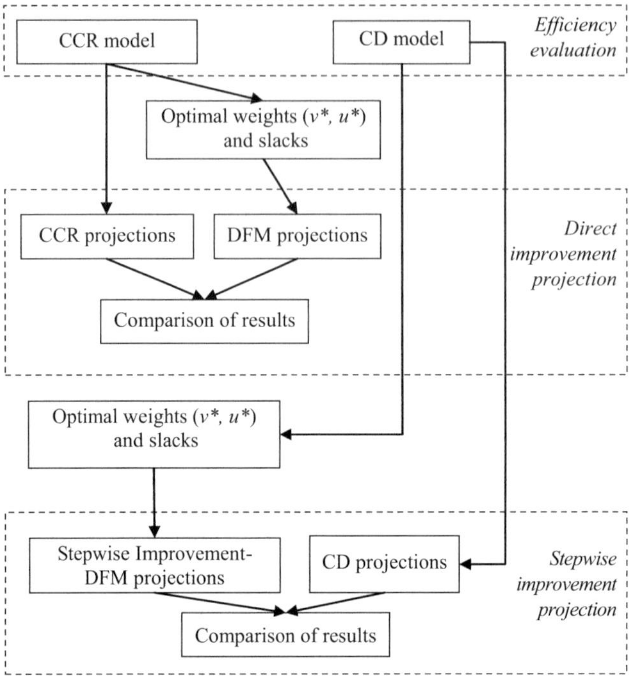

Fig. 7.1 Analysis framework of the Stepwise Improvement model

7.3 Performance Evaluation Based on the CCR Model

The efficiency evaluation results for the 25 public transport corporations based on the CCR model are given in Fig. 7.2. From Fig. 7.2, it can be seen that Keio and Tokyo Metro are efficiently operating firms. On the other hand, Kyoto has a low efficiency (i.e., an efficiency score around 50%). Furthermore, Kobe and Fukuoka also have a low efficiency.

It is noteworthy that the average efficiency level of urban transportation authorities is relatively low compared to major private railway companies. It seems thus plausible that apparently transportation authorities have still much room for further efficiently enhancing strategies.

7.4 Optimum Weights of Input and Output Items

The optimum weights of the input and output variables for the 25 public transport corporations based on the CCR model are given in Figs. 7.3 and 7.4, respectively.

It should be noted that (v^*, u^*) is the set of most favorable weights for each DMU, so that we can find the relative importance of each indicator with reference to

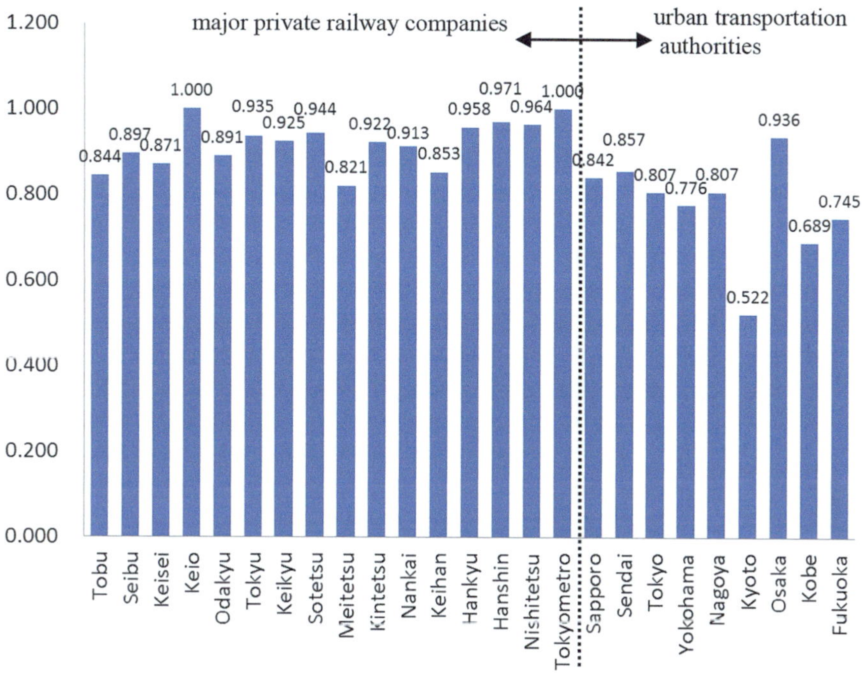

Fig. 7.2 Efficiency scores based on the CCR model

the value of each $v_m^* x_{mo}$ and $u_s^* y_{so}$ for each DMU. From these results, it can be seen that, for instance, Tokyu obtains a weight for operating cost equal to 0.455 and for railway business property equal to 0.545 in its inputs, while it obtains for operating revenues a weight of 0.935 in its output. These results offer meaningful insights for policies on efficiency improvement of public transport operation.

7.5 Performance Improvement Projection Based on CCR and DFM Model

The direct efficiency-improvement projection results based on the CCR and DFM model for inefficient public transport corporations (only of a non-slack type) are presented in Fig. 7.5.

In Fig. 7.5, it appears that the empirical ratios of change in the DFM projection are smaller than those in the CCR projection, as was to be expected. In Fig. 7.5, this applies particularly to Seibu, Tokyu, Keikyu, Hanshin, and Nishitetsu, which are apparently non-slack type (i.e., s^{-**} and s^{+**} are zero) corporations. The DFM projection involves both an input reduction and an output increase, and, clearly, the DFM projection does not involve a uniform ratio, because this model looks for

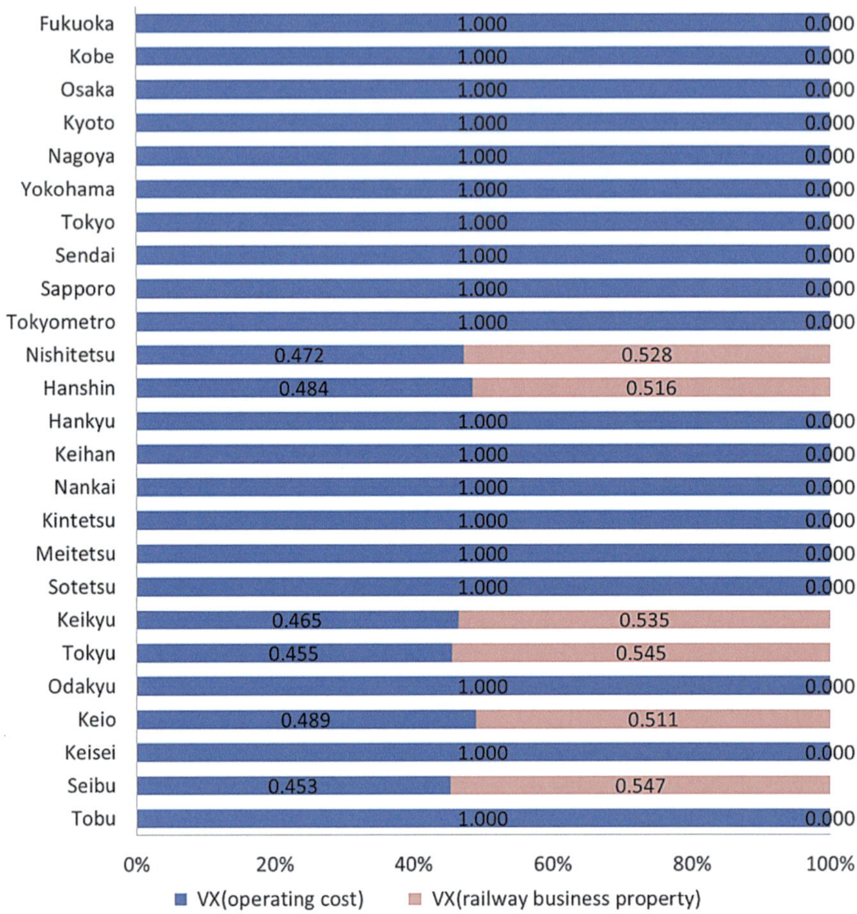

Fig. 7.3 Input optimum weights

the optimal input reduction (i.e., the shortest distance to the frontier, or distance friction minimization). For instance, the CCR projection shows that Seibu in Fig. 7.5 should reduce the operating cost and the railway business property by 10.34% in order to become efficient. On the other hand, the DFM results show that a reduction in railway business property of 9.96% and an increase in the operating revenues of 5.45% are required to become efficient. Apart from the practicality of such a solution, the models show clearly that a different – and perhaps more effective – solution is available than the standard CCR projection to reach the efficiency frontier.

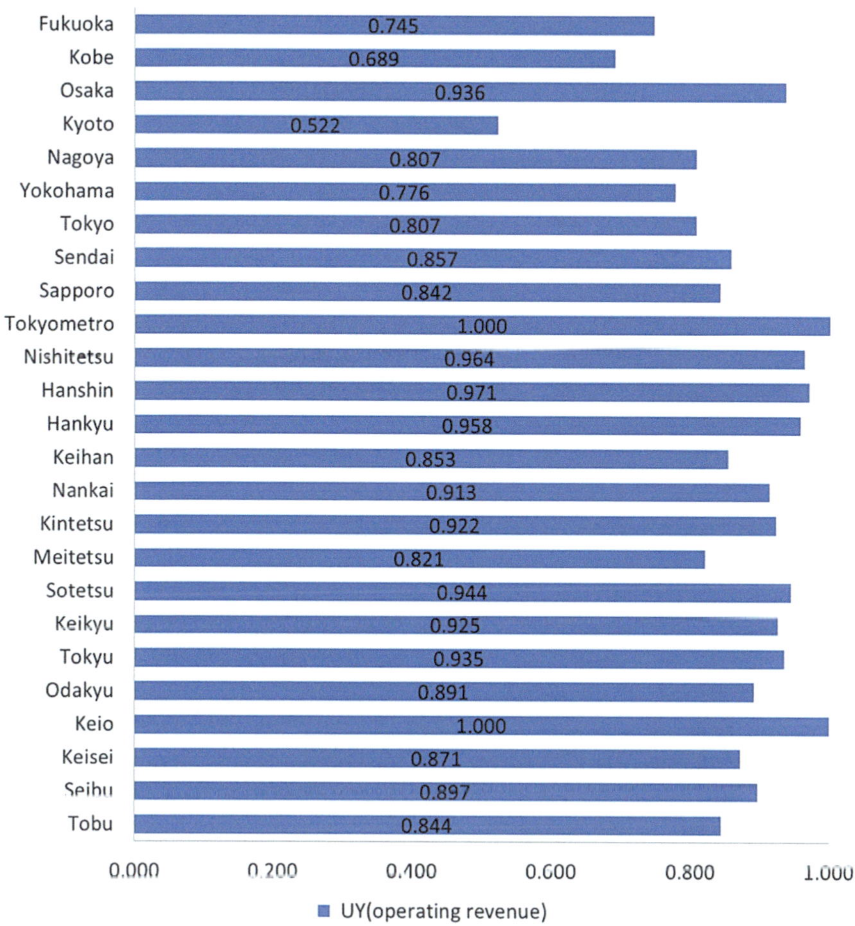

Fig. 7.4 Output optimum weights

7.6 Performance Improvement Projection Based on Stepwise Improvement Model

The efficiency-improvement projection results for the nearest upper level efficient frontier based on the CD and Stepwise Improvement model for inefficient public transport corporation (only of a non-slack type) are presented in Figs. 7.6, 7.7, and 7.8.

It appears that the ratios of change in the Stepwise Improvement projection are smaller than those in the CD projection, as was expected. In Figs. 7.6, 7.7, and 7.8, this particularly applies to Tobu, Seibu, Keisei, Odakyu, Tokyu, Keikyu, Meitetsu, Nankai, Keihan, Hanshin, Nishitetsu, Sapporo, Nagoya, and Kyoto, which are non-slack type (i.e., s^{-**} and s^{+**} are zero) corporations. Again, the

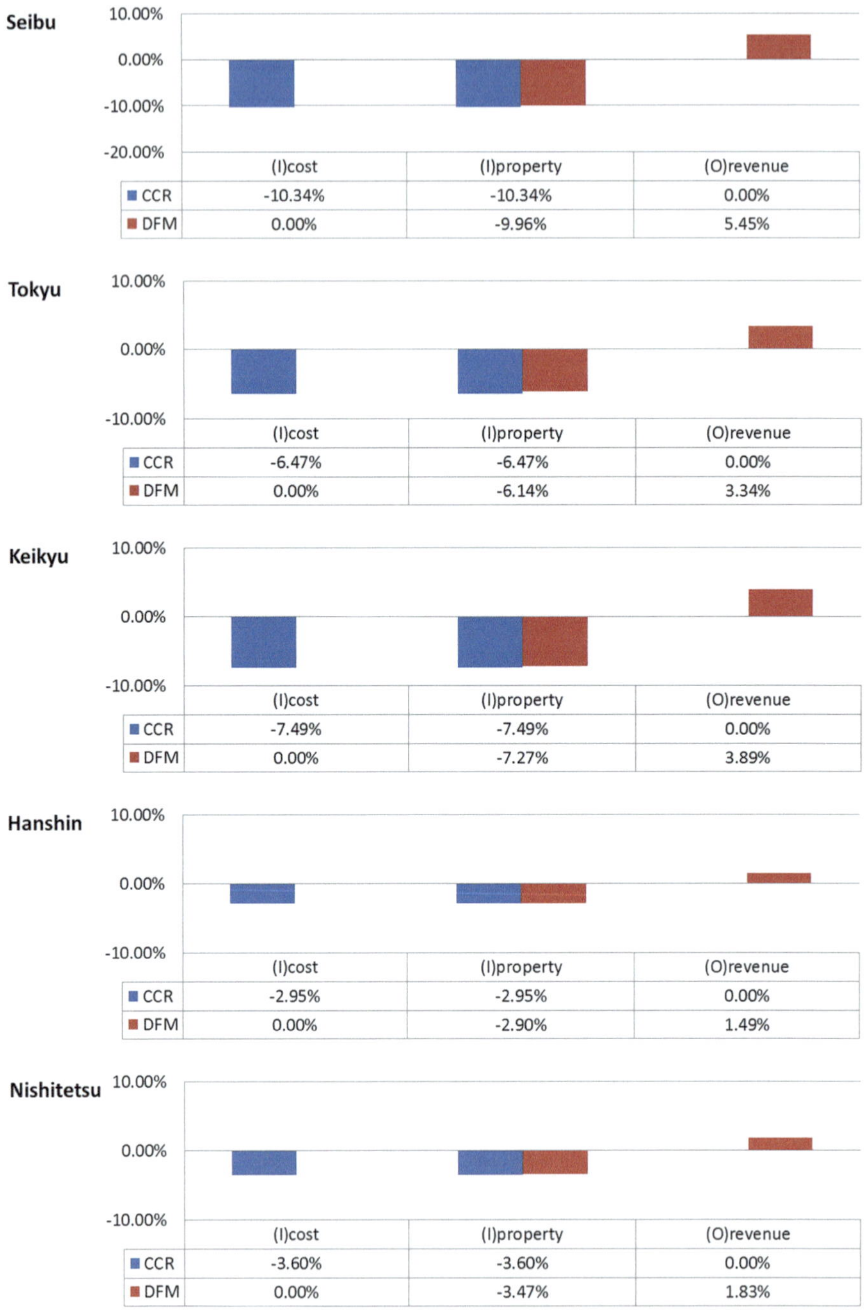

Fig. 7.5 Direct efficiency-improvement projection results of the CCR and DFM model

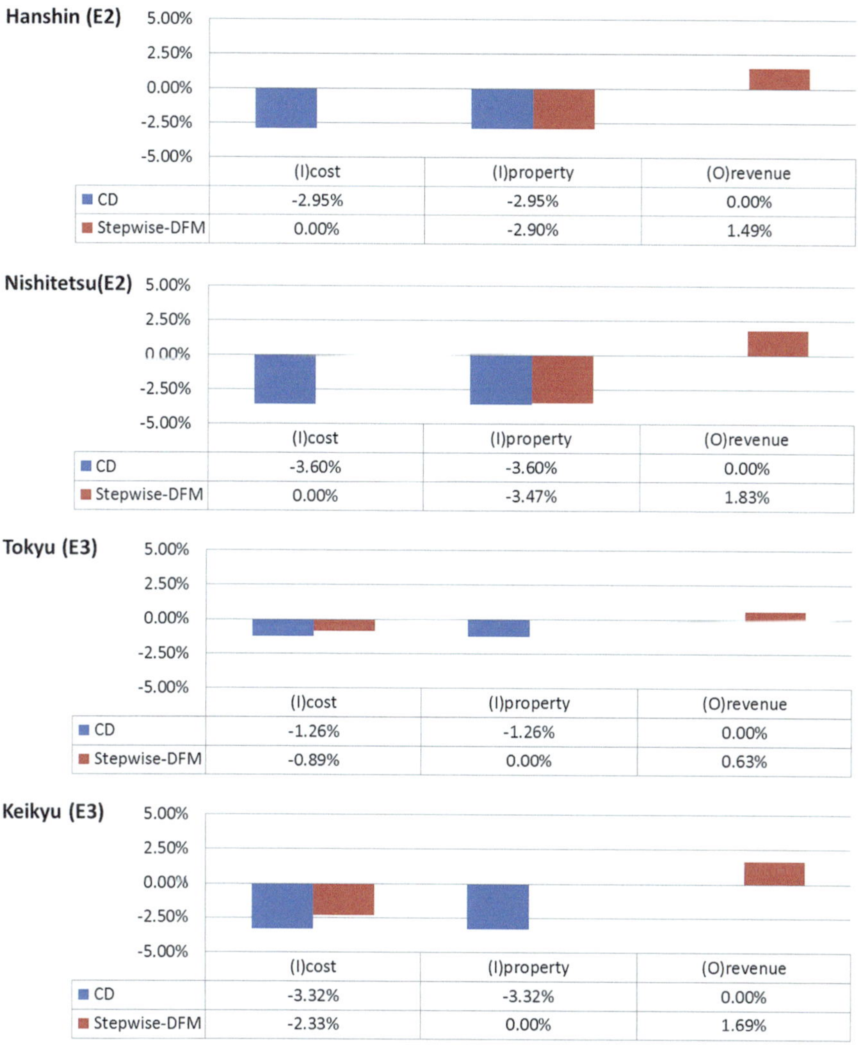

Fig. 7.6 Efficiency-improvement projection results for nearest upper level efficient frontier (E2–E3)

results of our model applications show clearly that a different – and perhaps more effective – solution may exist than the CD projection.

The Stepwise Improvement model appears to be able to present a more realistic efficiency-improvement plan, if we compare the results of Figs. 7.5, 7.6, and 7.7. For instance, the DFM results in Fig. 7.5 show that Keikyu should reduce the railway business property by 7.27% and an increase in the operating revenues of 3.89% in order to become efficient. On the other hand, the Stepwise Improvement results in Fig. 7.6 show that a reduction in operating cost of 2.33% and an

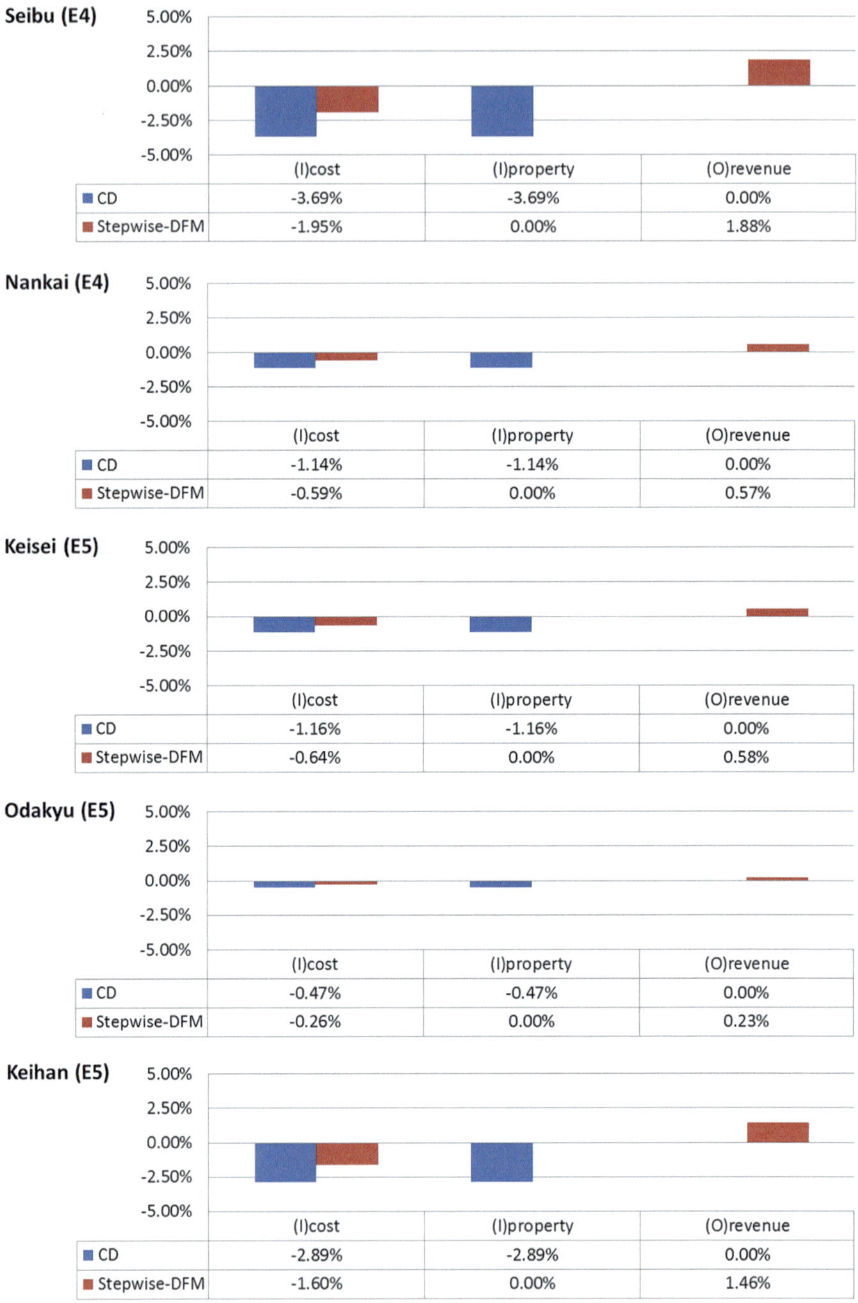

Seibu (E4)

	(I)cost	(I)property	(O)revenue
CD	-3.69%	-3.69%	0.00%
Stepwise-DFM	-1.95%	0.00%	1.88%

Nankai (E4)

	(I)cost	(I)property	(O)revenue
CD	-1.14%	-1.14%	0.00%
Stepwise-DFM	-0.59%	0.00%	0.57%

Keisei (E5)

	(I)cost	(I)property	(O)revenue
CD	-1.16%	-1.16%	0.00%
Stepwise-DFM	-0.64%	0.00%	0.58%

Odakyu (E5)

	(I)cost	(I)property	(O)revenue
CD	-0.47%	-0.47%	0.00%
Stepwise-DFM	-0.26%	0.00%	0.23%

Keihan (E5)

	(I)cost	(I)property	(O)revenue
CD	-2.89%	-2.89%	0.00%
Stepwise-DFM	-1.60%	0.00%	1.46%

Fig. 7.7 Efficiency-improvement projection results for nearest upper level efficient frontier (E4–E5)

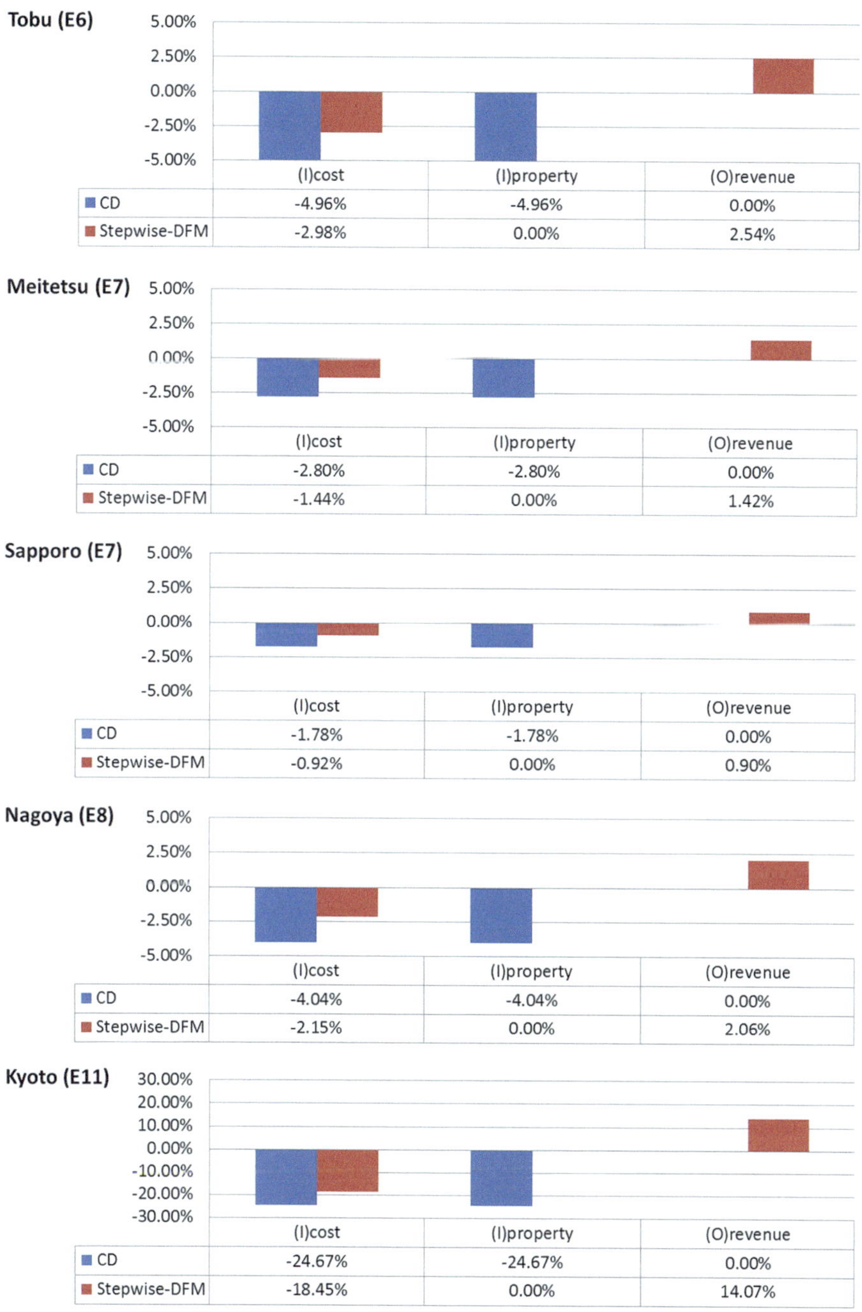

Fig. 7.8 Efficiency-improvement projection results for nearest upper level efficient frontier (E6–E11)

Table 7.2 Stepwise efficiency-improvement projection results for all level efficient frontier of Kyoto city

E-level		CD projection		Stepwise Improvement projection	
Score(θ*)	I/O	Difference	%	Difference	%
E1	(I)cost	−13,998,476	−47.82	−9,198,802	−31.43
0.522	(I)property	−431,710,412	−87.32	−412,015,460	−83.34
	(O)revenue	0	0.00	6,661,296	31.43
E2	(I)cost	−13,326,909	−45.53	−8,627,426	−29.47
0.545	(I)property	−409,592,737	−82.85	−384,602,214	−77.79
	(O)revenue	0	0.00	6,247,535	29.47
E3	(I)cost	−12,948,516	−44.24	−8,312,900	−28.40
0.558	(I)property	−320,952,550	−64.92	−271,699,932	−54.96
	(O)revenue	0	0.00	6,019,771	28.40
E4	(I)cost	−12,545,714	−42.86	−7,983,770	−27.27
0.571	(I)property	−388,368,792	−78.56	−359,453,901	−72.71
	(O)revenue	0	0.00	5,781,433	27.27
E5	(I)cost	−12,129,096	−41.44	−7,649,361	−26.13
0.586	(I)property	−403,618,629	−81.64	−379,900,020	−76.84
	(O)revenue	0	0.00	5,539,271	26.13
E6	(I)cost	−11,451,338	−39.12	−7,117,985	−24.32
0.609	(I)property	−264,143,086	−53.43	−208,155,744	−42.10
	(O)revenue	0	0.00	5,154,476	24.32
E7	(I)cost	−11,122,601	−38.00	−6,865,719	−23.46
0.620	(I)property	−262,795,274	−53.16	−208,476,027	−42.17
	(O)revenue	0	0.00	4,971,798	23.46
E8	(I)cost	−10,355,907	−35.38	−6,290,748	−21.49
0.646	(I)property	−253,569,768	−51.29	−201,816,843	−40.82
	(O)revenue	0	0.00	4,555,434	21.49
E9	(I)cost	−10,343,244	−35.34	−6,281,405	−21.46
0.647	(I)property	−208,797,137	−42.23	−147,513,278	−29.84
	(O)revenue	0	0.00	4,548,668	21.46
E10	(I)cost	−7,222,361	−24.67	−5,399,466	−18.45
0.753	(I)property	−121,982,117	−24.67	0	0.00
	(O)revenue	0	0.00	2,983,043	14.07

increase in the operating revenues of 1.69% are required to become efficient. The Stepwise Improvement model provides the policy decision maker with more flexible, practical, and transparent solutions that are available in the DFM projection to reach the nearest upper level efficiency frontier.

Finally, the stepwise efficiency-improvement projection results for all level efficient frontiers of Kyoto (lowest efficiency level DMU; E11) based on the CD and Stepwise Improvement model are presented in Table 7.2, while a comparative result of the Stepwise Improvement model for Kyoto is presented in Fig. 7.9.

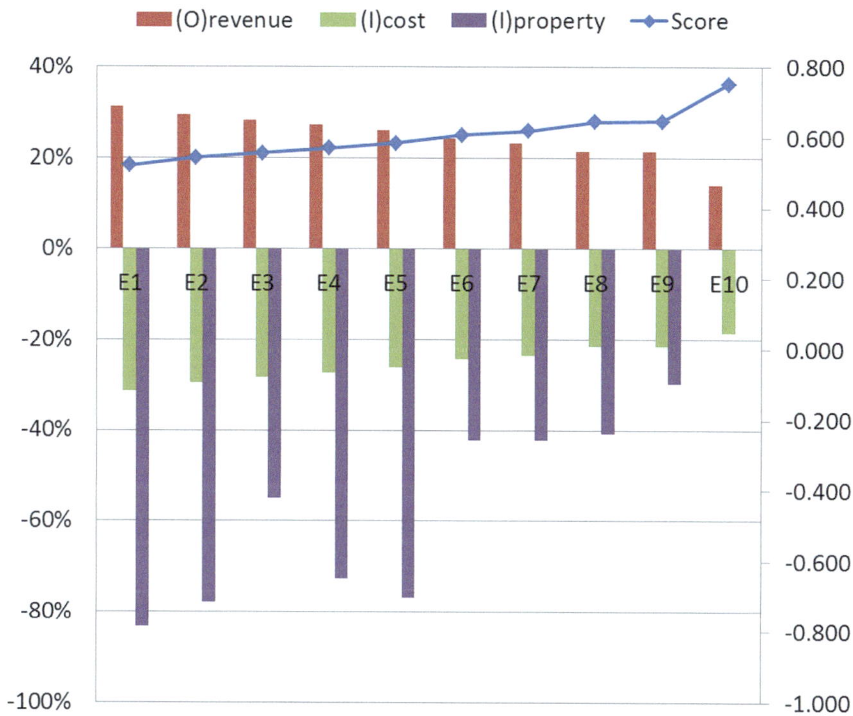

Fig. 7.9 Efficiency-improvement projection results based on the Stepwise Improvement model (Kyoto)

The findings from Fig. 7.9 illustrate, for instance, that, if Kyoto City wishes to implement an efficiency-improvement plan with a E10 level, only a reduction in the operating cost of 18.45% and an increase in operating revenue of 14.07% are required, while then the efficiency level rises to the E10 level efficient frontier.

These results offer a meaningful contribution to decision support and planning for the efficiency improvement of public transport operations. In conclusion, this Stepwise Improvement model may become a policy vehicle that may have great added value for decision making and planning of both public and private sectors.

7.7 Conclusion

In this chapter, we have presented a new methodology, the Stepwise Improvement model, which is integrated with a DFM and CD model. This new methodology does not require a uniform reduction of all inputs, as in the standard model. Instead, the new method minimizes the distance friction for each input and output separately. As a result, the reductions in inputs and increases in outputs do necessarily reach an efficiency frontier that is smaller than in the standard model. This offers more flexibility for the operational management of an organization. In addition, the Stepwise Improvement projection allows DMUs to include various levels of ambition regarding the ultimate performance in their strategic judgment. In conclusion, our Stepwise Improvement model is able to present a more realistic efficiency-improvement plan and may thus provide a meaningful contribution to decision making and planning for efficiency improvement of relevant agents.

References

Hirschhausena, C., & Cullmannc, A. (2010). A nonparametric efficiency analysis of German public transport companies. *Transportation Research Part E, 46*(3), 436–445.

Karlaftis, M. (2004). A DEA approach for evaluating the efficiency and effectiveness of urban transit systems. *European Journal of Operational Research, 152*(2), 354–364.

Kerstens, K. (1996). Technical efficiency measurement and explanation of French urban transit companies. *Transportation Research Part A, 30*(6), 431–452.

Piacenza, M. (2006). Regulatory contracts and cost efficiency: Stochastic frontier evidence from the Italian local public transport. *Journal of Productivity Analysis, 25*(3), 257–277.

Pina, V., & Torres, L. (2001). Analysis of the efficiency of local government services delivery. An application to urban public transport. *Transportation Research Part A, 35*(10), 929–944.

Seiford, L. M., & Zhu, J. (2003). Context-dependent data envelopment analysis – Measuring attractiveness and progress. *Omega, 31*, 397.

Suzuki, S., & Nijkamp, P. (2011). A stepwise-projection data envelopment analysis for public transport operations in Japan. *Letters in Spatial and Resource Sciences, 4*(2), 139–156.

Chapter 8
Performance Measurement of Global Cities: Combination of a Stepwise Improvement Model with an SE Model

Abstract This chapter aims to provide an empirical contribution to the rising literature on the relative performance and benchmarking of large cities in a competitive world. On the basis of a recent detailed database on many achievement criteria of 35 major cities in the world, it seeks to arrive at a relative performance ranking of these cities by using Data Envelopment Analysis (DEA). A novel element is the use of a new type of "Super-Efficiency DEA" to identify unambiguously the high performers in the group of world cities investigated. We also introduce an adjusted DEA model, emerging from a blend of a DFM and a context-dependent (CD) model, namely, a Stepwise Improvement model. This model can provide a stepwise efficiency-improvement projection to provide more practical and feasible solutions for realistic circumstances and requirements in an efficiency-improvement projection. In this chapter, we also make a new contribution to DEA analysis by combining a Super-Efficiency (SE) DEA with the Stepwise Improvement model. The above mentioned stepwise-projection model is next applied to a performance analysis in the context of an efficiency-improvement plan for inefficient global cities.

Keywords Data Envelopment Analysis (DEA) • Super-efficiency (SE) • Distance friction minimization (DFM) • Context-dependent (CD) • Stepwise projection • Global cities

8.1 Introduction

The structural and worldwide urbanization trend has prompted the emergence of metropolitan areas of an unprecedented scale. Especially in the current globalization age, such areas act as international power stations, with a rich pluriformity of centripetal and centrifugal economic, political, and technological forces. Such world cities have a strong global control and command impact, not only because of their sheer size but more so because of their innovative and creative potential (Glaeser and Kerr 2009; Sassen 1991; Shefer and Frenkel 1998). In this context, the local R&D, knowledge and learning base also plays an important role (Acs et al. 2002; van Geenhuizen and Nijkamp 2011; Kourtit et al. 2011).

S. Suzuki, P. Nijkamp, *Regional Performance Measurement and Improvement*, New Frontiers in Regional Science: Asian Perspectives 9,
DOI 10.1007/978-981-10-0242-7_8

World cities are increasingly also involved in fierce competition on global product and service markets, and consequently these metropolitan areas have to create favorable conditions for economic agents, such as a healthy entrepreneurial climate, a specialized basis of industrial clusters, a diversified economic structure, an ecologically sustainable urban environment, a high-quality research and educational infrastructure, a balanced population structure with sufficient skills, international accessibility through majors hubs, etc. (see also Cheshire and Magrini 2009). World cities are essentially involved in a permanent global battle that is concerned with the maximum development and exploitation of agglomeration externalities in international spatial networks.

An interesting question is now how global players and local experts view the potential and performance of these cities. In recent years, various attempts have been made to develop a classification or ranking of world cities based on their actual performance or their perceived success (see, e.g., Taylor et al. 2009; Grosveld 2002; Arribas-Bel et al. 2011; Kourtit et al. 2012; Suzuki et al. 2011). Especially the seminal work of Taylor and associates has gained worldwide recognition. A main challenge in empirical research is the development of a consistent, quantitative database that is appropriate for a comparative, strategic benchmark analysis.

One of the most detailed databases on world cities can be found in a recent study on the "Global Power City Index" (GPCI) undertaken by the Institute for Urban Strategies (2010). A thorough analysis of various world cities, 35 in total, was made in this study report, including not only the megacities of New York, London, Paris, Tokyo, or Beijing but also cities from emerging economies such as Sao Paulo, Mumbai, Kuala Lumpur, or Cairo. The GPCI database contains six major clusters of relevant information on these cities. We employ this database for a benchmark analysis of these cities, and, therefore, it is discussed in slightly greater detail in the next section.

The basic proposition of the present chapter is that a pure ranking of world cities on the basis of their weighted achievement scores does not tell us very much about their economic efficiency, which in the long run will be decisive for their prosperity and sustainability. Therefore, this chapter aims to provide a more critical analysis of the performance data on these 35 metropolitan areas by using Data Envelopment Analysis (DEA) to position these cities on the basis of their relative performance, i.e., by relating their output to their input. This ratio is much more informative about the actual economic profile of the city concerned.

We propose here a distance friction minimization (DFM) model in a DEA content that is based on a generalized distance friction function and serves to assist a DMU in improving its performance by an appropriate movement toward the efficiency frontier surface. This DFM approach aims to generate a new contribution to efficiency enhancement strategies by deploying a weighted projection function while at the same time it may address both an input reduction and an output increase as a strategy of a DMU. A general efficiency-improvement projection model including optional DFM model is able to calculate either an optimal input reduction value or an output increase value to reach a full efficiency score of 1, even though in reality this may be hard to achieve. It is therefore meaningful to develop a more practical and feasible efficiency-improvement projection model, based especially on the DFM model.

It should be noted here that Seiford and Zhu (2003) have developed a gradual improvement model for an inefficient DMU. This "context-dependent (CD)" DEA has an important merit, as it aims to reach a stepwise improvement through successive levels toward the efficiency frontier.

We introduce here an adjusted DEA model – emerging from a blend of the DFM and CD model – namely, a Stepwise Improvement model, in Sect. 5.2.2 (see also Suzuki et al. 2010). This model can provide a stepwise efficiency-improvement projection to provide more practical and feasible solutions for realistic circumstances and requirements in an efficiency-improvement projection.

In this chapter, we also make a new contribution to DEA analysis by combining a Super-Efficiency DEA (see Andersen and Petersen (1993) and Sect. 3.2) with a Stepwise Improvement model by introducing a new method for calculating and identifying superefficient actors (in our case, cities) (see Kourtit et al. 2013).

The abovementioned Stepwise Improvement projection model will be applied to a performance analysis in the context of an efficiency-improvement plan for inefficient global cities.

8.2 Database and Analysis Framework

For a systematic comparison of cities' performance analysis and their urban competitiveness, our empirical approach is based on a unique data set, the "Global Power City Index" (GPCI), produced by the Institute for Urban Strategies, under the aegis of the Mori Memorial Foundation (2010) in Tokyo for the year 2010.

The GPCI index is used, as a strategic tool, to evaluate and rank the comprehensive power determinants of 35 major cities worldwide, in terms of the strengths and weaknesses of their performance in creating wealth, enhancing social development, attracting investments, providing an open and attractive urban "milieu" or climate, offering access to social capital and networks, encouraging integrated sustainability, and harnessing both human and technological resources in productivity and competitiveness at local and global scales. In other words, the aim of these world cities is to maximize urban XXQ (the highest possible urban quality) which may strengthen their foundations for securing socioeconomic development and competitive advantage in a global playing field (Nijkamp 2008).

The comprehensive performance scores and rankings of these global cities in the GPCI data set are based on six main categories, namely, "Economy," "Research & Development," "Cultural Interaction," "Liveability," "Ecology & Natural Environment," and "Accessibility." Each of these main indicators was subdivided into relevant and measurable subindicators, so that finally a consistent and tested database on 69 subindicators for 35 world cities was created. Thus, we have a

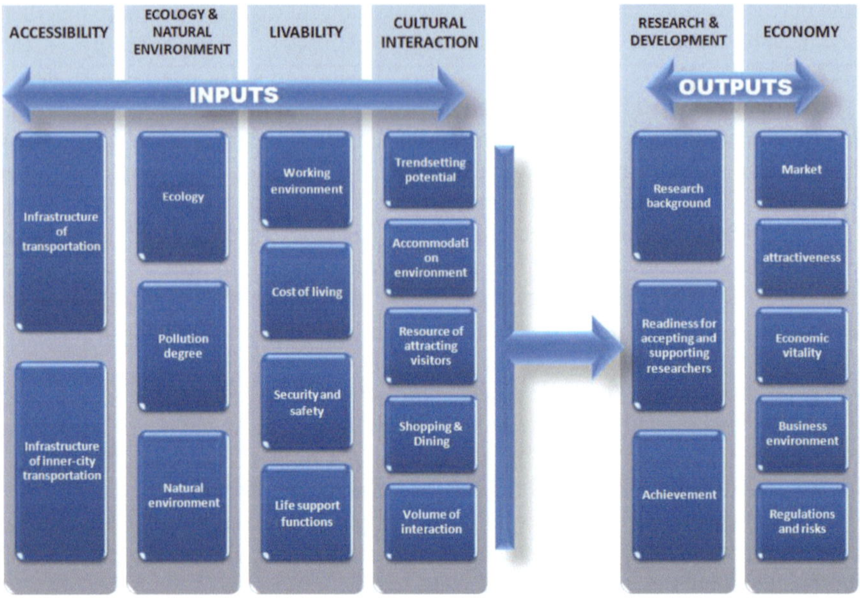

Fig. 8.1 An overview of the main categories of performance indicators used in GPCI 2010

complete, extensive, and quantitative database for a great variety of relevant urban (sub)indicators for all world cities under consideration.

Next, a set of five worldwide types of actors was identified: managers, researchers, artists, visitors, and residents. These people were asked to score the importance of each of these indicators, so that a weighted average importance score for each city could be calculated. All details can be found in the abovementioned GPCI 2010 report. See Annex A in this paper for more details of the ranking results of these cities as presented in the abovementioned study (more details can also be found in Arribas et al. 2013). Figure 8.1 provides a concise overview of the main categories of performance indicators used in the GPCI report.

8.3 Performance Evaluation Based on Super-Efficiency CCR-I Model

In our empirical application, we will use the GPCI 2010 database. But rather than seeking to achieve a ranking of cities based on a comprehensive set of indicators, we aim to look at the efficiency (or productivity) of these cities, by investigating more carefully the ratio between multi-attribute outputs and multi-attribute inputs. To that end, DEA is an appropriate tool.

In our application, we will first apply the CCR (see Charnes et al. 1978) model and the Super-Efficiency model in our search for exceptional world cities based on

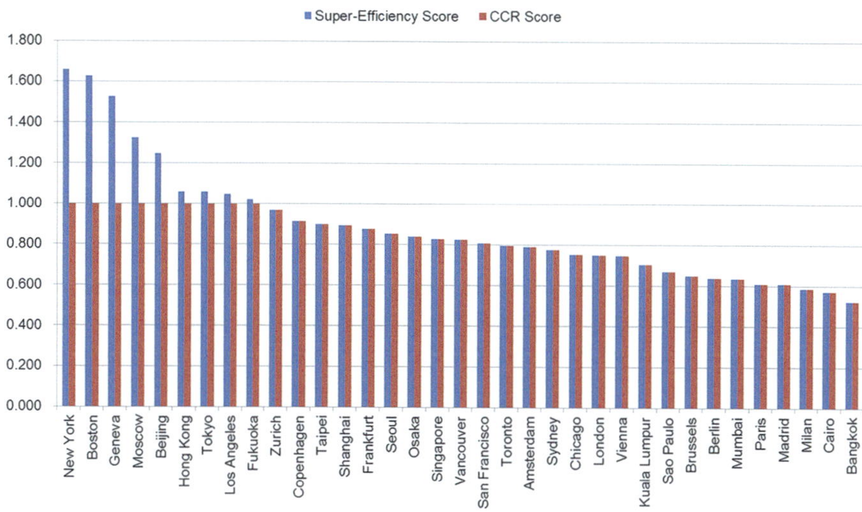

Fig. 8.2 Efficiency score based on the CCR model and the Super-Efficiency model

a Super-Efficiency DEA. In addition, we will apply the CD model based on the superefficiency concept; in this way, the cities in our sample can be categorized according to efficiency levels based on successive levels of efficient frontiers.

The efficiency evaluation results for the 35 world cities based on the CCR model and the Super-Efficiency model using four inputs ("Cultural Interaction," "Liveability," "Ecology & Natural Environment," "Accessibility") and two outputs ("Economy," "Research & Development") are given in Fig. 8.2. The standard CCR model assigns an equal efficiency to nine world cities, viz., New York, Boston, Genève, Moscow, Beijing, Hong Kong, Tokyo, Los Angeles, and Fukuoka, so that it is not possible to discriminate among these cities. However, by applying a Super-Efficient DEA model, a clear difference in performance of these nine cities can be observed (see Fig. 8.2).

In Fig. 8.2, the rankings of the superefficiency values for 9 of the 35 world cities (i.e., New York, 1.659; Boston, 1.628; Geneva, 1.527; Moscow, 1.325; Beijing, 1.248; Hong Kong, 1.060; Tokyo, 1.059; Los Angeles, 1.048; and Fukuoka, 1.022) were identified on the basis of their high superefficiency score. It is noteworthy that in our analysis "New York" is the "exceptional world city" based on the Super-Efficiency model. This is an unambiguous result that originates from the advantages of the design of the Super-Efficiency model.

It should be added that these results differ quite considerably from those achieved in the original GPCI 2010 report. The reason is that our productivity-based analysis allows non-megacities (such as Boston or Geneva) to achieve a favorable efficiency outcome, in which size and agglomeration effects are combined with smart management of the urban area concerned. Nevertheless, metropolitan areas like New York or Tokyo have managed to maintain their high ranking

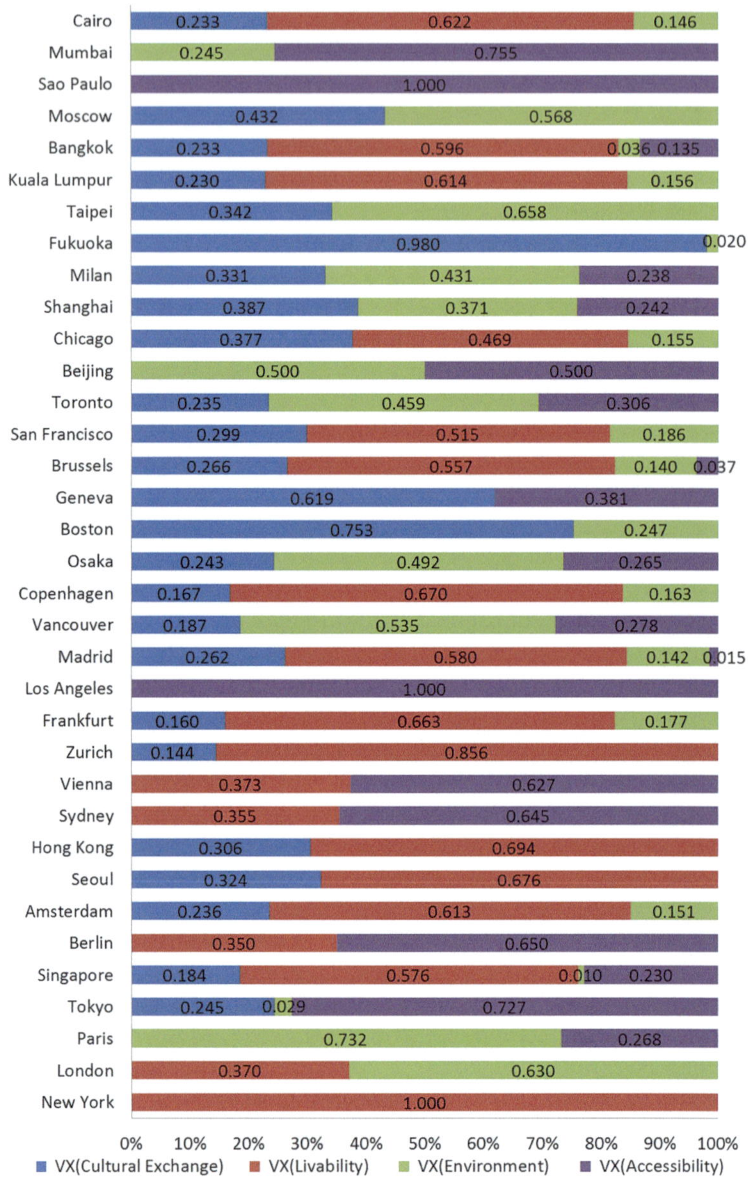

Fig. 8.3 Input optimum weights

in our efficiency analysis. Clearly, there are economies of scale for world cities, but some medium-sized world cities appear to perform exceptionally well.

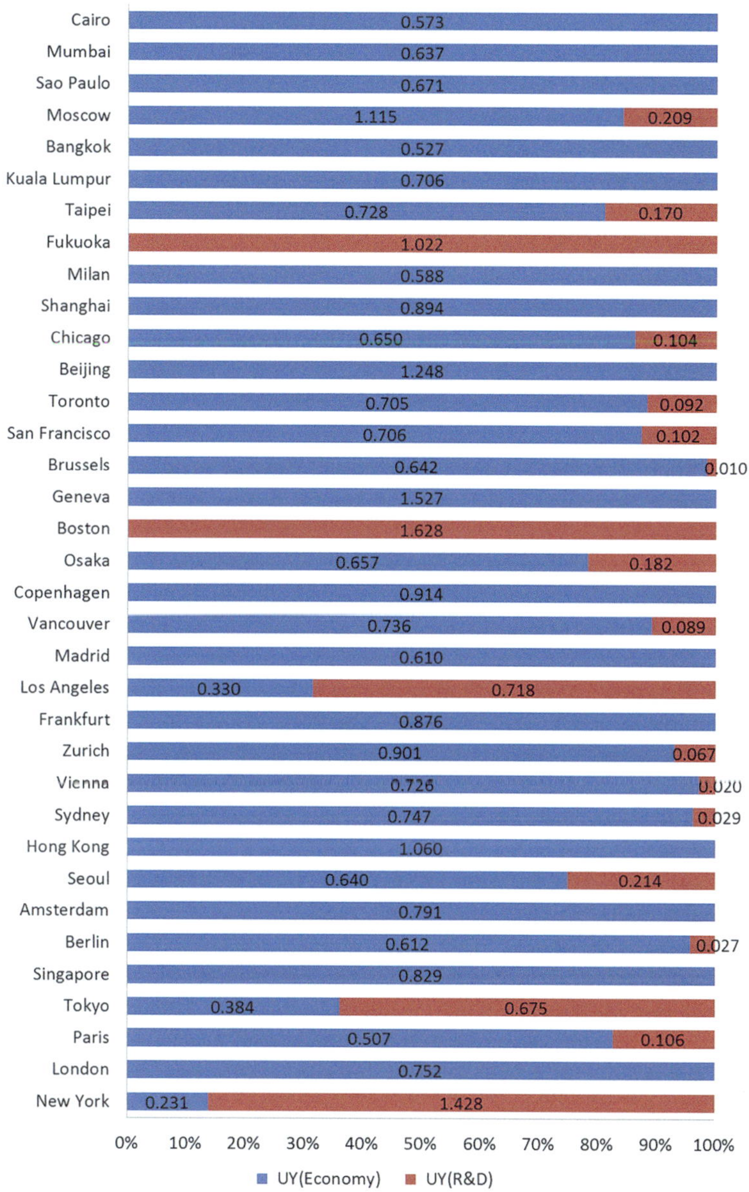

Fig. 8.4 Output optimum weights

8.4 Optimum Weights of Input and Output Items

The optimum weights of the input and output variables for the 35 world cities based on the CCR model are given in Figs. 8.3 and 8.4, respectively.

It should be noted that (v^*, u^*) is the set of most favorable weights for each DMU, so that we can find the relative importance of each indicator with reference to the value of each $v_m^* \, x_{mo}$ and $u_s^* \, y_{so}$ for each DMU. From these results, it can be seen that, for instance, Tokyo obtains a weight for Cultural Exchange equal to 0.245, for Environment equal to 0.029, and for Accessibility equal to 0.727 in its inputs, while it obtains for Economy a weight of 0.384 and for R&D a weight of 0.675 in its outputs. These results offer meaningful insights for policies on efficiency improvement of city.

8.5 Performance Assessment Based on a Context-Dependent Super-Efficiency Model

The detailed efficiency evaluation results for the 35 world cities based on the CD Super-Efficiency model with the six performance categories E (Efficiency level)1–E6 are given in Fig. 8.5.

In Fig. 8.5, the DMUs in set E1 (New York, Boston, Geneva, Moscow, Beijing, Hong Kong, Tokyo, Los Angeles, and Fukuoka) are the most high-level efficient cities. These are identified on the basis of the super-efficient DMUs.

The DMUs in set E2 (Zurich, Copenhagen, Taipei, Shanghai, Seoul, Singapore, San Francisco, and London) take the second-level efficient cities group, after the exclusion of the first-level efficient cities. The DMUs in set E3 (Vancouver, Osaka, Sydney, Paris, Chicago, Toronto, and Frankfurt) relate to the third-level efficient cities, after the exclusion of the second-level efficient cities. The DMUs in set E4 (Vienna, Amsterdam, Sao Paulo, Brussels, and Berlin) are fourth-level efficient cities, while the DMUs in set E5 (Mumbai, Milan, Kuala Lumpur, and Madrid) and the DMUs in set E6 (Bangkok and Cairo) represent the fifth-level and sixth-level efficient cities, respectively.

On the basis of these more differentiated performance categories, we will now compute an efficiency-improvement projection for the nearest upper-level efficient frontier cities for inefficient cities in the next section.

8.6 Direct Efficiency-Improvement Projection Based on SE and SE-DFM Models

The direct efficiency improvement projection results based on the SE and the SE-DFM model for inefficient Asian cities are presented in Fig. 8.6.

We will now offer a concise interpretation of the results presented in these tables. We will take Singapore as an illustrative example. From Fig. 8.6.a, the SE projection shows that, for instance, Singapore – in order to achieve a superefficiency state – should reduce its input volumes Cultural Exchange,

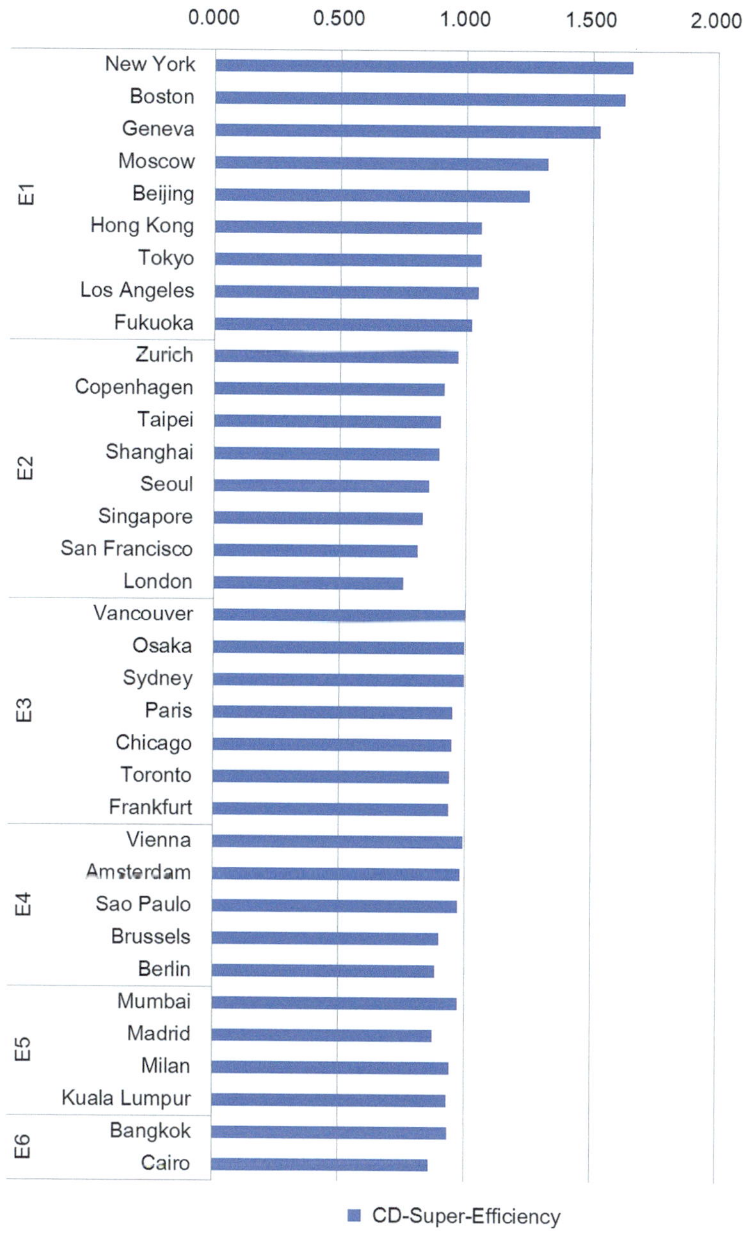

Fig. 8.5 Efficiency scores and categorizations based on CD Super-Efficiency

Liveability, Environment, and Accessibility by 17.1% and increase its volumes Economy of 9.4% in order to become efficient. On the other hand, the SE-DFM projection results show that a reduction in the Liveability of 16.3% and an increase in the Economy of 9.4% is required to become efficient. It should be added that in a deterministic DEA model, these findings are numerically correct but that in policy practice such accurate adjustments will hardly be achieved. Nevertheless, this

Fig. 8.6 Efficiency improvement projection of the SE and SE-DFM model

b

Taipei

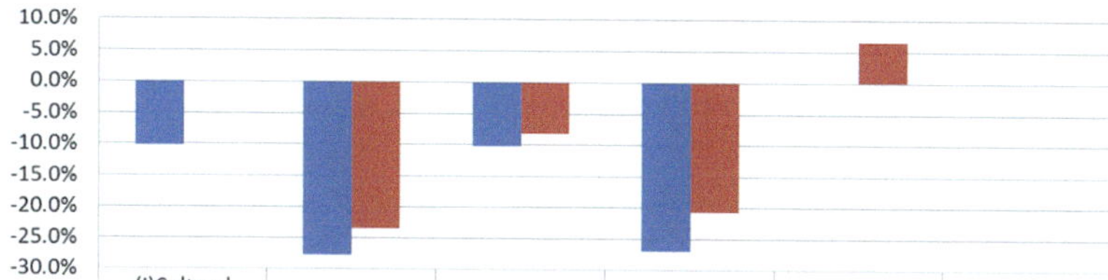

	(I)Cultural Exchange	(I)Livability	(I)Environment	(I)Accessibility	(O)Economy	(O)R&D
SE	-10.1%	-27.7%	-10.1%	-27.0%	0.0%	0.0%
SE-DFM	0.0%	-23.5%	-8.1%	-20.7%	6.6%	0.0%

Kuala Lumpur

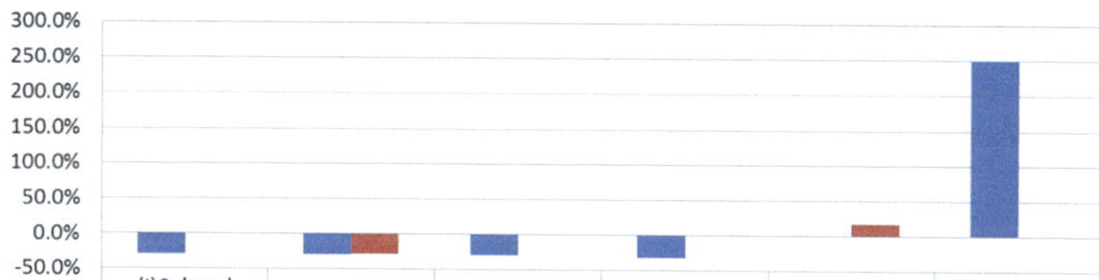

	(I)Cultural Exchange	(I)Livability	(I)Environment	(I)Accessibility	(O)Economy	(O)R&D
SE	-29.4%	-29.4%	29.4%	-31.2%	0.0%	250.6%
SE-DFM	0.0%	-28.1%	0.0%	0.0%	17.2%	0.0%

Bangkok

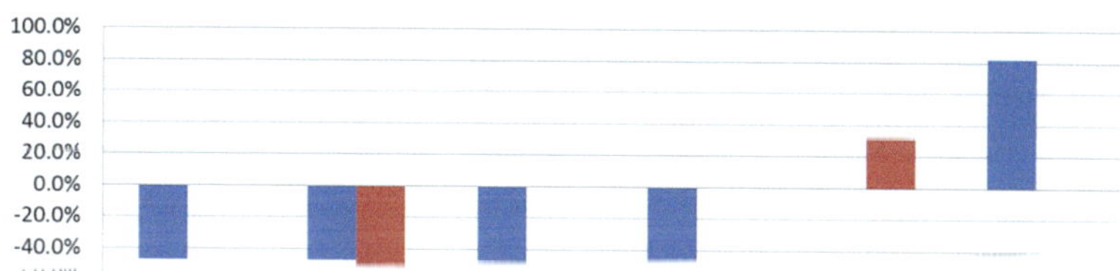

	(I)Cultural Exchange	(I)Livability	(I)Environment	(I)Accessibility	(O)Economy	(O)R&D
SE	-47.3%	-47.3%	-47.3%	-47.3%	0.0%	82.1%
SE-DFM	0.0%	-52.0%	0.0%	0.0%	31.0%	0.0%

Mumbai

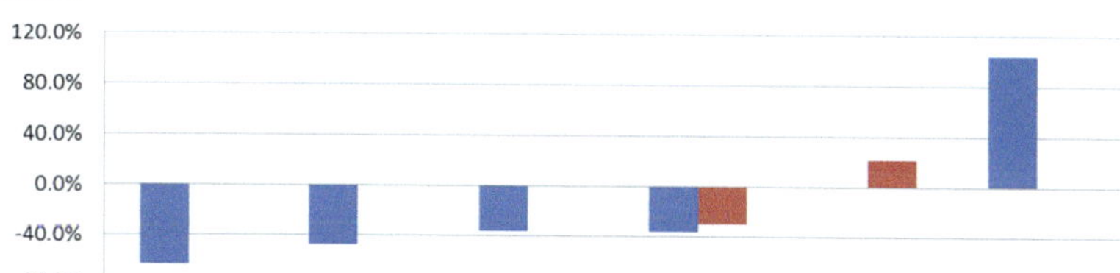

	(I)Cultural Exchange	(I)Livability	(I)Environment	(I)Accessibility	(O)Economy	(O)R&D
SE	-63.3%	-47.2%	-36.3%	-36.3%	0.0%	104.0%
SE-DFM	0.0%	0.0%	0.0%	-29.3%	22.2%	0.0%

Fig. 8.6 (continued)

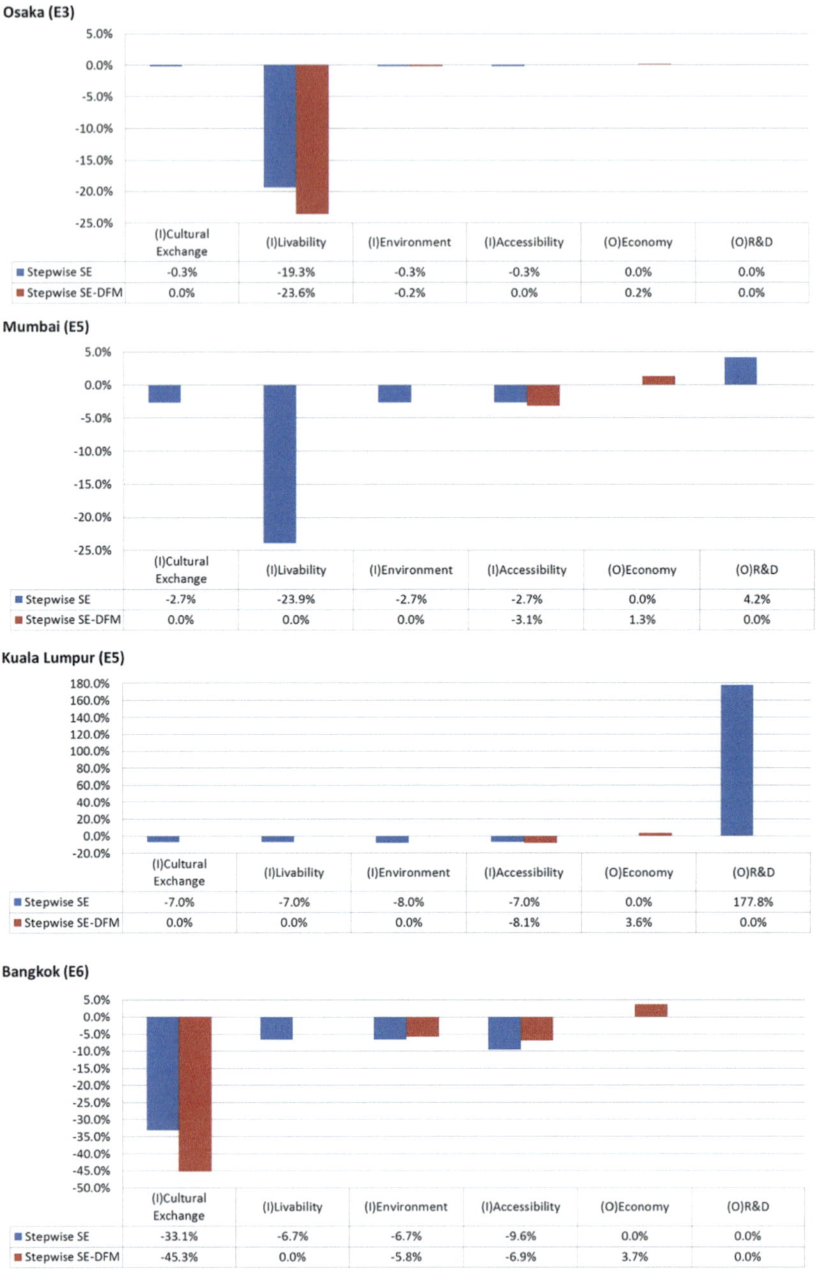

Osaka (E3)

	(I)Cultural Exchange	(I)Livability	(I)Environment	(I)Accessibility	(O)Economy	(O)R&D
Stepwise SE	-0.3%	-19.3%	-0.3%	-0.3%	0.0%	0.0%
Stepwise SE-DFM	0.0%	-23.6%	-0.2%	0.0%	0.2%	0.0%

Mumbai (E5)

	(I)Cultural Exchange	(I)Livability	(I)Environment	(I)Accessibility	(O)Economy	(O)R&D
Stepwise SE	-2.7%	-23.9%	-2.7%	-2.7%	0.0%	4.2%
Stepwise SE-DFM	0.0%	0.0%	0.0%	-3.1%	1.3%	0.0%

Kuala Lumpur (E5)

	(I)Cultural Exchange	(I)Livability	(I)Environment	(I)Accessibility	(O)Economy	(O)R&D
Stepwise SE	-7.0%	-7.0%	-8.0%	-7.0%	0.0%	177.8%
Stepwise SE-DFM	0.0%	0.0%	0.0%	-8.1%	3.6%	0.0%

Bangkok (E6)

	(I)Cultural Exchange	(I)Livability	(I)Environment	(I)Accessibility	(O)Economy	(O)R&D
Stepwise SE	-33.1%	-6.7%	-6.7%	-9.6%	0.0%	0.0%
Stepwise SE-DFM	-45.3%	0.0%	-5.8%	-6.9%	3.7%	0.0%

Fig. 8.7 Stepwise efficiency-improvement projections based on SE and DFM

information is indicative for the direction and intensity of necessary policy handles for a city to become efficient. This result clearly shows that a different – and more efficient and effective – solution is available than the SE projection to reach the efficiency frontier.

8.7 Stepwise Efficiency-Improvement Projection Based on SE and SE-DFM Models

The stepwise efficiency-improvement projection results based on the SE and SE-DFM model for inefficient Asian cities are presented in Fig. 8.7.

In Fig. 8.7, it appears that the ratios of change in the Stepwise Improvement SE-DFM projection are smaller than those in the Stepwise Improvement SE projection, as might be expected. In Fig. 8.7, this particularly applies to Mumbai and Kuala Lumpur, which are non-slack type DMUs (i.e., $s-^{**}$ and $s+^{**}$ are zero). Apart from the practicality of such a solution, the models show clearly that a different – and perhaps more efficient – solution is available than the Stepwise Improvement SE projection to reach the efficiency frontier.

The more advanced Stepwise Improvement SE-DFM model is able to present a more realistic efficiency-improvement result, which we can compare with the results of Fig. 8.6b. For instance, the SE-DFM results in Fig. 8.6b show that Mumbai should reduce its accessibility indicator by 29.3% and increase the Economy by 22.2% in order to become entirely efficient. On the other hand, the Stepwise Improvement SE-DFM results in Fig. 8.7 show that a reduction in Accessibility of 3.1% and an increase in the Economy of 1.3% are required to become efficient (this means that Mumbai can attain the E4 level efficient frontier moving up from the E5 level). It should be noted that also in this case the same proviso on the interpretation holds, as indicated above.

8.8 Conclusion

The DEA analysis in this chapter has aimed to shed new light on the rankings of world cities. Most comparative studies are based on an aggregate (weighted or unweighted) average of a set of background factors that have been translated into operational indicators. The approach adopted in the present study has focused attention much more on the efficiency and productivity of large world cities, using a comparative data set. These research presented in the present study has offered interesting insights into the benchmark position of world cities, based on an extensive data set. Our findings reveal striking differences compared with standard ranking and benchmarking procedures. In particular, the new methods to arrive at unambiguous DEA ranking results provide promising findings.

The Stepwise Improvement SE-DFM model provides the policy-maker with practical and transparent solutions that are available in the SE-DFM projection to reach the nearest upper-level efficiency frontier. These results offer a meaningful contribution to decision support and planning for the efficiency improvement of strategic urban policy. And therefore, this Stepwise Improvement SE-DFM model may become a policy vehicle that may have great added value for operational decision making and planning in cities. Clearly, cities have the possibility to increase their potential. This improvement potential differs for each city, but our results offer operational guidelines on a case-by-case city basis.

In this chapter, we have in particular presented a new methodology, the SE-DFM and Stepwise Improvement SE-DFM model, which integrates a Super-Efficiency model, a DFM model, and a CD model. The new method minimizes the distance friction for each input and output separately. As a result, the combined reductions in inputs and increases in outputs that are necessary to reach an efficiency frontier are smaller than in the standard model. Furthermore, the new model could be adapted to reflect realistic conditions in an efficiency-improvement projection. In addition, the stepwise projection allows DMUs to include various levels of ambition regarding the ultimate performance in their strategic judgment. Clearly, our deterministic DEA modeling results have to be interpreted with some caution, as the level of precision implied by our findings is in practical situations not achievable. Nevertheless, our results offer an indication of the level of intensity and the direction of policy efforts that are needed to upgrade the efficiency profile of world cities. In conclusion, our Stepwise Improvement SE-DFM model is able to present a more realistic efficiency-improvement urban policy strategy and may thus provide a significant support contribution to decision making and planning for the efficiency improvement of the relevant agents involved.

References

Acs, Z. J., FitzRoy, F. R., & Smith, I. (2002). High technology employment and R&D in cities: Heterogeneity vs specialization. *The Annals of Regional Science, 36*, 373–386.

Andersen, P., & Petersen, N. (1993). A procedure for ranking efficient units in data envelopment analysis. *Management Science, 39*, 1261–1264.

Arribas, D., Kourtit, K., & Nijkamp, P. (2013). Benchmarking of world cities through self-organizing maps. *Cities, 31*, 248–257.

Arribas-Bel, D., Nijkamp, P., & Scholten, H. (2011). Multidimensional urban sprawl in Europe: A self-organizing map approach, computers. *Environment and Urban Systems, 35*(4), 263–275.

Charnes, A., Cooper, W. W., & Rhodes, E. (1978). Measuring the efficiency of decision making units. *European Journal of Operational Research, 2*, 429–444.

Cheshire, P. C., & Magrini, S. (2009). Urban growth drivers in a continent of sticky people and implicit boundaries. *Journal of Economic Geography, 9*, 85–115.

Glaeser, E., & Kerr, W. R. (2009). Local industrial conditions and entrepreneurship: How much of the spatial distribution can we explain? *Journal of Economics and Management Strategy, 18*(3), 623–663.

Grosveld, H. (2002) The leading cities of the world and their competitive advantages, PhD dissertation, University of Amsterdam.

Institute for Urban Strategies. (2010). *Global power city index*. Tokyo: The Mori Memorial Foundation.

Kourtit, K., Nijkamp, P., & Stough, R. (Eds.). (2011). *Drivers of innovation, entrepreneurship and regional dynamics*. Berlin: Springer.

Kourtit, K., Nijkamp, P., & Arribas, D. (2012). Smart cities perspective – A comparative european study by means of self-organizing maps. *The European Journal of Social Science Research, 25* (2), 229–246.

Kourtit, K., Nijkamp, P., & Suzuki, S. (2013). The rat race between world cities: In search of exceptional places by means of super-efficient data development analysis. *Computers, Environment and Urban Systems, 38*, 67–77.

Nijkamp, P. (2008). XXQ factors for sustainable urban development: A systems economics view. *Romanian Journal of Regional Science, 2*(1), 1–34.

Sassen, S. (1991). *The global city*. Princeton: Princeton University Press.

Seiford, L. M., & Zhu, J. (2003). Context-dependent data envelopment analysis – measuring attractiveness and progress. *Omega, 31*, 397.

Shefer, D., & Frenkel, A. (1998). Local milieu and innovations: Some empirical results. *The Annals of Regional Science, 32*, 185–200.

Suzuki, S., Nijkamp, P., Rietveld, P., & Pels, E. (2010). A distance friction minimization approach in data envelopment analysis: A comparative study on airport efficiency. *European Journal of Operational Research, 207*, 1104–1115.

Suzuki, S., Nijkamp, P., & Rietveld, P. (2011). Regional efficiency improvement by means of data envelopment analysis through Euclidean distance minimization including fixed input factors: An application to tourist regions in Italy. *Papers in Regional Science, 90*(1), 67–89.

Taylor, P. J., Ni, P., Derudder, B., Hoyler, M., Huang, J., Lu, F., Pain, K., Witlox, F., Yang, X., Bassens, D., & Shen, W. (2009). Measuring the world city network: New developments and results. *GaWC Research Bulletin, 300*.

van Geenhuizen, M., & Nijkamp, P. (2011). *The creative knowledge city*. Cheltenham: Edward Elgar.

Chapter 9
An Energy-Environment Performance Analysis After the Fukushima Disaster in Japan: Combination of a Target-Oriented Model with an SE Model

Abstract The aim of this chapter is to apply an extended DEA model – emerging from a blend of a distance friction minimization (DFM) and a Target-Oriented (TO) approach based on a Super-Efficiency (SE) model – for generating an appropriate efficiency-improvement projection model. The DFM model is able to calculate an optimal input reduction value and an optimal output increase value in order to reach an efficiency score of 1.0, even though in reality this may be hard to achieve for low-efficiency DMUs. In contrast, high-efficiency DMUs might find it easier to reach an efficiency score of 1.0 or, in the case of a Super-Efficiency DEA, a score above 1.0. The TO approach specifies a Target-Efficiency Score (TES) for inefficient DMUs. This approach can compute an input reduction value and an output increase value in order to achieve a higher TES. The abovementioned TO-DFM model will be applied to an efficiency analysis of the energy-environment interface for ten regions in Japan. The focus will be on one input cost criterion (viz., expenditures) and two output-based performance criteria (viz., electricity generation and CO2 emission). Based on an extensive database, a comparative performance analysis of ten Japanese regions under consideration will be pursued.

Keywords Data Envelopment Analysis (DEA) • Distance friction minimization (DFM) • Super-Efficiency (SE) • Target-Oriented (TO) • Energy-environment efficiency

9.1 Introduction

Japan is faced with the "Fukushima" problem, meaning that a recent serious single nuclear accident has led to a drastic electrical power shortage in the country. Japan had until recently 54 nuclear plants, but almost all have in the meantime stopped generating power owing to the strong backlash of public opinion. The ten regional electrical companies in Japan have now permission to increase thermal power generation based on coal, oil, and LNG (liquefied natural gas) in order to compensate for the shortfall caused by the accident. A comparison of electrical power supply between the case before and after the accident in Japan is presented in Fig. 9.1.

S. Suzuki, P. Nijkamp, *Regional Performance Measurement and Improvement*, New Frontiers in Regional Science: Asian Perspectives 9,
DOI 10.1007/978-981-10-0242-7_9

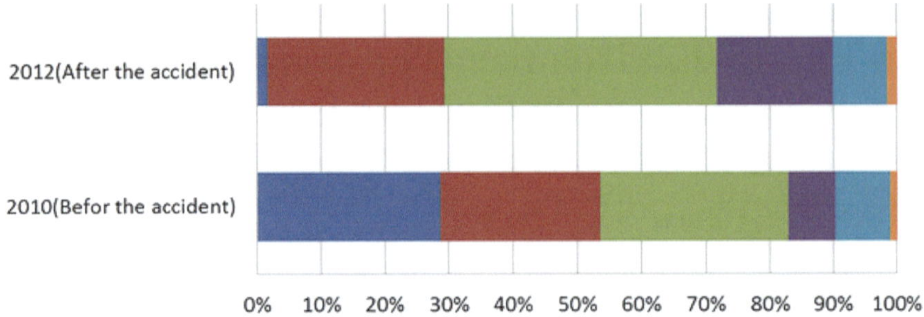

	2010(Befor the accident)	2012(After the accident)
Nuclear	28.6	1.7
Coal	25.0	27.6
LNG	29.3	42.5
Oil	7.5	18.3
Hydraulic	8.5	8.4
New Energy	1.1	1.6

Fig. 9.1 A comparison of electric power supply before and after the nuclear accident in Japan

This creates the problem of an increase in electricity cost and CO2 emission, which is also related to a non-balanced energy-environment policy. Although it is difficult at this stage to develop a robust strategy, it is necessary to make an effort to achieve a more efficient and sustainable energy-environment outcome in Japan, even though Japan has decided to withdraw from the Kyoto Protocol.

A standard tool by which to judge efficiency among different actors is Data Envelopment Analysis (DEA), proposed by Charnes et al. (1978). There are in the meantime also several studies that have applied DEA models to measure energy efficiency in the context of regions and power companies. For example, Martínez (2011) measures energy efficiency development in non-energy-intensive sectors (NEISs) in Germany and Colombia, based on a DEA model. Wu et al. (2014) apply a DEA model and related Malmquist indices for an efficiency evaluation of regions in China, while Li et al. (2014) apply a DEA model to efficiency measurement of electric power supply companies in China. This list of studies shows that comparative efficiency analysis in the energy-environment sector using DEA models has increasingly become an important research issue in recent years.

We propose here a distance friction minimization (DFM) model that is based on a generalized distance function and serves to improve the performance of a DMU by identifying the most appropriate movement toward the efficiency frontier surface. The DFM model is able to calculate either an optimal input reduction value or an output increase value in order to reach an efficiency score of 1.000, even though in reality this might be hard to achieve for low-efficiency DMUs. There is a wealth of DEA models and applications, but most DEA models have intrinsic limitations or weaknesses.

We introduce now an adjusted DEA model, emerging from a blend of the DFM and the Target-Oriented (TO) approach based on a Super-Efficiency model (Andersen and Petersen (1993), in order to generate a more appropriate efficiency-improvement projection model, in Sect. 5.2.3 (see also Suzuki et al. 2015). The TO approach specifies a Target Efficiency Score (TES) for each DMU. This approach can compute an input reduction value and an output increase value in order to achieve a TES for the efficiency improvement of a DMU. The abovementioned TO-DFM model is applied to an efficiency analysis of the energy-environment sector for the ten regions related to the management zones of the ten electrical power companies in Japan. Based on the efficiency results and the efficiency-improvement projections, we aim to highlight a variation of the energy-environment efficiency between the situation before (2010) and after (2011) the accident, while we also aim to assist target setting for energy-environment policy in Japan.

9.2 Database and Analysis Framework

A comparative performance analysis calls for detailed information. We use the following input and output data for a set of ten regions (Hokkaido, Tohoku, Tokyo, Chubu, Hokuriku, Kansai, Chugoku, Shikoku, Kyushu, and Okinawa) related to each of the management zones for the ten electrical power companies in Japan (see the map in Fig. 9.2).

The DMUs used in our analysis are listed in Table 9.1.

As shown in Table 9.1, we will compare an efficiency score from before the Fukushima accident (in 2010) with the efficiency score after the accident (in 2011).

We consider in our DEA study one input (I):

(I1) Expenditure of electricity company (including fuel and labor cost) (million yen/year),

while two outputs (o) are incorporated:

(O1) Electricity generated (million kWh/year).

(O2) CO2 emission (1,000,000,000 t/year).
CO2 emission is denoted as a multiplicative inverse of the "bad" output to make it a "good" output (for details, see also Scheel (2001) and Seiford (2002)).

All datasets were obtained from the "Electrical Power Industry Handbook" in 2010 and 2011.

In our application, we first employed the Super-Efficiency CCR-I model, while next the results were used to determine the CCR-I, DFM, and TO-DFM projections. Additionally, we applied the TO-DFM model using Hokuriku 2010 as a reference region.

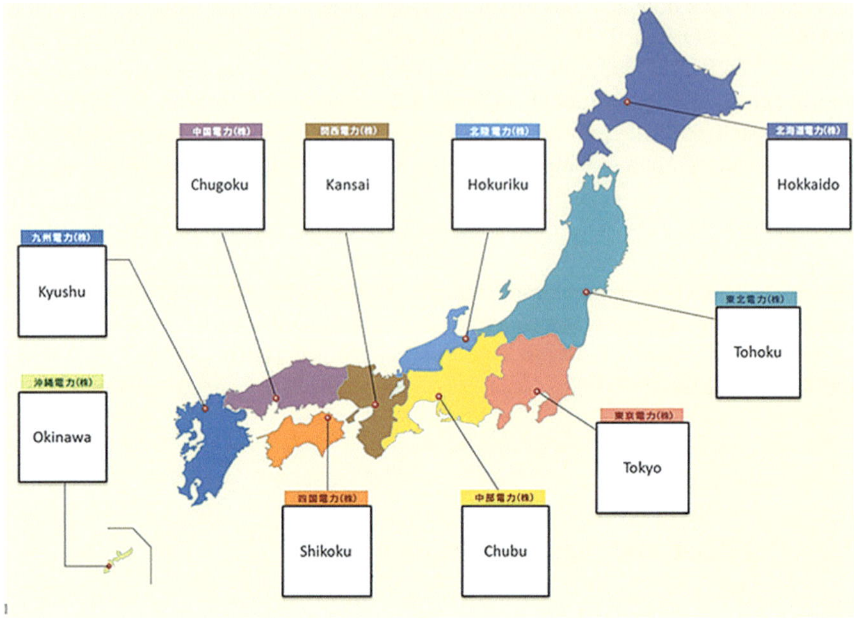

Fig. 9.2 Ten electrical companies in Japan

Table 9.1 A list of DMUs

No	DMUs (before Fukushima accident)	No	DMUs (after Fukushima accident)
1	Hokkaido 2010	11	Hokkaido 2011
2	Tohoku 2010	12	Tohoku 2011
3	Tokyo 2010	13	Tokyo 2011
4	Chubu 2010	14	Chubu 2011
5	Hokuriku 2010	15	Hokuriku 2011
6	Kansai 2010	16	Kansai 2011
7	Chugoku 2010	17	Chugoku 2011
8	Shikoku 2010	18	Shikoku 2011
9	Kyushu 2010	19	Kyushu 2011
10	Okinawa 2010	20	Okinawa 2011

9.3 Performance Evaluation Based on an SE-CCR-I Model

The efficiency evaluation result for the ten regions in 2010 and 2011 (a total of 20 DMUs) based on the Super-Efficiency CCR-I model is presented in Fig. 9.3.

From Fig. 9.3, it can be seen that Hokuriku 2010 and Okinawa 2010 may be regarded as super-efficient DMUs.

On the other hand, we notice that the efficiency score of all 2011 DMUs decreases significantly compared with each of the 2010 DMUs. A reason for the

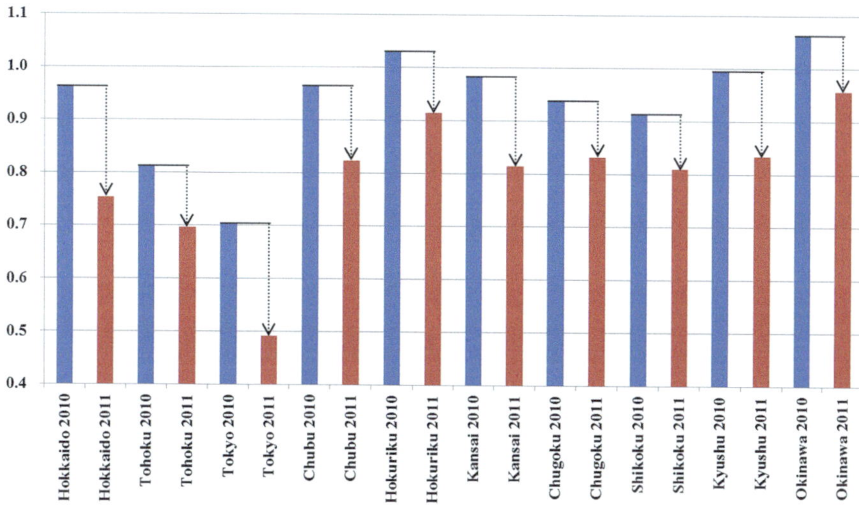

Fig. 9.3 Efficiency scores based on the Super-Efficiency CCR-I model

decrease is definitely the adverse influence of the Fukushima disaster, which meant that all regional electricity companies compensated for the electrical shortage by increased thermal power generation based on coal, oil, and LNG (liquefied natural gas), which caused an increased fuel cost and a rapid rise in CO2 emissions from 2010 to 2011.

It is also noteworthy that Hokkaido's performance fell rapidly from a score of 0.964 to 0.754. The reason for this is its heavy dependency on nuclear power generation, which was 44% in 2010, the highest level of dependency in Japan. Given the above findings, it is necessary to make an effort for efficiency improvement of the energy-environment balance in each region.

9.4 Optimum Weights of Input and Output Items

The optimum weights of the input and output variables for the ten regions based on the SE-CCR-I model are given in Figs. 9.4 and 9.5, respectively.

It should be noted that (v^*, u^*) is the set of most favorable weights for each DMU, so that we can find the relative importance of each indicator with reference to the value of each $v_m^* x_{mo}$ and $u_s^* y_{so}$ for each DMU. From these results, it can be seen that, for instance, Okinawa 2010 obtains a weight for expenditure equal to 1.000 in its input, while it obtains for electricity a weight of 0.805 and for CO2 emission a weight of 0.257 in its outputs. These results offer meaningful insights for policies on efficiency improvement of regional energy-environment.

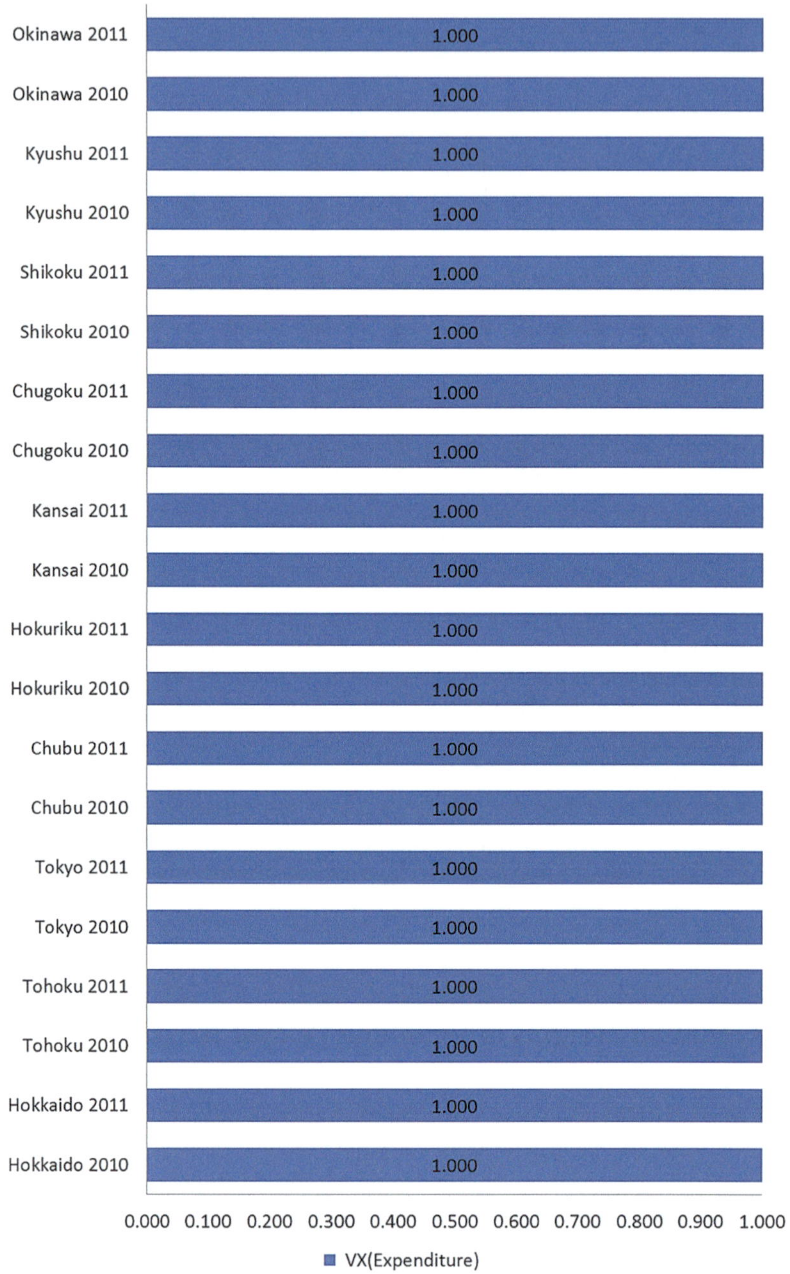

Fig. 9.4 Input optimum weights

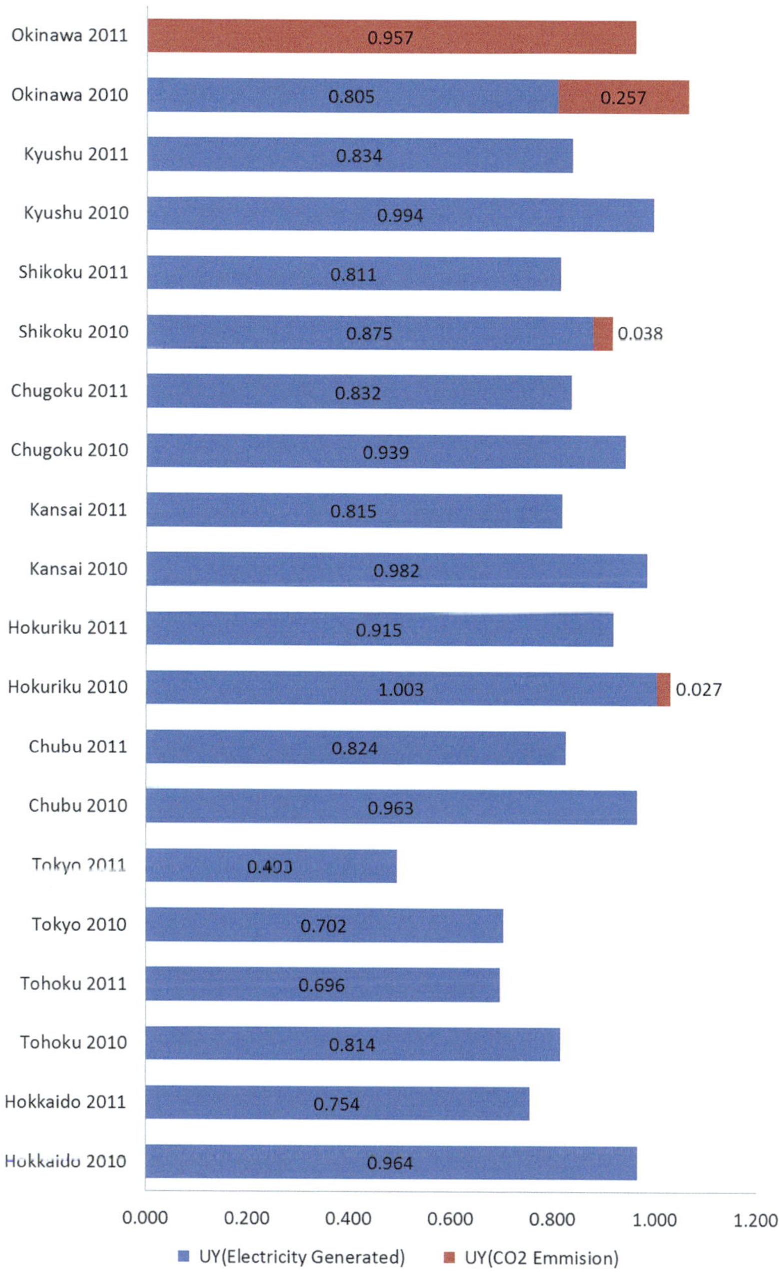

Fig. 9.5 Output optimum weights

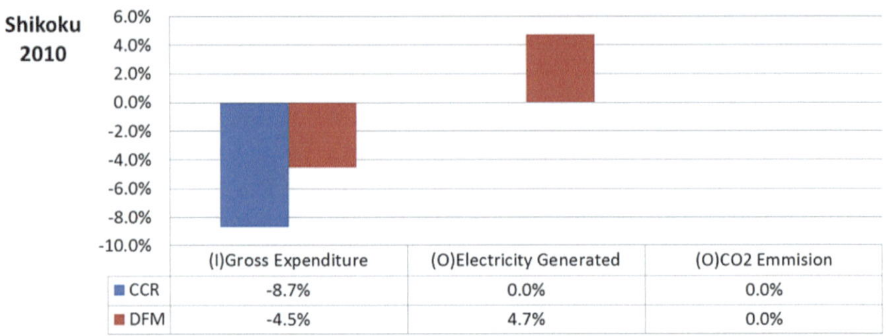

Fig. 9.6 Efficiency-improvement projection results of the CCR and DFM models for 2010 DMUs (Shikoku 2010)

9.5 Performance Improvement Projection Based on CCR, DFM, and TO-DFM Model

The results of an efficiency improvement projection based on the CCR and DFM models for the 2010 inefficient DMUs (only of a non-slack type) are presented in Fig. 9.6.

It appears that, as expected, the empirical ratios of change in the DFM projection are smaller than in the CCR projection. In Fig. 9.6, this particularly applies to Shikoku, which is apparently a non-slack type (i.e., s−** and s + ** are zero) region. Apart from the practicality of such a solution, the models clearly show that a different – and perhaps more efficient – solution than the standard CCR projection is available for reaching the efficiency frontier. For instance, the CCR projection shows that Shikoku should reduce its expenditures by 8.7%, in order to become efficient. On the other hand, the DFM results show that a reduction in expenditures by 4.5%, together with an increase in the electricity generated of 4.7%, is required to become efficient.

The results of the efficiency-improvement projection based on the CCR, DFM, and TO-DFM models for the 2011 DMUs are presented in Fig. 9.7.

In the case of the TO-DFM model, we will set a TES target for each 2011 DMU in comparison to the super-efficiency score in 2010 before the Fukushima disaster, as represented in Fig. 9.3. For example, for Hokkaido, this score was 0.964 in 2010. To achieve this score using the DFM approach, a reduction in expenditures of 14.0% and an increase in electricity generated of 14.0% and in CO_2 emission (inverse number) of 58.3% are required. It thus appears that the TO-DFM result is able to present a realistic efficiency-improvement plan, compared with the CCR and DFM approach for the DMUs with an efficiency score below 1 in the initial situation.

a

Hokkaido 2011

	(I)Gross Expenditure	(O)Electricity Generated	(O)CO2 Emmision
CCR	-24.6%	0.0%	38.9%
DFM	-14.0%	14.0%	58.3%
TO-DFM (2010 Level)	-12.2%	12.2%	0.0%

Tohoku 2011

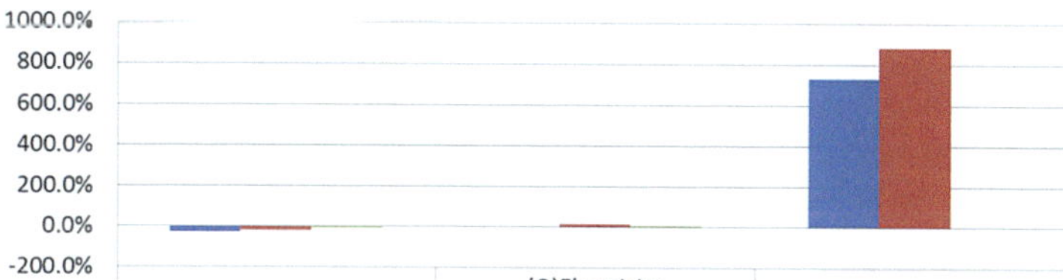

	(I)Gross Expenditure	(O)Electricity Generated	(O)CO2 Emmision
CCR	-30.4%	0.0%	730.5%
DFM	-17.9%	17.9%	879.3%
TO-DFM (2010 Level)	-7.8%	7.8%	0.0%

Tokyo 2011

	(I)Gross Expenditure	(O)Electricity Generated	(O)CO2 Emmision
CCR	-50.7%	0.0%	8730.7%
DFM	-34.0%	34.0%	11731.0%
TO-DFM (2010 Level)	-17.5%	17.5%	0.0%

Chubu 2011

	(I)Gross Expenditure	(O)Electricity Generated	(O)CO2 Emmision
CCR	-17.6%	0.0%	2148.9%
DFM	-9.7%	9.7%	2366.3%
TO-DFM (2010 Level)	-7.8%	7.8%	0.0%

Fig. 9.7 Efficiency-improvement projection results of the CCR, DFM, and TO-DFM models for 2011 DMUs

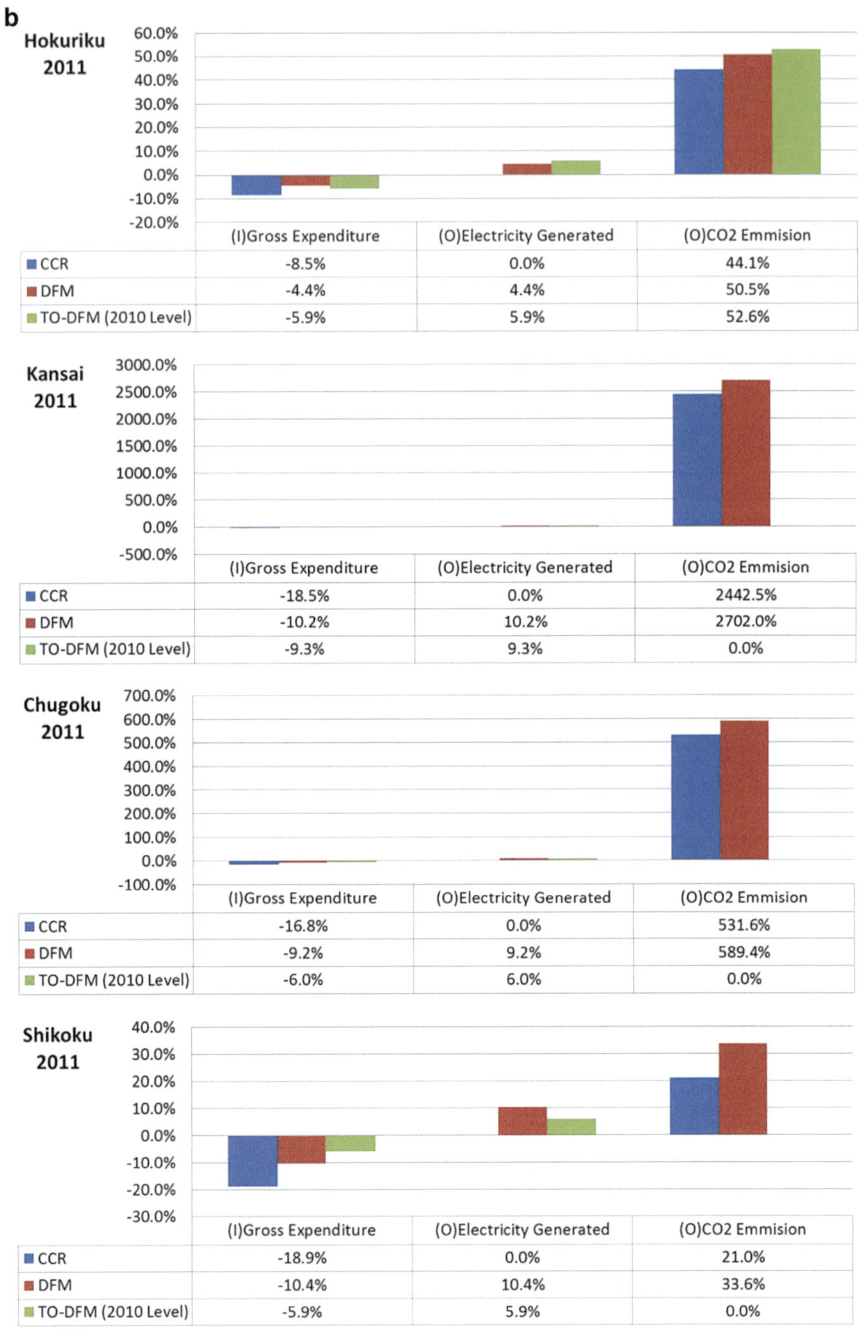

Hokuriku 2011

	(I)Gross Expenditure	(O)Electricity Generated	(O)CO2 Emmision
CCR	-8.5%	0.0%	44.1%
DFM	-4.4%	4.4%	50.5%
TO-DFM (2010 Level)	-5.9%	5.9%	52.6%

Kansai 2011

	(I)Gross Expenditure	(O)Electricity Generated	(O)CO2 Emmision
CCR	-18.5%	0.0%	2442.5%
DFM	-10.2%	10.2%	2702.0%
TO-DFM (2010 Level)	-9.3%	9.3%	0.0%

Chugoku 2011

	(I)Gross Expenditure	(O)Electricity Generated	(O)CO2 Emmision
CCR	-16.8%	0.0%	531.6%
DFM	-9.2%	9.2%	589.4%
TO-DFM (2010 Level)	-6.0%	6.0%	0.0%

Shikoku 2011

	(I)Gross Expenditure	(O)Electricity Generated	(O)CO2 Emmision
CCR	-18.9%	0.0%	21.0%
DFM	-10.4%	10.4%	33.6%
TO-DFM (2010 Level)	-5.9%	5.9%	0.0%

Fig. 9.7 (continued)

c

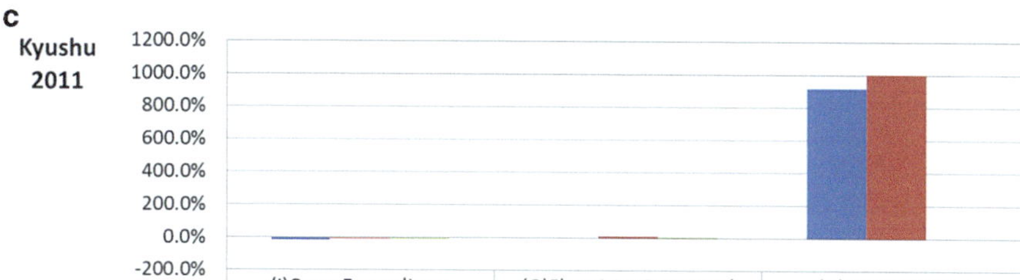

	(I)Gross Expenditure	(O)Electricity Generated	(O)CO2 Emmision
CCR	-16.6%	0.0%	911.5%
DFM	-9.0%	9.0%	1002.8%
TO-DFM (2010 Level)	-8.7%	8.7%	0.0%

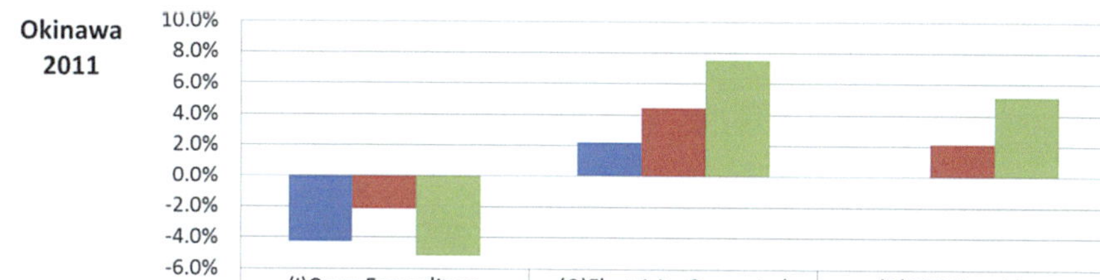

	(I)Gross Expenditure	(O)Electricity Generated	(O)CO2 Emmision
CCR	-4.3%	2.2%	0.0%
DFM	-2.2%	4.4%	2.2%
TO-DFM (2010 Level)	-5.2%	7.5%	5.2%

Fig. 9.7 (continued)

9.6 Performance Improvement Projection Based on Target-Oriented DFM Model

In this subsection, we will use the prefecture of Hokuriku 2011 as an illustrative case and point of reference and present an efficiency-improvement projection result based on the TO-DFM model. The 2011 efficiency value is 0.915 (see Fig. 9.3). We consider now the steps to improve efficiency toward 0.940, 0.970, and 1.000 and furthermore toward the 2010 super-efficiency level of 1.030. The resulting input reduction values and the output increase values based on the TO-DFM model are presented in Fig. 9.8.

These results show that if Hokuriku implements an efficiency-improvement plan with a TES amounting to 0.970, a reduction in expenditures of 2.9% and an increase in electricity generated of 2.9% are required. Furthermore, for a plan to achieve again the super-efficiency level of 2010 with a TES of 1.030, a reduction in expenditure of 5.9% and an increase in the electricity generated of 5.9% and in the CO2 emission (inverse number) of 52.6% would be required.

From these results, we notice that a normal DFM model can only compute TES = 1.000 projections. Our new proposed TO-DFM model based on a Super-Efficiency CCR model can compute a stepwise projection below 1.000 levels but is also able to compute an outcome beyond an efficiency frontier projection in order to reach the performance before the accident level. If we would have used a normal

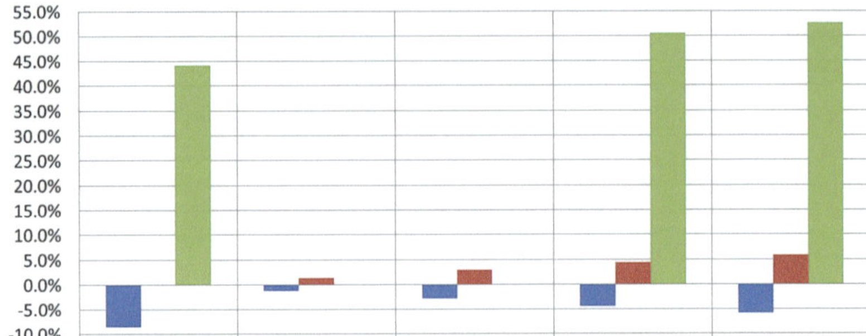

	CCR-I (Score=1.000)	TES=0.940	TES=0.970	TES=1.000 (Normal DFM)	TES=1.030 (2010Hokuriku Level)
(I)Gross Expenditure	-8.5%	-1.4%	-2.9%	-4.4%	-5.9%
(O)Electricity Generated	0.0%	1.4%	2.9%	4.4%	5.9%
(O)CO2 Emmision (inverse number)	44.1%	0.0%	0.0%	50.5%	52.6%

Fig. 9.8 Efficiency-improvement projection results based on the TO-DFM (Hokuriku 2011)

CCR model, it would not have been possible to find a real projection to recover from before the accident.

In order to achieve an efficiency improvement in the energy-environment situation in Japan, it becomes clear that an "aggressive" introduction of new energy is needed, in particular by a radical replacement of old thermal power stations to obtain a reduction of CO2 emission. As mentioned in relation to Fig. 9.1, we notice that the share of new energy such as solar, wind, geothermal, and small-scale hydroelectric and biomass energy is dramatically smaller (1.6% in 2012) than thermal power generation based on coal, oil, and LNG (liquefied natural gas). Conversely, if new energy can be introduced at a large scale, we may expect both a cost reduction through innovation and a CO2 reduction by replacement of the old thermal power generation.

This finding underlines that the TO-DFM can be used for both the formulation of efficiency-improvement policies in the short run and for more ambitious policies in the longer run.

9.7 Conclusion

In this chapter, we have presented a new methodology, the TO-DFM model. Its feasibility was tested for the Japanese energy sector. The new model was tested in realistic circumstances, based on regional efficiency-improvement projections in the post-Fukushima situation in Japan.

The results appear to offer a meaningful contribution to decision making and planning for an efficiency improvement in the energy-environment sector for each region in Japan. These findings are mapped out in a detailed way in the present study. This new model has the potential to become a policy instrument that could offer great benefits for combined environmental-energy decision making and planning. For example, for an agreement on energy-environment sustainability policy, all inefficient regions have to pursue improvements in efficiency (to reach a higher target score). This framework might prompt a new concept like a "regional Kyoto Protocol" for each relevant area in Japan.

References

Andersen, P., & Petersen, N. (1993). A procedure for ranking efficient units in data envelopment analysis. *Management Science, 39*, 1261–1264.

Charnes, A., Cooper, W. W., & Rhodes, E. (1978). Measuring the efficiency of decision making units. *European Journal of Operational Research, 2*, 429–444.

Li, J., Li, J., & Zheng, F. (2014). Unified efficiency measurement of electric power supply companies in China. *Sustainability, 6*(2), 779–793.

Martínez, P. (2011). Energy efficiency development in German and Colombian non energy-intensive sectors: A non-parametric analysis. *Energy Efficiency, 4*(1), 115–131.

Scheel, H. (2001). Undesirable outputs in efficiency valuations. *European Journal of Operational Research, 132*(2), 400–410.

Seiford, L., & Zhu, J. (2002). Modeling undesirable factors in efficiency evaluation. *European Journal of Operational Research, 142*(1), 16–20.

Suzuki, S., Nijkamp, P., & Rietveld, P. (2015). A target-oriented data envelopment analysis for energy-environment efficiency improvement in Japan. *Energy Efficiency, 8*(3), 433–446.

Wu, A., Cao, Y., & Liu, B. (2014). Energy efficiency evaluation for regions in China: An application of DEA and Malmquist indices. *Energy Efficiency, 7*(3), 429–439.

Chapter 10
The Need for a New Energy Performance Balance in Japan: Combination of an Adjusted-Improvement Model with a CCR Model

Abstract This chapter aims to present an application result of the Adjusted-Improvement (AI) approach to DEA for generating an appropriate efficiency-improvement projection model. We propose a Target-Oriented (TO) DFM model that allows reference points that remain below the efficiency frontier. Our TO-DFM model specifies a Target Efficiency Score (TES) for inefficient DMUs. This model is able to compute an improvement projection based on an input reduction value and an output increase value in order to achieve a TES. However, in reality, these values may represent an infeasible case; for example, a Networking Rate may be required of more than 100% in the improvement projection, but this would exceed a physical limit. Therefore, we propose an Adjusted-Improvement (AI) approach based on the TO-DFM model. The AI approach specifies an adjustment in input/output items based on the absence or presence of a DMU's improvement limit. This approach can compute an input reduction value and an output increase value in order to achieve a TES that maintains an improvement limit condition. This chapter evaluates the efficiency of new energy in Japan based on DEA and the abovementioned Adjusted-Improvement TO-DFM model to produce a realistic efficiency-improvement projection. The focus will be on three input cost criteria (cost of power generation, energy payback time, and CO2 emissions) and one output performance criterion (Networking Rate). Based on the results of the performance analysis and the efficiency-improvement projection of new energy performance needs in Japan, we offer a quantitative contribution to efficiency rise in energy-environment policy in Japan.

Keywords Data Envelopment Analysis (DEA) • Distance friction minimization • Adjusted-Improvement (AI) model • Target-Oriented (TO) • New energy

10.1 Introduction

Japan is, nowadays, confronted with "the post-Fukushima problem," in which a single nuclear accident has caused drastic electrical power shortages. Due to the strong backlash of public opinion, almost all of Japan's 54 nuclear plants had to suspend their operations. Japan has now permission to increase thermal power

S. Suzuki, P. Nijkamp, *Regional Performance Measurement and Improvement*, New Frontiers in Regional Science: Asian Perspectives 9,
DOI 10.1007/978-981-10-0242-7_10

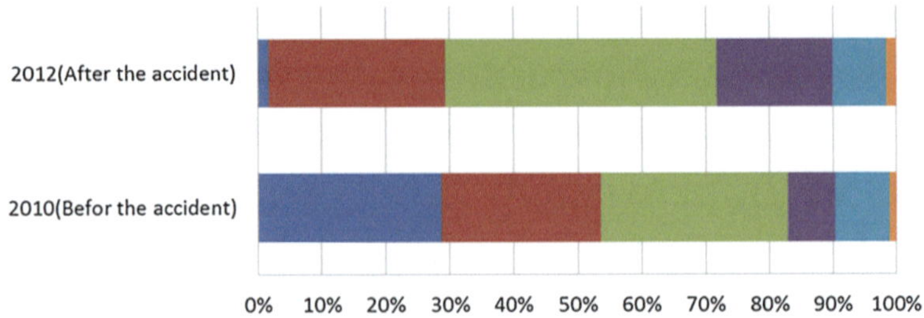

	2010(Befor the accident)	2012(After the accident)
Nuclear	28.6	1.7
Coal	25.0	27.6
LNG	29.3	42.5
Oil	7.5	18.3
Hydraulic	8.5	8.4
New Energy	1.1	1.6

Fig. 10.1 A comparison of electronic power supply between before and after the accident in Japan

generation based on coal, oil, and LNG (liquefied natural gas) in order to compensate for the shortfall following the accident, as presented in Fig. 10.1. An intensive search for alternative forms of energy – ranging from fossil fuels to new energy, such as solar, wind, geothermal, and small-scale hydroelectric and biomass energy – has started. There is no clear-cut direction for energy policy, as each option involves costs and CO2 consequences and Japan has even withdrawn from the Kyoto Protocol. A policy that balances energy and the environment is difficult to achieve in the short term; therefore, there is an urgent need for a comprehensive efficiency and performance analysis of new energy in Japan.

A standard tool by which to judge efficiency is Data Envelopment Analysis (DEA), proposed by Charnes et al. (1978). Suzuki et al. (2010) proposed a distance friction minimization (DFM) model that is based on a generalized distance function and serves to improve the performance of a DMU by identifying the most appropriate movement toward the efficiency frontier surface. The DFM model is able to calculate either an optimal input reduction value or an output increase value in order to reach an efficiency score of 1.000, even though in reality this might be hard to achieve for low-efficiency DMUs.

To produce a more realistic improvement plan, we need a method that allows reference points that remain below the efficiency frontier. A Target-Oriented (TO) DFM model which was proposed by Suzuki et al. (2015) specifies a Target Efficiency Score (TES) for inefficient DMUs. This model is able to compute an input reduction value and an output increase value in order to achieve a TES. The TO-DFM result is able to present a more realistic efficiency-improvement plan than those of the original DEA model and the original DFM model for DMUs with an efficiency score below 1 in the initial situation.

The TO-DFM model calculates an optimal input reduction value and an output increase value in order to reach a TES, but in reality these values may represent an infeasible case, for example, a Networking Rate may be required of more than 100% in the improvement projection, but then it exceeds a physical limit.

Therefore, we proposed an Adjusted-Improvement (AI) approach (see Sect. 5.3.1) based on the TO-DFM model. The AI approach specifies adjustment in input/output items based on the absence or presence of a DMU's improvement limit. This approach can compute an input reduction value and an output increase value in order to achieve a TES that maintains an improvement limit condition.

This chapter aims to present an application result of the Adjusted-Improvement (AI) approach, for generating an appropriate efficiency-improvement projection model. The AI approach specifies an adjustment input/output items based on absence or presence of DMU's improvement limit. This approach can compute an input reduction value and an output increase value in order to achieve a TES that maintains an improvement limit condition.

This study evaluates the efficiency of new energy in Japan based on DEA, and the abovementioned Adjusted-Improvement TO-DFM model based on the CCR model is applied to produce a realistic efficiency-improvement projection. The focus will be on the three input cost criteria (cost of power generation, energy payback time, and CO2 emissions) and output performance criterion (Networking Rate). Based on the results of the performance analysis and the efficiency-improvement projection of new energies in Japan, this study will offer a quantitative contribution to energy-environment policy in Japan.

10.2 Analysis Framework and Database

We use the following input and output data for a set of eight types of new energy in Japan. Figure 10.2 presents the inputs and outputs considered in this analysis of new energy efficiency.

We consider three inputs (I):

(I1) Cost (including construction, fuel, and operating cost) (yen/kWh)
(I2) Energy payback time (year)
(I3) CO2 emission (Kg-CO2/kWh)

While one output is incorporated:

(O2) Networking Rate (%)

Datasets (I1) were obtained from the "report of commission for cost verification, energy, and environment conference, Japan Cabinet Secretariat," and "Japan Geothermal Developers' Council." Datasets (I2) were obtained from the report of "Mizuho Information & Research Institute" and "The National Institute of Advanced Industrial Science and Technology (AIST) in Japan." Datasets (I3) were obtained from the report of "Central Research Institute of Electric Power Industry (CRIEPI) in Japan" and "AIST in Japan." Datasets (O1) were obtained from the "report of commission for cost verification, energy, and

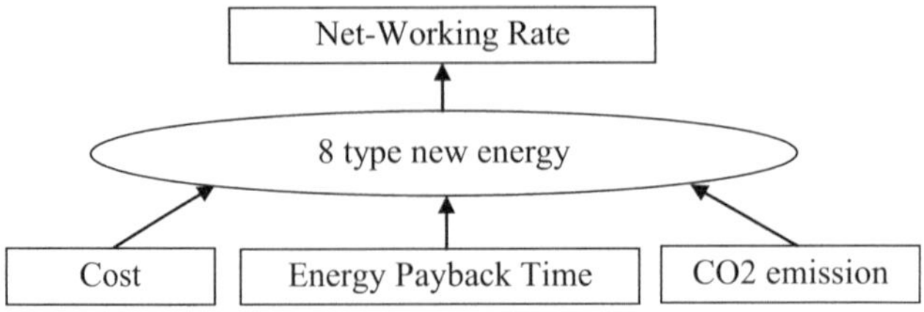

Fig. 10.2 Inputs and outputs of new energy efficiency

Table 10.1 A listing of DMUs and datasets

No.	DMU	(Input) cost	(Input) energy payback time	(Input) CO2 emission	(Output) Networking Rate
1	Household solar (HS)	18.70	2.20	38.00	12.00
2	Mega solar (MS)	22.10	2.58	55.20	12.00
3	Geothermal (GT)	14.80	0.97	15.00	80.00
4	Woody biomass (WB)	24.80	3.60	44.00	80.00
5	Biogas (BG)	26.29	3.40	54.97	90.00
6	Small hydroelectric (SH)	20.55	0.60	5.50	60.00
7	Wind on the land (WL)	13.05	0.68	29.00	20.00
8	Wind on the ocean (WO)	15.95	0.68	29.00	30.00

environment conference, Japan Cabinet Secretariat," and "BTS Japan website (http://bts.jpn.com/)."

The DMUs and these datasets used in analysis are listed in Table 10.1.

In our application, we first applied the CCR-I model, while then the results were used to determine the CCR-I, DFM, TO-DFM, and AI-TO-DFM projections.

10.3 Performance Evaluation Based on the CCR Model

An efficiency evaluation result for eight types of new energy based on the CCR model is presented in Fig. 10.3. From Fig. 10.3, it can be seen that small hydroelectric (1.000) and geothermal (1.00) are efficient DMUs. On the other hand, we noticed that mega solar (0.100), household solar (0.119), wind on the land (0.342), and wind on the ocean (0.490) have low efficiency than biogas (0.633) and woody biomass (0.597). In general, solar and wind energies are expected to lead as new energy sources in Japan; nevertheless the Networking Rate of these energies is in a lower level as shown in Table 1, and then efficiency scores of solar and wind are evaluated as low efficiency. From these facts, it is considered that output fluctuation

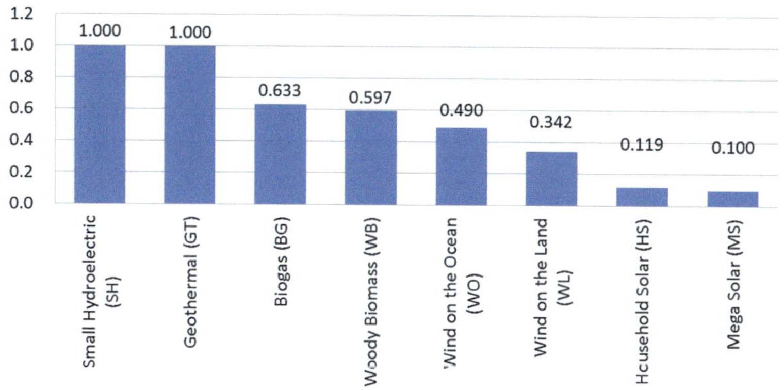

Fig. 10.3 Efficiency scores based on the Super-Efficiency CCR-I model

and its stabilization of new energy are important factors for new energy policy in Japan. Given the above findings, it is necessary to make an effort in efficiency improvement of the new energy.

10.4 Optimum Weights of Input and Output Items

The optimum weights of the input and output variables for the eight types of new energy based on the Super-Efficiency CCR model are given in Figs. 10.4 and 10.5, respectively.

It should be noted that (v^*, u^*) is the set of most favorable weights for each DMU, so that we can find the relative importance of each indicator with reference to the value of each $v_m^* \ x_{mo}$ and $u_s^* \ y_{so}$ for each DMU. From these results, it can be seen that, for instance, wind on the land obtains a weight for cost equal to 0.206 and for energy payback time equal to 0.794 in its inputs, while it obtains for Networking Rate a weight of 0.342 in its output. These results offer meaningful insights for policies on efficiency improvement of new energy.

10.5 Performance Improvement Projection Based on CCR, DFM, and Target-Oriented DFM Model

The results of efficiency-improvement projection based on the CCR, DFM, and TO-DFM models for inefficient DMUs are presented in Fig. 10.6.

It appears that, as expected, the empirical ratios of change in the DFM projection are smaller than in the CCR projection. In Fig. 10.6, this particularly applies to wind on the ocean, which is apparently a non-slack type (i.e., s−** and s + ** are zero) energy. Apart from the practicality of such a solution, the models clearly show that

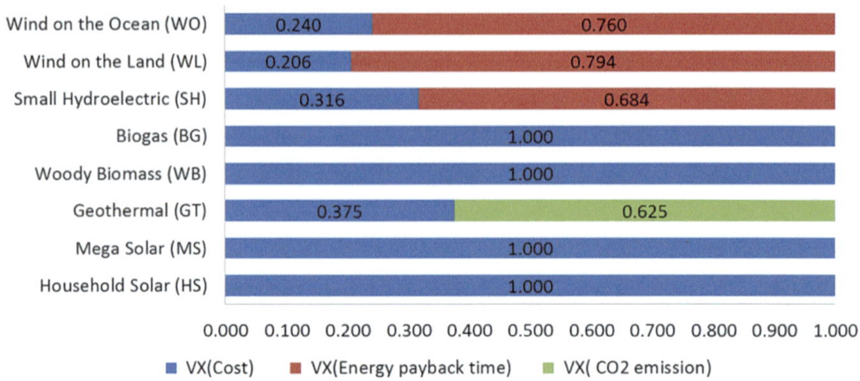

Fig. 10.4 Input optimum weights

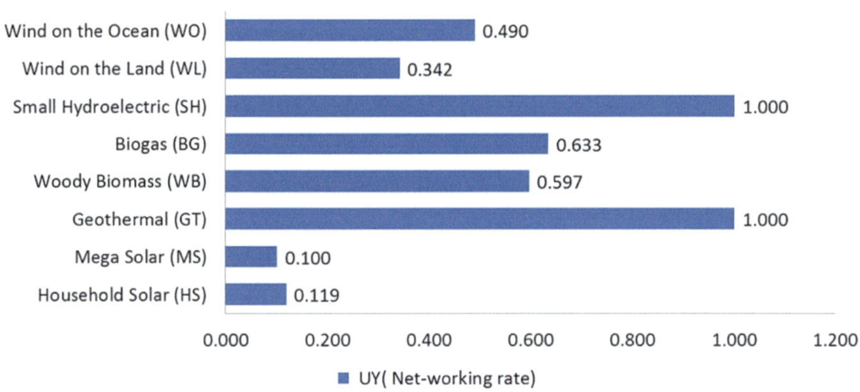

Fig. 10.5 Output optimum weights

a different – and perhaps more efficient – solution than the standard CCR projection is available for reaching the efficiency frontier. For instance, the CCR projection shows that wind on the ocean should reduce its cost by 51.0%, its energy payback time by 51.0%, and its energy CO2 emission by 85.4%, in order to become efficient. On the other hand, the DFM results show that a reduction in energy payback time of 45.1%, together with an increase in the Networking Rate of 34.2%, is required to become efficient.

In the case of the TO-DFM model, the Target Efficiency Score (TES) for each inefficient DMU is set an efficiency score of proximate upper-level DMU. For example, woody biomass score was 0.597. To achieve a biogas score (0.633) using the TO-DFM model, a reduction in cost of 3.0% and an increase in Networking Rate of 3.0% are required. It thus appears that the TO-DFM result is able to present a realistic efficiency-improvement plan, compared with the CCR and DFM approach for the DMUs with an efficiency score below 1 in the initial situation.

Woody Biomass(WB)

	(I)cost	(I)energy payback time	(I)CO2 emission	(O)net-working rate
CCR	-40.3%	-73.1%	-65.9%	0.0%
DFM	-25.3%	-66.3%	-57.3%	25.3%
TO-DFM	-3.0%	0.0%	0.0%	3.0%

BioGas(BG)

	(I)cost	(I)energy payback time	(I)CO2 emission	(O)net-working rate
CCR	-36.7%	-67.9%	-69.3%	0.0%
DFM	-22.4%	-60.7%	-62.4%	22.4%
TO-DFM	-11.6%	0.0%	0.0%	11.6%

Wind on the Land (WL)

	(I)cost	(I)energy payback time	(I)CO2 emission	(O)net-working rate
CCR	-65.84%	-65.84%	-88.66%	0.00%
DFM	0.0%	-61.8%	0.0%	49.1%
TO-DFM	0.0%	-22.5%	0.0%	17.8%

Wind on the Ocean (WO)

	(I)cost	(I)energy payback time	(I)CO2 emission	(O)net-working rate
CCR	-51.0%	-51.0%	-85.4%	0.0%
DFM	0.0%	-45.1%	0.0%	34.2%
TO-DFM	0.0%	-12.9%	0.0%	9.8%

Fig. 10.6 Efficiency-improvement projection results of the CCR, DFM, and TO-DFM models

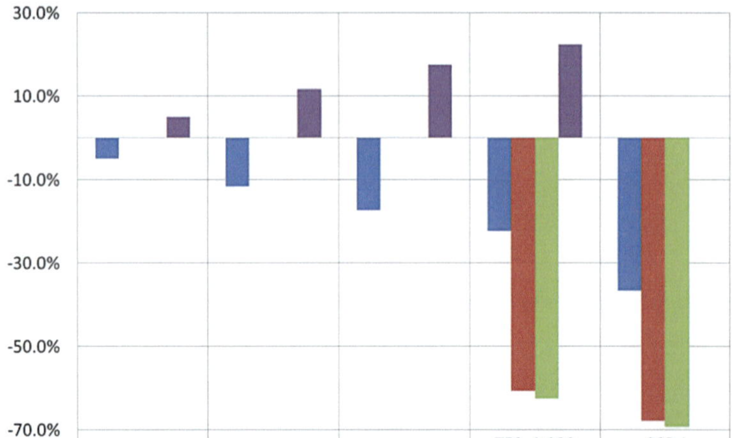

	TES=0.700	TES=0.800	TES=0.900	TES=1.000 (Normal DFM)	CCR-I (Score=1.000)
(I)Cost	-5.0%	-11.6%	-17.4%	-22.4%	-36.7%
(I)Energy payback time	0.0%	0.0%	0.0%	-60.7%	-67.9%
(I)CO2 emission	0.0%	0.0%	0.0%	-62.4%	-69.3%
(O)Net-working rate	5.0%	11.6%	17.4%	22.4%	0.0%

Fig. 10.7 Efficiency-improvement projection results (%) based on TO-DFM (biogas)

10.6 Performance Improvement Projection Based on an Adjusted-Improvement Target-Oriented DFM Model

In this subsection, we will use the biogas as example and present an efficiency-improvement projection result based on the TO-DFM model. Efficiency score of biogas is 0.633 (see Fig. 10.3). We consider steps to improve efficiency toward 0.7, 0.8, 0.9, and 1.0. The resulting input reduction percentage and the output increase percentage based on the TO-DFM model are presented in Fig.10.7.

These results show that if it implements an efficiency-improvement plan with a TES amounting to 0.7, a reduction in cost of 5.0% and an increase in Networking Rate of 5.0% are required. Furthermore, for a plan to achieve a TES of 1.000, a reduction in cost of 22.4%, in energy payback time of 60.7%, and in CO 2 emission of 62.4% and an increase in Networking Rate of 22.4% would be required.

Projection results on actual number based on the TO-DFM model are presented in Fig. 10.8.

From Fig. 10.8, it appears that value of Networking Rate exceeds 100(%) in the case of TES = 0.8–1.0. It is clearly an infeasible solution.

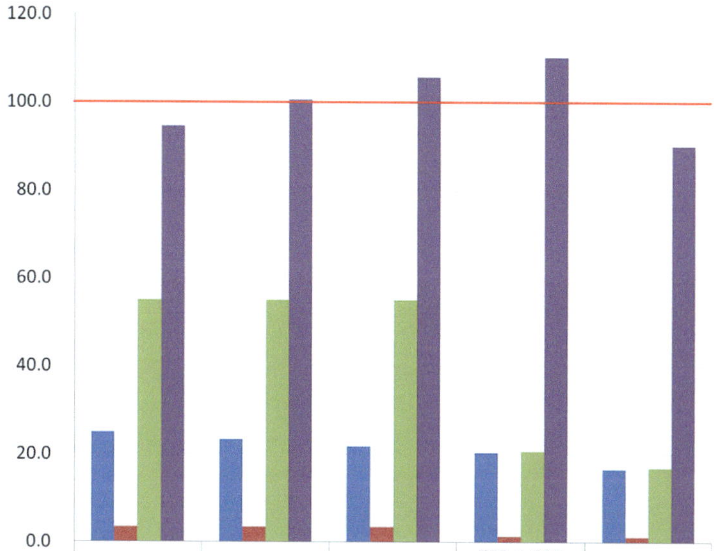

	TES=0.700	TES=0.800	TES=0.900	TES=1.000 (Normal DFM)	CCR-I (Score=1.000)
(I)Cost	25.0	23.2	21.7	20.4	16.7
(I)Energy payback time	3.4	3.4	3.4	1.3	1.1
(I)CO2 emission	55.0	55.0	55.0	20.7	16.9
(O)Net-working rate	94.5	100.5	105.6	110.2	90.0

Fig. 10.8 Efficiency-improvement projection results (actual number) based on TO-DFM (biogas)

10.7 Efficiency Improvement Projection of the Adjusted-Improvement TO-DFM Model

In this subsection, we will use the biogas as example and present an efficiency-improvement projection result based on the Adjusted-Improvement TO-DFM model. As we confirmed the infeasible case in subsection 10.6, that Networking Rate exceeds 100(%) in the case of TES = 0.8 to 1.0, then we set out Networking Rate as restricted output item. This study assumed that improvement limitation of Networking Rate is set out to 95(%).

The efficiency score of biogas is 0.633 (see Fig. 10.3). We consider steps to improve efficiency toward 0.7, 0.8, 0.9, and 1.0. The projection result of input reduction percentage and the output increase percentage, also each actual number, based on the AI-TO-DFM model are presented in Figs. 10.9 and 10.10.

From Figs. 10.9 and 10.10, it can be confirmed that an efficiency improvement plan with a TES amounting from 0.8 to 1.0, an increase percentage in Networking Rate of 5.6%, and its actual number of 95(%) are adjusted. From this fact, it appears that AI-TO-DFM model can produce more realistic efficiency-improvement projection than DFM and TO-DFM model.

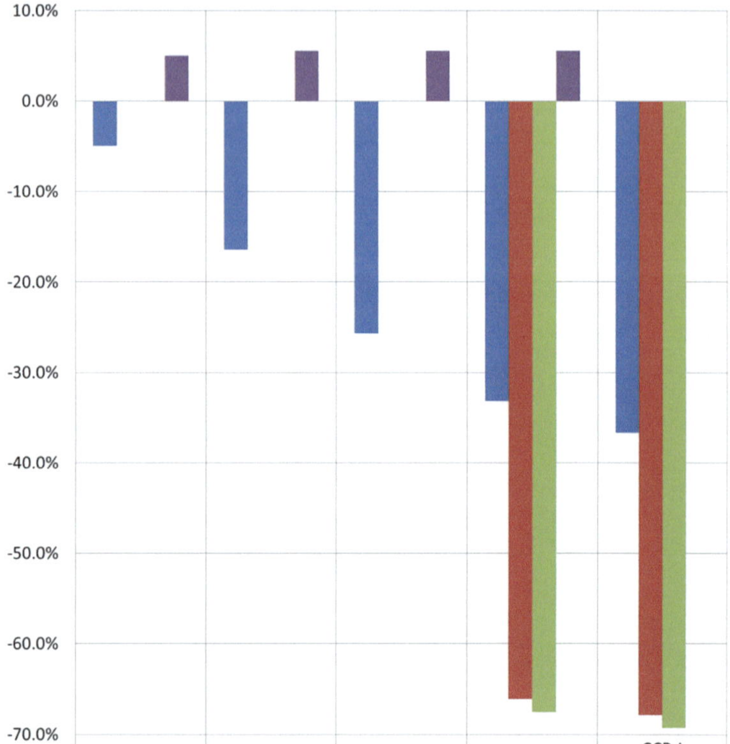

	TES=0.700	TES=0.800	TES=0.900	TES=1.000	CCR-I (Score=1.000)
(I)Cost	-5.0%	-16.4%	-25.7%	-33.1%	-36.7%
(I)Energy payback time	0.0%	0.0%	0.0%	-66.1%	-67.9%
(I)CO2 emission	0.0%	0.0%	0.0%	-67.6%	-69.3%
(O)Net-working rate	5.0%	5.6%	5.6%	5.6%	0.0%

Fig. 10.9 Efficiency-improvement projection results (%) based on the AI-TO-DFM (biogas)

10.8 Conclusion

In this chapter, we have presented a new DEA methodology, the AI-TO-DFM model. Its feasibility was tested for the new energy performance balance in Japan; the new model was applied in rather realistic circumstances in Japan.

The results appear to offer a meaningful contribution to decision making and planning for an efficiency improvement in the energy-environment sector in Japan. These findings are mapped out in a detailed way in the present study. This model has the potential to become a policy instrument that could offer great benefits for combined environmental-energy decision making and planning in Japan and elsewhere.

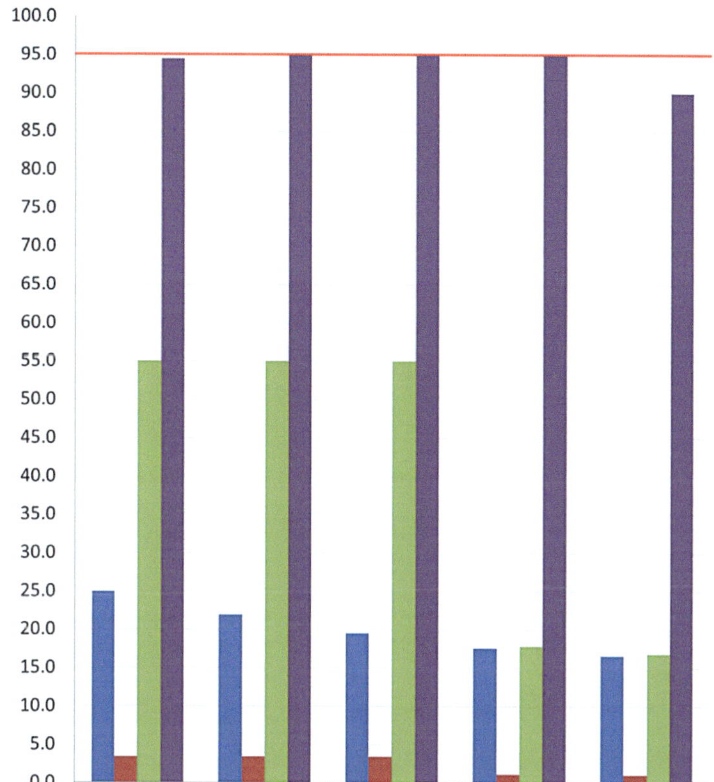

	TES=0.700	TES=0.800	TES=0.900	TES=1.000	CCR-I (Score=1.000)
(I)Cost	25.0	22.0	19.5	17.6	16.7
(I)Energy payback time	3.4	3.4	3.4	1.2	1.1
(I)CO2 emission	55.0	55.0	55.0	17.8	16.9
(O)Net-working rate	94.5	95.0	95.0	95.0	90.0

Fig. 10.10 Efficiency-improvement projection results (actual number) based on AI-TO-DFM (biogas)

References

Charnes, A., Cooper, W. W., & Rhodes, E. (1978). Measuring the efficiency of decision making units. *European Journal of Operational Research, 2*, 429–444.

Suzuki, S., Nijkamp, P., & Rietveld, P. (2015). A target-oriented data envelopment analysis for energy-environment efficiency improvement in Japan. *Energy Efficiency, 8*(3), 433–446.

Suzuki, S., Nijkamp, P., Rietveld, P., & Pels, E. (2010). A distance friction minimization approach in data envelopment analysis: A comparative study on airport efficiency. *European Journal of Operational Research, 207*, 1104–1115.

Chapter 11
Measurement of Energy-Environment-Economic Performance for EU, APEC, and ASEAN Countries: Combination of a Fixed-Factor Model with an SE Model

Abstract The aim of this chapter is to apply an extended DEA model – emerging from a blend of a distance friction minimization (DFM) and a target-oriented (TO) with a fixed (inflexible) factor (FF) approach based on a super-efficiency (SE) model – for generating an appropriate efficiency-improvement projection model. The DFM model is able to calculate an optimal input reduction value and an optimal output increase value in order to reach an efficiency score of 1.0, even though in reality this may be hard to achieve for low-efficiency DMUs. To design a feasible improvement strategy for low-efficiency DMUs, we develop here a target-oriented (TO) DFM model. However, in many real-world cases input factors may not be flexibly adjusted in the short run. We integrate here the TO-DFM model with a fixed (inflexible) factor (FF) approach to cope with such more realistic circumstances. Super-efficiency DEA is next used in our comparative study on the efficiency assessment of energy-environment-economic targets for the EU, APEC, and ASEAN (A&A) countries, employing appropriate data sets from the years 2003 to 2012. We consider two inputs (primary energy consumption and population) and two outputs (CO2 and GDP), including a fixed input factor (viz., population). On the basis of our DEA analysis results, EU countries appear to exhibit generally a higher efficiency than A&A countries. The above-mentioned TO-DFM-FF projection model is able to address realistic circumstances and requirements in an operational sustainability strategy for efficiency improvement in inefficient countries in the A&A region.

Keywords Data Envelopment Analysis (DEA) • Distance friction minimization (DFM) • Target-oriented (TO) • Fixed factor (FF) • Energy-environment-economic efficiency • EU, APEC, ASEAN countries

11.1 Introduction

It is nowadays widely accepted that balanced economic growth has to be accompanied simultaneously by resource and environment conservation in a sustainable world. In 2014, the "International Energy Efficiency Scorecard," published by American Council for an Energy-Efficient Economy (ACEEE) (2014), pointed

S. Suzuki, P. Nijkamp, *Regional Performance Measurement and Improvement*, New Frontiers in Regional Science: Asian Perspectives 9,
DOI 10.1007/978-981-10-0242-7_11

out that "Countries can preserve their resources, address global warming, stabilize their economies, and reduce the costs of their economic outputs by using energy more efficiently—an eminently achievable goal." This report analyzed the world's 16 largest economies (countries/regions). The report looked at 31 criteria, divided roughly in half between policies and quantifiable performance in order to evaluate how efficiently these economies use energy. The scores for the policy criteria were based on the presence in a country/region of a best-practice policy. However, this evaluation relied heavily on rather subjective policy criteria. Therefore, the actual conditions of energy efficiency for each country/region were not evaluated in an appropriate or testable manner.

A standard tool by which to judge efficiency among different actors is Data Envelopment Analysis (DEA), proposed by Charnes, Cooper, and Rhodes (CCR) (1978). This has become over the past decades an established quantitative assessment method in the evaluation literature. Nowadays, there are also in a sustainability context several assessment studies that have applied DEA models to measure aggregate energy-environment-economic efficiency among countries or regions, regarded as decision-making units (DMUs). For example, Zhou et al. (2008) presented a literature survey on the application of DEA to energy and environmental (E&E) studies, followed by a classification of 100 publications in this field. This study argues that all this research which provides lists of DMUs is confined to just one country or major region, such as the OECD, the APEC, and the EU, or developing countries, but without a rigorous cross-regional comparison, for example, the EU vs. APEC and ASEAN (hereafter A&A). The A&A countries are regions where remarkable economic development is taking place, but comparing them from the viewpoint of energy-environment-economic efficiency with the performance of EU countries brings to light often contrasting findings. Martínez (2011) measures energy-efficiency development in nonenergy-intensive sectors (NEISs) in both Germany and Colombia, based on a DEA model. And Wu et al. (2014) apply a DEA model – and calculate related Malmquist indices – for an efficiency evaluation of regions in China. The above list of studies shows that comparative efficiency analysis in the energy-environment sector using DEA models has increasingly become an important research topic in recent years.

We apply in the present study a distance friction minimization (DFM) model that is based on a generalized distance function and serves to improve the performance of a DMU by identifying the most appropriate movement toward the efficiency frontier surface. The DFM model is able to calculate either an optimal input reduction value or an optimal output increase value in order to reach an efficiency score of 1.000, even though in reality this might be hard to achieve for low-efficiency DMUs. We also presented an adjusted DEA model, emerging from a blend of the DFM and the target-oriented (TO) approach based on a Super-Efficiency model, for generating an appropriate efficiency-improvement projection model. The TO approach specifies a Target Efficiency Score (TES) for inefficient DMUs. This approach can compute an input reduction value and an output increase value in order to achieve a higher TES. However, in many cases, the input factor may not be flexible or adjustable due to the indivisible nature or inertia in the input or output factor. Usually, the DEA model does not allow for such a noncontrollable or a fixed input factor.

We introduce now an adjusted DEA model-emerging blend of the TO-DFM model and a fixed factor (FF) model, in Sect. 5.4 (see also Suzuki and Nijkamp (2016)) which has an advantage in that policy implications by the approach can be more realistic than given in any other DEA approaches. A comparative assessment of real-world choices in which fixed factors beyond a DMU's control exist and data for a DEA efficiency analysis are wide-ranging calls for a new research approach.

We will compute the empirical results from a comparative assessment on energy efficiency in various countries, by our TO-DFM-FF model in order to cope with realistic choice conditions in our search for a feasible efficiency-improvement projection. After the description of the methodology adopted here, a Super-Efficiency model (Andersen and Petersen 1993) for DEA is used in our comparative study on the efficiency assessment of energy-environment-economic goals for EU and A&A countries, using appropriate data sets ranging from 2003 to 2012. As mentioned above, the A&A countries are regions where remarkable economic development is taking place, but comparing them from the viewpoint of energy-environment-economic efficiency with the performance of EU countries brings to light often contrasting and sometimes disappointing findings. From this viewpoint, the present chapter takes for granted that EU countries are operating at significantly higher efficiency levels than A&A countries.

In this chapter, due to comparative data limitations, we consider two inputs (primary energy consumption and population) and two outputs (CO2 and GDP), including a fixed (inflexible) input factor related to population. In this comparative analysis, we will conceive of "population" as a production factor that cannot be flexibly adjusted in a short period of time. The abovementioned TO-DFM-FF projection model is then used to consider realistic circumstances and to address requirements in an operational strategy for a feasible efficiency improvement in inefficient countries in A&A. Clearly, the number of inputs and outputs considered here is rather low, and this may reduce the flexibility in adjustment mechanisms, but the advantage is that it focuses the attention on critical variables that are common in all countries considered.

11.2 Database and Analysis Framework

There is a vast difference in energy use, environmental quality, economic growth, and demographic composition in many countries. It may be interesting to obtain new insights from a comparative study on energy efficiency in such countries, which may provide lessons for national sustainability policies. From that perspective, we have to look at input-output ratios as measures of efficiency or productivity, using the DEA framework sketched out above.

We use for our analysis the following relevant input and output data from the years 2003 to 2012 for a set of 27 EU countries (Austria, Belgium, Bulgaria,

Table 11.1 A list of DMUs

No.	EU	No.	A&A
1	Austria	28	Australia
2	Belgium	29	Brunei
3	Bulgaria	30	Cambodia
4	Croatia	31	Canada
5	Cyprus	32	Chile
6	Czech	33	China
7	Denmark	34	Indonesia
8	Estonia	35	Japan
9	Finland	36	Korea
10	France	37	Malaysia
11	Germany	38	Mexico
12	Greece	39	Myanmar
13	Hungary	40	New Zealand
14	Ireland	41	Peru
15	Italy	42	Philippines
16	Latvia	43	Russia
17	Lithuania	44	Singapore
18	Luxembourg	45	Thailand
19	Netherlands	46	USA
20	Poland	47	Vietnam
21	Portugal		
22	Romania		
23	Slovak		
24	Slovenia		
25	Spain		
26	Sweden		
27	UK		

Croatia, Cyprus, Czech, Denmark, Estonia, Finland, France, Germany, Greece, Hungary, Ireland, Italy, Latvia, Lithuania, Luxembourg, the Netherlands, Poland, Portugal, Romania, Slovakia, Slovenia, Spain, Sweden, and the UK) and 20 ASEAN and APEC (A&A) countries (Australia, Brunei, Cambodia, Canada, Chile, China, Indonesia, Japan, Korea, Malaysia, Mexico, Myanmar, New Zealand, Peru, the Philippines, Russia, Singapore, Thailand, the USA, and Vietnam) to evaluate and compare their energy-environment-economic efficiency. The DMUs used in our analysis are listed in Table 11.1.

As shown in Table 11.1, we regard as DMUs the 27 EU countries and 20 A&A countries. We note that Lao People's Democratic Republic, Papua New Guinea, China, Hong Kong, and Taiwan are omitted in the list for reason of data restrictions. Malta is omitted in the list for a reason of too much small data. In our subsequent DEA context, we will focus on both input and output variables.

For our comparative sustainability analysis of various countries, we consider two inputs (I):

(I1) Population (thousands) (Reference: UN Statistics Division)
(I2) Energy consumption (Peta Joule) (Reference: International Energy Agency)

while also two outputs (O) are incorporated:

(O1) GDP (at constant 2005 prices – hundred million US dollars) (Reference: UN Statistics Division)
(O2) CO2 emission (million tons) (Reference: International Energy Agency)
CO2 emission in our study is defined as a multiplicative inverse of the "bad" output (actual CO2 emission) in order that a decrease in the actual CO2 emission ("good output") indicates an increase in variable CO2 (for details, see also Scheel (2001) and Seiford (2002)).

In our application, we first employed the Super-Efficiency CCR-I model, while next the results were used to determine the CCR-I, DFM, and TO-DFM-FF projections. Additionally, we applied the TO-DFM-FF model using Japan 2012 as a reference country for our benchmark experiment.

11.3 Performance Evaluation Based on a Combined SE-CCR-I Model

The efficiency evaluation result for the 47 countries from 2003 to 2012 based on the Super-Efficiency CCR-I model is presented in Fig. 11.1 (EU countries) and Fig. 11.2 (A&A countries).

From Figs. 11.1 and 11.2, it can be seen that Luxembourg, Cyprus, Ireland, and Brunei may be regarded as super-efficient DMUs. It also can be seen that the efficiency scores of EU countries are higher on average than the A&A countries. We can also compare an average score between the EU and A&A countries, based on a two-sample T-test (statistical significance test for differences in the average efficiency score between the EU and A&A countries), as shown in Fig. 11.3.

From Fig. 11.3, we notice that the gap between the average scores for EU and A&A countries has narrowed from 2003 to 2005, but, after 2006, the gap has widened year by year. In particular, the gap in 2011 and 2012 shows a statistical significance (in Fig. 11.3, * means: 5 significant at a 5% level). This result offers policy-relevant information on energy-environment-economic efficiency in a cross-regional comparison of EU vs. A&A countries. This finding supports the hypothesis that EU countries are significantly performing at higher efficiency levels than A&A countries.

Given the above findings, it is clear that a serious effort should be made for the efficiency improvement of the energy-environment-economic performance in APEC and ASEAN countries.

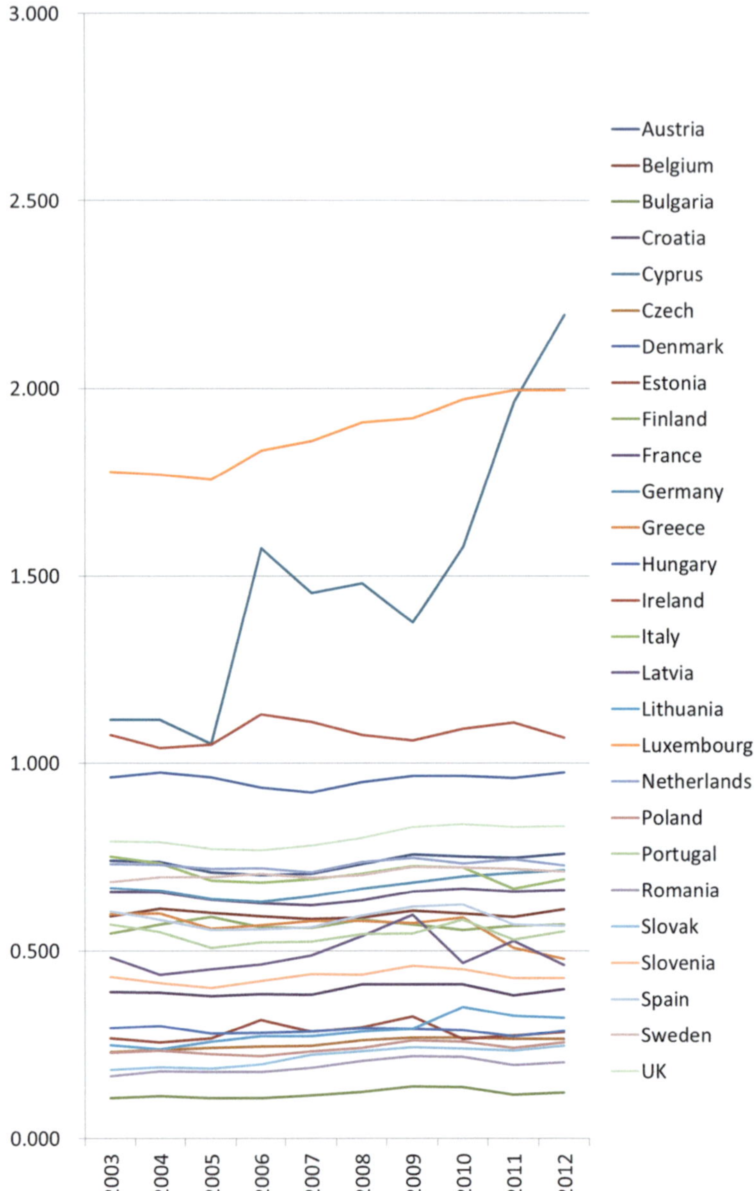

Fig. 11.1 Efficiency scores based on the Super-Efficiency CCR-I model (EU countries)

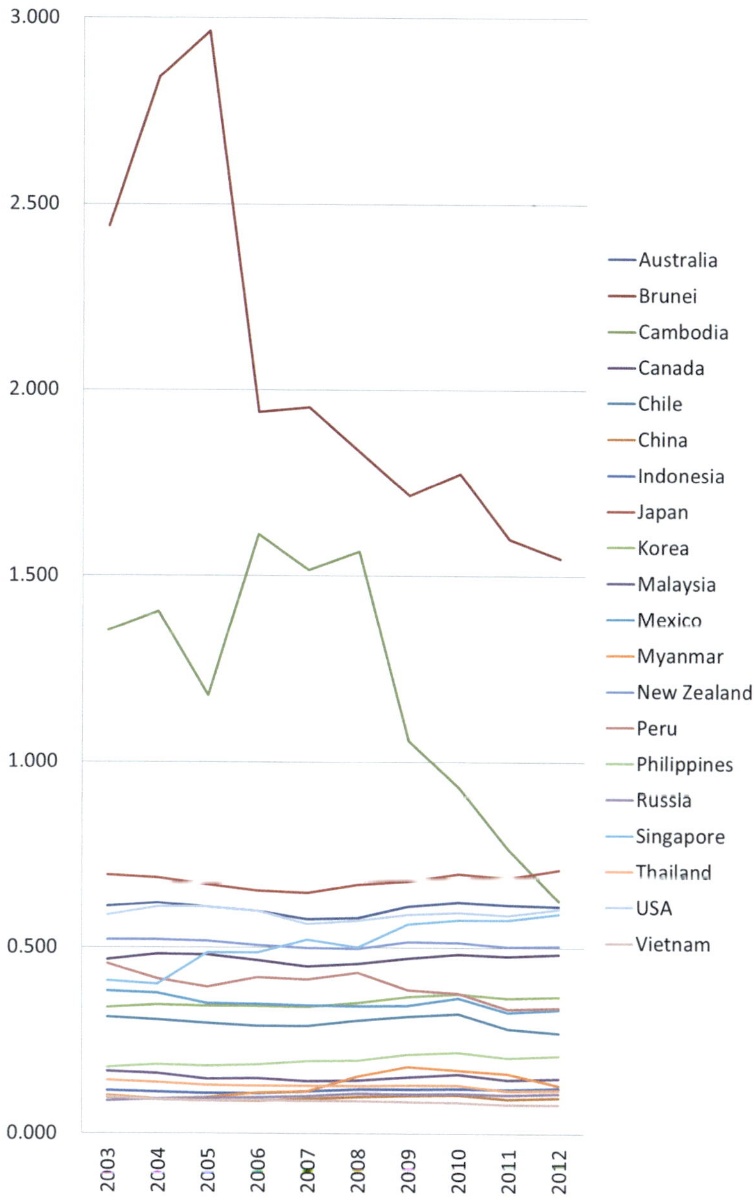

Fig. 11.2 Efficiency scores based on the Super-Efficiency CCR-I model (A&A countries)

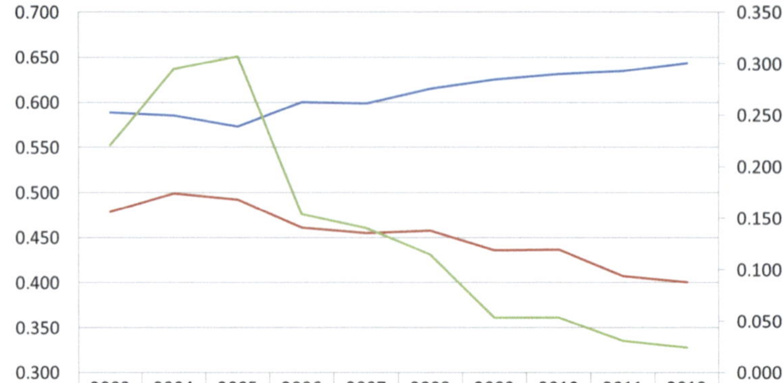

	2003	2004	2005	2006	2007	2008	2009	2010	2011	2012
EU	0.589	0.585	0.573	0.600	0.599	0.615	0.625	0.631	0.634	0.644
A&A	0.478	0.499	0.492	0.461	0.455	0.457	0.436	0.437	0.407	0.400
T-test	0.221	0.294	0.307	0.154	0.140	0.114	0.053	0.054	0.031*	0.025*

Fig. 11.3 Average scores of EU and A&A countries, and T-test values

11.4 Optimum Weights of Input and Output Items

The optimum weights of the input and output variables for the 27 EU countries and 20 A&A countries in 2012 based on the SE-CCR-I model are given in Figs. 11.4 and 11.5, respectively.

It should be noted that (v^*, u^*) is the set of most favorable weights for each DMU, so that we can find the relative importance of each indicator with reference to the value of each $v_m^* x_{mo}$ and $u_s^* y_{so}$ for each DMU. From these results, it can be seen that, for instance, Japan obtains a weight for population equal to 0.532 and for energy consumption equal to 0.468 in its inputs, while it obtains for GDP a weight of 0.711 in its output. These results offer meaningful insights for policies on efficiency improvement of energy-environment-economic of country.

11.5 Performance Improvement Projection Based on the Combined CCR, DFM, and TO-DFM Model

The results of an efficiency-improvement projection based on the application of CCR-I and DFM models for inefficient A&A countries in 2012 are presented in Table 11.2.

In regard to Table 11.2, we note that the results of an efficiency-improvement projection for CO2 may be difficult to understand as a consequence of the use of "inverse" numbers (translating the "bad" output into a "good" output). And, therefore, we have recalculated the results into normal numbers, as presented in Table 11.3.

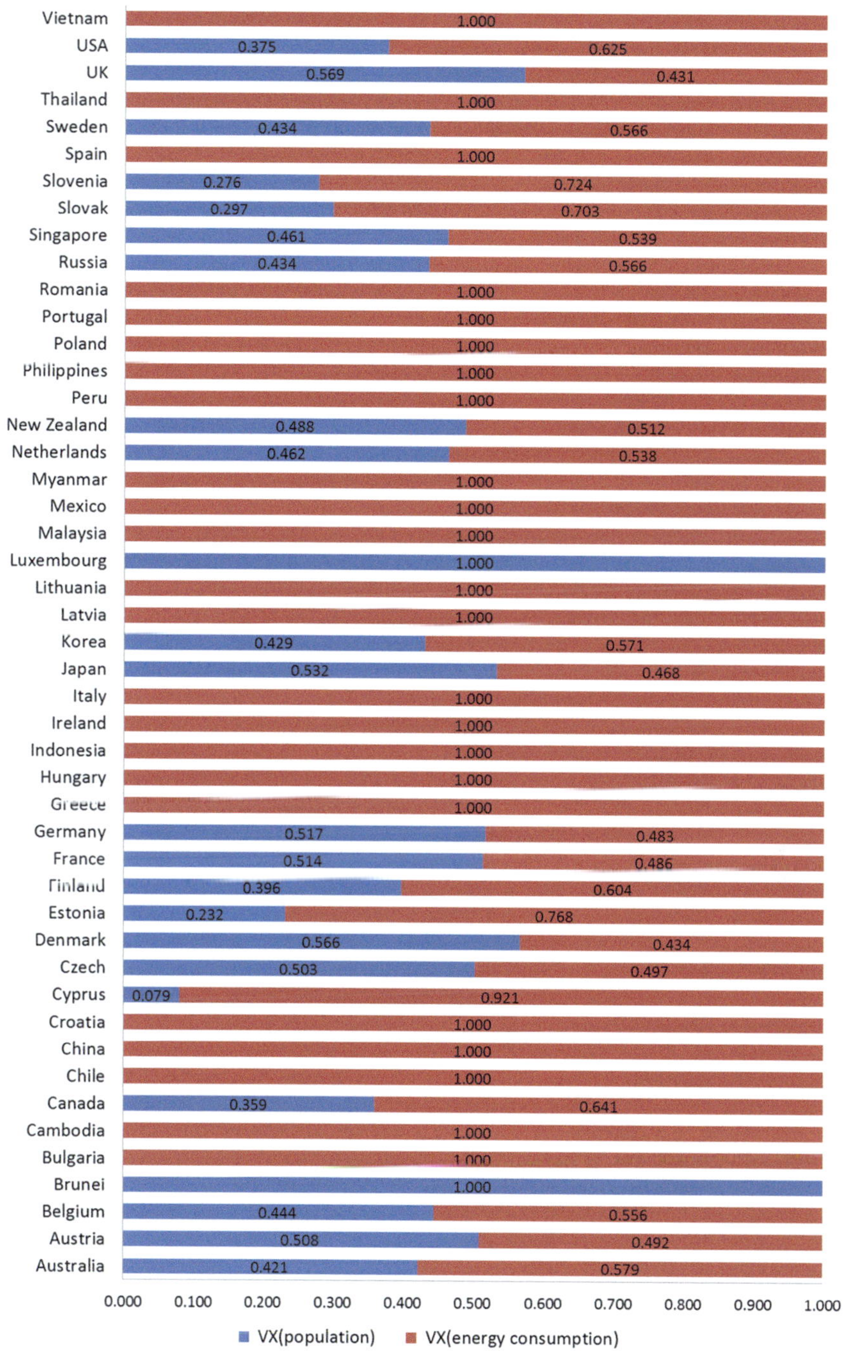

Fig. 11.4 Input optimum weights

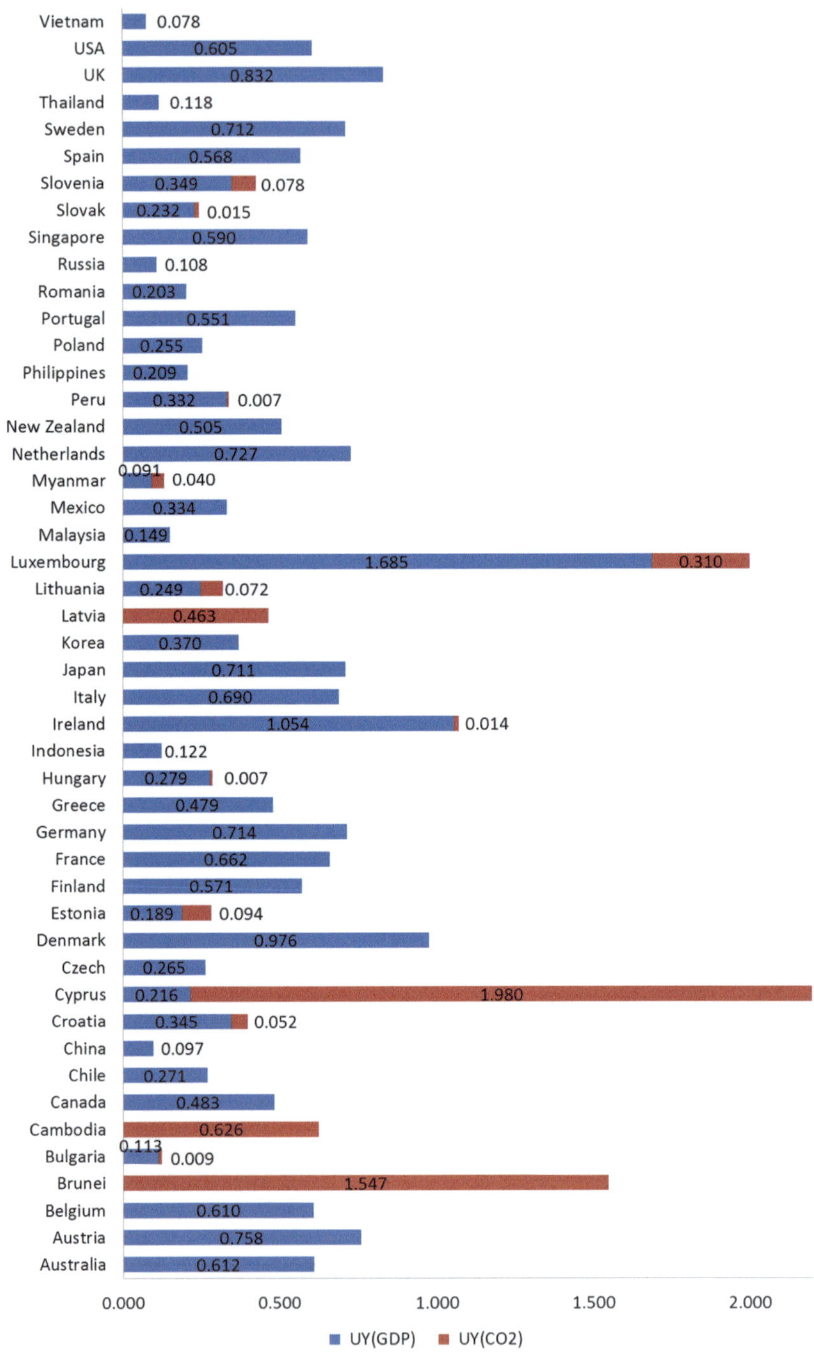

Fig. 11.5 Output optimum weights

Table 11.2 Efficiency-improvement projection results of CCR, DFM, and TO-DFM-FF models (A&A countries)

		CCR model		DFM model		TO-DFM-FF model	
DMU	Score	Score(θ**)		Score(θ**)		Score(θ**)	
I/O	Data	Difference	%	Difference	%	Difference	%
Australia	0.612	1.000		1.000		0.644	(EU Ave level)
(FI)Population	23050.0	−8948.3	−38.8%	−2262.6	−9.8%	0.000	0.0%
(I)Energy consumption	5371.0	−2085.1	−38.8%	−1850.7	−34.5%	−174.151	−3.2%
(O)GDP	9253.4	0.0	0.0%	2228.7	24.1%	300.035	3.2%
(O)CO_2 (inverse)	0.00259	1.5	56847.0%	1.0	38824.6%	0.000	0.0%
Cambodia	0.626	1.000		1.000		0.644	(EU Ave level)
(FI)Population	14865.0	−13532.7	−91.0%	−13226.7	−89.0%	0.000	0.0%
(I)Energy consumption	230.0	−85.9	−37.4%	−52.8	−23.0%	−3.135	−1.4%
(O)GDP	99.9	189.4	189.6%	255.8	256.1%	0.000	0.0%
(O)CO_2 (inverse)	0.23981	0.0	0.0%	0.1	23.0%	0.003	1.4%
Canada	0.483	1.000		1.000		0.644	(EU Ave level)
(FI)Population	34838.0	−17994.4	−51.7%	−3249.9	−9.3%	0.000	0.0%
(I)Energy consumption	10514.0	−5430.7	−51.7%	−5164.6	−49.1%	−1880.593	−17.9%
(O)GDP	12941.9	0.0	0.0%	4506.1	34.8%	2314.865	17.9%
(O)CO_2 (inverse)	0.00187	2.8	148344.7%	1.5	81630.8%	0.000	0.0%
Chile	0.271	1.000		1.000		0.644	(EU Ave level)
(FI)Population	17465.0	−13985.3	−80.1%	−11989.0	−68.6%	0.000	0.0%
(I)Energy consumption	1558.0	−1136.0	−72.9%	−893.8	−57.4%	−635.113	−40.8%
(O)GDP	1649.3	0.0	0.0%	946.2	57.4%	672.327	40.8%
(O)CO_2 (inverse)	0.01286	0.0	66.4%	0.0	161.8%	0.000	0.0%
China	0.097	1.000		1.000		0.644	(EU Ave level)
(FI)Population	1377065.0	−1280474.3	−93.0%	−1200913.3	−87.2%	0.000	0.0%
(I)Energy consumption	121178.0	−109463.0	−90.3%	−99813.4	−82.4%	−89532.486	−73.9%

(continued)

Table 11.2 (continued)

DMU	Score	CCR model Score(θ**)		DFM model Score(θ**)		TO-DFM-FF model Score(θ**)	
I/O	Data	Difference	%	Difference	%	Difference	%
(O)GDP	45781.7	0.0	0.0%	37710.0	82.4%	33825.839	73.9%
(O)CO_2 (inverse)	0.00012	0.6	487129.7%	1.1	888457.3%	0.000	0.0%
Indonesia	0.122	1.000		1.000		0.644	(EU Ave level)
(FI)Population	246864.0	−237842.2	−96.4%	−230787.6	−93.5%	0.000	0.0%
(I)Energy consumption	8942.0	−7847.8	−87.8%	−6992.2	−78.2%	−6085.349	−68.1%
(O)GDP	4276.1	0.0	0.0%	3343.7	78.2%	2910.062	68.1%
(O)CO_2 (inverse)	0.00230	0.1	2315.1%	0.1	4203.6%	0.000	0.0%
Japan	0.711	1.000		1.000		0.750	(Arbitrary level)
(FI)Population	127250.0	−36757.0	−28.9%	−27895.2	−21.9%	0.000	0.0%
(I)Energy consumption	18936.0	−5469.8	−28.9%	−2110.3	−11.1%	−692.874	−3.7%
(O)GDP	46953.6	0.0	0.0%	7926.2	16.9%	1718.044	3.7%
(O)CO_2 (inverse)	0.00082	2.7	336289.2%	4.8	589089.6%	0.000	0.0%
Korea	0.370	1.000		1.000		0.644	(EU Ave level)
(FI)Population	49003.0	−30888.2	−63.0%	−18198.5	−37.1%	0.000	0.0%
(I)Energy consumption	11030.0	−6952.6	−63.0%	−5813.3	−52.7%	−4101.349	−37.2%
(O)GDP	11652.6	0.0	0.0%	5362.6	46.0%	4332.847	37.2%
(O)CO_2 (inverse)	0.00169	1.8	104690.8%	1.5	88440.6%	0.000	0.0%
Malaysia	0.149	1.000		1.000		0.644	(EU Ave level)
(FI)Population	29240.0	−25053.5	−85.7%	−21954.7	−75.1%	0.000	0.0%
(I)Energy consumption	3401.0	−2893.2	−85.1%	−2517.4	−74.0%	−2120.415	−62.3%
(O)GDP	1984.3	0.0	0.0%	1468.8	74.0%	1237.145	62.3%
(O)CO_2 (inverse)	0.00510	0.0	404.1%	0.0	777.3%	0.000	0.0%
Mexico	0.334	1.000		1.000		0.644	(EU Ave level)

(FI)Population	120847.0	−99132.7	−82.0%	−88288.8	−73.1%	0.000	0.0%
(I)Energy consumption	7888.0	−5254.4	−66.6%	−3939.2	−49.9%	−2500.020	−31.7%
(O)GDP	10292.1	0.0	0.0%	5139.7	49.9%	3261.960	31.7%
(O)CO_2 (inverse)	0.00229	0.1	5717.0%	0.2	8621.9%	0.000	0.0%
Myanmar	0.131	1.000		1.000		0.644	(EU Ave level)
(FI)Population	52797.0	−52058.0	−98.6%	−51497.7	−97.5%	0.000	0.0%
(I)Energy consumption	639.0	−555.5	−86.9%	−491.3	−76.9%	−423.383	−66.3%
(O)GDP	230.2	0.0	0.0%	191.9	83.4%	174.281	75.7%
(O)CO_2 (inverse)	0.08584	0.0	0.0%	0.1	62.1%	0.038	44.7%
New Zealand	0.505	1.000		1.000		0.644	(EU Ave level)
(FI)Population	4460.0	−2207.3	−49.5%	−1389.9	−31.2%	0.000	0.0%
(I)Energy consumption	794.0	−393.0	−49.5%	−274.1	−34.5%	−131.828	−16.6%
(O)GDP	1276.2	0.0	0.0%	419.6	32.9%	211.882	16.6%
(O)CO_2 (inverse)	0.03111	0.1	306.3%	0.1	378.3%	0.000	0.0%
Peru	0.339	1.000		1.000		0.644	(EU Ave level)
(FI)Population	29988.0	−27442.0	−91.5%	−26217.4	−87.4%	0.000	0.0%
(I)Energy consumption	909.0	−600.7	−66.1%	−448.5	−49.3%	−281.624	−31.0%
(O)GDP	1197.6	0.0	0.0%	603.6	50.4%	379.006	31.6%
(O)CO_2 (inverse)	0.02182	0.0	0.0%	0.0	7.0%	0.000	0.0%
Philippines	0.209	1.000		1.000		0.644	(EU Ave level)
(FI)Population	96707.0	−93643.4	−96.8%	−91537.0	−94.8%	0.000	0.0%
(I)Energy consumption	1782.0	−1410.4	−79.2%	−1157.1	−65.5%	−910.014	−51.1%
(O)GDP	1452.1	0.0	0.0%	951.0	65.5%	741.519	51.1%
(O)CO_2 (inverse)	0.01258	0.0	49.6%	0.0	147.6%	0.000	0.0%
Russia	0.108	1.000		1.000		infeasible case	
(FI)Population	143170.0	−127776.1	−89.3%	−111111.0	−77.6%		
(I)Energy consumption	31677.0	−28271.0	−89.3%	−26247.8	−82.9%		

(continued)

Table 11.2 (continued)

DMU	Score	CCR model		DFM model		TO-DFM-FF model	
		Score(θ**)		Score(θ**)		Score(θ**)	
I/O	Data	Difference	%	Difference	%	Difference	%
(O)GDP	9806.1	0.0	0.0%	7902.1	80.6%		
(O)CO_2 (inverse)	0.00060	1.4	240447.8%	1.6	257732.1%		
Singapore	0.590	1.000		1.000		0.644	(EU Ave level)
(FI)Population	5303.0	−2173.5	−41.0%	−1036.1	−19.5%	0.000	0.0%
(I)Energy consumption	1049.0	−430.0	−41.0%	−326.4	−31.1%	−59.993	−5.7%
(O)GDP	1873.9	0.0	0.0%	483.0	25.8%	107.167	5.7%
(O)CO_2 (inverse)	0.02010	0.2	1045.0%	0.2	929.0%	0.000	0.0%
Thailand	0.118	1.000		1.000		0.644	(EU Ave level)
(FI)Population	66785.0	−61645.2	−92.3%	−57587.5	−86.2%	0.000	0.0%
(I)Energy consumption	5299.0	−4675.6	−88.2%	−4183.5	−78.9%	−3661.454	−69.1%
(O)GDP	2436.1	0.0	0.0%	1923.3	78.9%	1683.290	69.1%
(O)CO_2 (inverse)	0.00390	0.0	710.9%	0.1	1351.1%	0.000	0.0%
USA	0.605	1.000		1.000		0.644	(EU Ave level)
(FI)Population	317505.0	−125551.5	−39.5%	0.0	0.0%	0.000	0.0%
(I)Energy consumption	89623.0	−35439.8	−39.5%	−35337.8	−39.4%	−3484.242	−3.9%
(O)GDP	141377.6	0.0	0.0%	34841.3	24.6%	5496.286	3.9%
(O)CO_2 (inverse)	0.00020	28.4	14407875.2%	15.8	8040357.1%	0.000	0.0%
Vietnam	0.078	1.000		1.000		0.644	(EU Ave level)
(FI)Population	90796.0	−89043.9	−98.1%	−87546.3	−96.4%	0.000	0.0%
(I)Energy consumption	2715.0	−2502.5	−92.2%	−2320.9	−85.5%	−2126.349	−78.3%
(O)GDP	830.4	0.0	0.0%	709.9	85.5%	650.381	78.3%
(O)CO_2 (inverse)	0.00700	0.0	53.9%	0.0	185.4%	0.000	0.0%

Table 11.3 Efficiency-improvement projection results for CO2 in 'normal' numbers

DMU	Score	Data (O)CO2 (inverse)	Data (O) CO2	CCR Projection	CCR Difference	CCR %	DFM Projection	DFM Difference	DFM %	TO-EDM-FF Projection	TO-EDM-FF Difference	TO-EDM-FF %
Australia	0.612	0.002589	386.27	0.678	−385.592	−99.824%	0.992	−385.278	−99.743%	386.270	0.000	0.000%
Cambodia	0.626	0.239808	4.17	4.170	0.000	0.000%	3.391	−0.779	−18.680%	4.114	−0.056	−1.345%
Canada	0.483	0.001874	533.74	0.360	−533.380	−99.933%	0.653	−533.087	−99.878%	533.740	0.000	0.000%
Chile	0.271	0.012858	77.77	46.750	−31.020	−39.886%	29.707	−48.063	−61.801%	77.770	0.000	0.000%
China	0.097	0.000122	8205.86	1.684	−8204.176	−99.979%	0.924	−8204.936	−99.989%	8205.860	0.000	0.000%
Indonesia	0.122	0.002296	435.48	18.031	−417.449	−95.859%	10.119	−425.361	−97.676%	435.480	0.000	0.000%
Japan	0.711	0.000817	1223.30	0.364	−1222.936	−99.970%	0.208	−1223.092	−99.983%	1223.300	0.000	0.000%
Korea	0.370	0.001687	592.92	0.566	−592 354	−99.905%	0.670	−592.250	−99.887%	592.920	0.000	0.000%
Malaysia	0.149	0.005105	195.89	38.858	−157 032	−80.164%	22.329	−173.561	−88.601%	195.890	0.000	0.000%
Mexico	0.334	0.002295	435.79	7.492	−428.298	−98.281%	4.996	−430.794	−98.853%	435.790	0.000	0.000%
Myanmar	0.131	0.085837	11.65	11.650	0.000	0.000%	7.186	−4.464	−38.321%	8.051	−3.599	−30.894%
New Zealand	0.505	0.031114	32.14	7.910	−24.230	−75.388%	6.719	−25.421	−79.094%	32.140	0.000	0.000%
Peru	0.339	0.021825	45.82	45.820	0.000	0.000%	42.806	−3.014	−6.578%	45.820	0.000	0.000%
Philippines	0.209	0.012585	79.46	53.101	−26.359	−33.173%	32.086	−47.374	−59.620%	79.460	0.000	0.000%
Russia	0.108	0.000603	1659.03	0.690	−1658.340	−99.958%	0.643	−1658.387	−99.961%			
Singapore	0.590	0.020101	49.75	4.345	−45.405	−91.266%	4.835	−44.915	−90.282%	49.750	0.000	0.000%
Thailand	0.118	0.003896	256.65	31.651	−224.999	−87.668%	17.687	−238.963	−93.109%	256.650	0.000	0.000%
USA	0.605	0.000197	5074.14	0.035	−5074.105	−99.999%	0.063	−5074.077	−99.999%	5074.140	0.000	0.000%
Vietnam	0.078	0.007000	142.85	92.849	−50.001	−35.002%	50.058	−92.792	−64.957%	142.850	0.000	0.000%

From Table 11.2, it appears that the DFM model clearly shows that a different – and likely more efficient – solution than the standard CCR-I projection is available for reaching the efficiency frontier. In this particular case, we could not identify a non-slack type (i.e., s-** and s + ** are zero) country; this is particularly confirmed for the USA. For instance, the CCR-I projection in Tables 11.2 and 11.3 shows that the USA would have to reduce its population and energy consumption by 39.5%, together with an increase in the (inverse) CO2 of 14407875.2% (−99.999% in "normal numbers"), in order to become efficient (variable, CO2 emission, in our study is defined as a multiplicative inverse of the "bad" output (actual CO2 emission) in order that a decrease in the actual CO2 emission ("good output") indicates an increase in variable CO2. Accordingly, "normal numbers" are changes in percentage in the actual CO2 emission.

On the other hand, the DFM results show that a reduction in energy consumption by 39.4%, together with an increase in the GDP of 24.6% and in the CO2 (inverse) of 8040357.1% (−99.999% in "normal numbers"), is required to become really efficient.

The results of the efficiency-improvement projection based on the TO-DFM-FF model for inefficient A&A countries are presented in Tables 11.2 and 11.3. The parameter θ** in the results of TO-DFM-FF in Table 11.2 expresses a target efficiency score (TES) based on the EU average score level (0.644), while Japan is set at 0.750 as an arbitrary level, because the current score is already exceeded (0.711). The anomalous result of Russia was at the end regarded as an infeasible case. More specifically, the computed necessary reduction value for energy consumption (35973.710 Peta Joule) appeared to exceed the current level (316677.000 Peta Joule). Clearly, the number of policy instruments (only due input factor) appears which is a limitation here.

The TO-DFM-FF model is clearly able to present a more realistic efficiency-improvement energy plan, to be compared with the results of the DFM model in Tables 11.2 and 11.3. For instance, the DFM results in Tables 11.2 and 11.3 show that Korea should reduce its population by 37.1% and its energy consumption by 52.7% and increase its GDP by 46.0% and its CO2 level (inverse) by 88440.6% (−99.887% in "normal numbers") in order to become efficient. On the other hand, the TO-DFM-FF results in Table 11.2 show that a reduction in energy consumption of 37.2% and an increase in GDP of 37.2% are required to reach the EU average level (0.644). Note also that population is interpreted in our application as a fixed factor in the TO-DFM-FF model.

We also remark that the efficiency-improvement levels of CO2 in our CCR-I and DFM models seem to offer unrealistic outcomes, like 14407875.2%, (−99.999% in "normal numbers"), 8040357.1% (−99.999% in "normal numbers"), and 88440.6% (−99.887% in "normal numbers") caused by the existence of "slack," as a result of vast differences in absolute numbers of relevant variables in the countries under consideration (e.g., Russia or the USA vs. Luxembourg or Cyprus). On the other hand, our TO-DFM-FF results seem to offer more realistic outcomes than found in previous models. The TO-DFM-FF model provides policy-makers with practical and transparent directions for operational solutions that are available in the DFM projection to reach the target efficiency level. These results provide a meaningful contribution to decision support and planning for the efficiency improvement of the countries' energy-environment-economic resources.

11.6 Performance Improvement Projection Based on the TO-DFM-FF Model

In this subsection, we will use Japan 2012 as an illustrative case and point of reference and present an efficiency improvement projection result based on the TO-DFM-FF model. The 2012 efficiency value is 0.711 (see Table 11.2). We now consider the steps to improve efficiency toward 0.750, 0.800, 0.850, 0.900, 0.950, and 1.000. The resulting input reduction values and the output increase values based on the TO-DFM-FF model are presented in Fig. 11.6.

These results show that, if Japan implements an efficiency-improvement plan with a TES amounting to 0.850, a reduction in energy consumption of 12.5% and an increase in GDP of 12.5% are required.

Furthermore, the normal DFM results in Fig. 11.6 show that Japan should reduce its population by 21.9% and the energy consumption by 11.1% and increase its GDP by 16.9% and the CO2 (inverse) with 589089.6% (−99.983% in "normal numbers" in Table 11.3) in order to become efficient. On the other hand, the TES = 1.000 (TO-DFM-FF) results in Fig. 11.6 show that a reduction in energy consumption of 24.5% and an increase in GDP of 24.5% would be needed. From the above finding, we note that the TO-DFM-FF model is able to present a more realistic efficiency-improvement plan, compared with the normal DFM. Note also here that population is interpreted in the application as a fixed factor in the TO-DFM-FF model, which reduces the degree of freedom in implementing policy instruments.

Our new proposed TO-DFM-FF model cannot only compute a stepwise projection that falls below the 1.000 levels, but it is also able to compute an outcome just to reach the efficiency frontier (TES = 1.000). From this fact, it appears that the TO-DFM-FF model can produce a more realistic efficiency-improvement projection than the previous CCR-I, DFM, and TO-DFM models.

11.7 Interpretation and Conclusion

This chapter has presented the evaluation results of energy-environment-economic efficiency in a cross-regional comparison, in particular the EU vs. APEC and ASEAN countries.

Based on these results, it is clear that the new proposed TO-DFM-FF model is able to suggest a more realistic efficiency-improvement energy plan, compared to

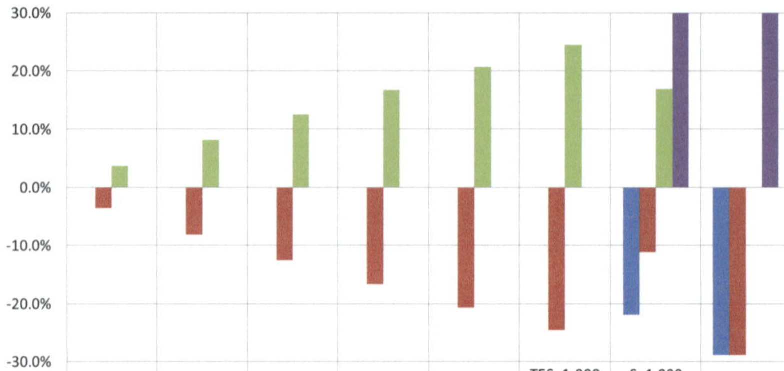

	TES=0.750	TES=0.800	TES=0.850	TES=0.900	TES=0.950	TES=1.000 (TO-DFM-FF)	S=1.000 (Normal DFM)	CCR-I (S=1.000)
(FI)population	0.0%	0.0%	0.0%	0.0%	0.0%	0.0%	-21.9%	-28.9%
(I)energy consumption	-3.7%	-8.2%	-12.5%	-16.7%	-20.7%	-24.5%	-11.1%	-28.9%
(O)GDP	3.7%	8.2%	12.5%	16.7%	20.7%	24.5%	16.9%	0.0%
(O)CO2 (inverse)	0.0%	0.0%	0.0%	0.0%	0.0%	0.0%	589089.6%	336289.2%

Fig. 11.6 Efficiency-improvement projection results based on the TO-DFM-FF model (Japan 2012)

the results of the CCR-I, DFM, and TO-DFM model. It also supports the hypothesis that EU countries are operating as significantly higher efficiency levels than A&A countries.

An examination of the strengths and shortcomings of the new model brings to light that a strength can incorporate the idea of target setting by a decision or policy-maker while taking into account a fixed factor. A shortcoming is that the model cannot incorporate the transition path toward a make efficient solution.

Based on these results, it is evident that more case studies on cross-regional comparisons are needed, including also dynamic transitions in the analytic modeling of sustainability trajectories of countries.

On the basis of our DEA analysis results, it can be seen that Luxembourg, Cyprus, Ireland, and Brunei may be regarded as super-efficient DMUs. It also can be seen that the efficiency scores of EU countries are higher on average than the A&A countries. We also compared an average score between the EU and A&A countries, based on a two-sample T-test. From these results, we noticed that the gap between the average scores for EU and A&A countries has narrowed from 2003 to 2005, but, after 2006, the gap has widened year by year. In particular, the gap in 2011 and 2012 shows a statistical significance. Given the above findings, it seems necessary to make a serious effort for the efficiency improvement of the energy-environment-economic efficiency for APEC and ASEAN countries.

In this chapter, we have presented a new DEA methodology, the TO-DFM-FF model. Its feasibility was tested for improving energy-environment-economic efficiency for the APEC and ASEAN countries; the new model was examined on the basis of real-world information on relevant indicators. This new analytical tool combines both flexibilities in energy-environment-economic strategies while considering also a fixed input constellation such as population. The results show that in many cases there is considerable scope for improvement along various strategic paths in the various countries under consideration.

The application of the proposed approach to the energy efficiency-improvement argument among countries has successfully shown the advantage and usefulness over the other approaches of DEA. Especially, in a situation in which policy- or decision-maker has to compromise between a several competing objectives, the TO-DFM-FF approach can give useful and helpful step-by-step policy-making information to DMUs.

Regarding actual policy implications based on our TO-DFM-FF results, we may need more careful considerations. For example, the relation between GDP and CO2 emission is a sort of complementary one. An increase in GDP while keeping the CO2 emission constant means that the current energy technologies must be replaced by renewable ones or that more energy-efficient production technologies must be adopted or both. Additionally, IEA (2015) has reported that global emissions of carbon dioxide from the energy sector stabilized in 2014, marking the first time in 40 years in which there was a halt or reduction in emissions of the greenhouse gas that was not tied to an economic downturn. It also attributes the halt in emission growth to changing patterns of energy consumption in China and OECD countries. In China, the year 2014 saw a larger generation of electricity from renewable sources, such as hydropower, solar and wind, and less burning of coal. In the OECD economies, recent efforts to promote more sustainable growth – including greater energy efficiency and more renewable energy – are producing a new trend toward decoupling economic growth from greenhouse gas emissions. It is clear that from these results that the direction a country might or should go is dependent on the current sustainability efforts, which may be different for each country. Our TO-DFM-FF approach has attained interesting results and useful suggestions which are directly conceivable and implementable by policy- or decision-makers in charge of strategic planning of energy transformation. The application results show that also the proposed approach needs further refinement and development, especially such as the complementary relation between GDP and CO2 emission and the number of instruments (input factors).

The results appear to offer a meaningful contribution to sustainable decision-making and planning aiming at an efficiency improvement in the energy-environment-economic sector in the countries concerned. These findings are mapped out in a detailed way in the present chapter. This model is still elementary, but has the potential to become a policy instrument that could offer great benefits for combined energy-environment-economic decision-making and planning strategies at national or sectoral policy levels. An important caveat of the present approach is noteworthy, viz., large-scale differences in relevant policy variables of the DMUs considered may cause flaws in the outcomes.

References

American Council for an Energy-Efficient Economy. (2014). 2014 International Energy Efficiency Scorecard

Anderson, P., & Petersen, N. (1993). A procedure for ranking efficient units in data envelopment analysis. *Management Science, 39*, 1261–1264.

Charnes, A., Cooper, W. W., & Rhodes, E. (1978). Measuring the efficiency of decision making units. *European Journal of Operational Research, 2*, 429–444.

International Energy Agency (IEA). (2015). News (Global energy-related emissions of carbon dioxide stalled in 2014- Preliminary IEA data point to emissions decoupling from economic growth for the first time in 40 years -), http://www.iea.org/newsroomandevents/news/2015/march/global-energy-related-emissions-of-carbon-dioxide-stalled-in-2014.html

Martínez, P. (2011). Energy efficiency development in German and Colombian non-energy-intensive Sectors: A non-parametric analysis. *Energy Efficiency, 4*(1), 115–131.

Scheel, H. (2001). Undesirable outputs in efficiency valuations. *European Journal of Operational Research, 132*(2), 400–410.

Seiford, L., & Zhu, J. (2002). Modeling undesirable factors in efficiency evaluation. *European Journal of Operational Research, 142*(1), 16–20.

Suzuki, S., & Nijkamp, P. (2016). An evaluation of energy-environment-economic efficiency for EU, APEC and ASEAN countries: Design of a target-oriented DFM model with fixed factors in data envelopment analysis. *Energy Policy, 88*, 100–112.

Wu, A., Cao, Y., & Liu, B. (2014). Energy efficiency evaluation for regions in China: An application of DEA and Malmquist indices. *Energy Efficiency, 7*(3), 429–439.

Zhou, P., Ang, B. W., & Poh, K. L. (2008). A survey of data envelopment analysis in energy and environmental studies. *European Journal of Operational Research, 189*, 1–18.

Chapter 12
Performance Measurement of Airport Operations in Japan: Combination of a Stepwise Improvement Model with a Fixed-Factor Model

Abstract The aim of this chapter is to apply an extended DEA model emerging from a blend of a Stepwise Improvement-distance friction minimization (DFM) model and a Fixed-Factor (FF) model, for generating an appropriate efficiency-improvement projection model. A DFM model serves to improve the performance of business activities by identifying the most appropriate movement toward the efficiency frontier surface. Likewise, a context-dependent (CD) model seeks to reach efficient frontiers in a series of steps. A Stepwise Improvement-DFM model will be integrated here with a DFM and CD model. An extension of a Stepwise Improvement-DFM model is next achieved by including an FF. DEA is used in our comparative study on the efficiency assessment of airport operations in Japan. We consider three inputs (nonlabor material costs, labor input, and total runway length) and one output (operating airport revenues), including a fixed input factor (viz., total runway length). The abovementioned Stepwise Improvement-DFM-FF projection model is next illustrated on the basis of a comparative study regarding an efficiency assessment of airports in Japan.

Keywords Data Envelopment Analysis (DEA) • Distance friction minimization (DFM) • Stepwise Improvement projection • Context-dependent (CD) model • Fixed Factor (FF) • Airport operation

12.1 Introduction

In the spirit of the deregulation movement, Japan is faced with an "Asia open sky" agreement which favors liberalization in international airline services. This means an end to Japan's aviation policy of isolation. In association with this policy change, environmental concerns have also become increasingly urgent for small local or regional airports. Consequently, there is a need for an objective and transparent analysis of the performance and efficiency of airport operations in Japan.

A standard tool to judge the efficiency of such agencies is Data Envelopment Analysis (DEA, see Charnes et al. 1978). DEA was developed to analyze the relative efficiency of a decision making unit (DMU), by constructing a piecewise linear production frontier and projecting the performance of each DMU onto the

S. Suzuki, P. Nijkamp, *Regional Performance Measurement and Improvement*, New Frontiers in Regional Science: Asian Perspectives 9,
DOI 10.1007/978-981-10-0242-7_12

frontier. A DMU that is located on the frontier is efficient, while a DMU that is not on the frontier is inefficient. An inefficient DMU can become efficient by reducing its inputs or increasing its outputs.

DEA has frequently been employed in the analysis of airport efficiency. For instance, Adler and Golany (2001) apply a DEA-Principal Component Analysis to hub-and-spoke airline network in the Western Europe. Fernandes and Pacheco (2002) apply the BCC model to Brazilian airports. Bazargan and Vasigh (2003) apply the CCR model to US airports, and Martín and Román (2001) and Pels et al. (2003) apply the BCC model to Spanish and European airports, respectively. Yoshida and Fujimoto (2004) analyze the efficiency of Japanese airports using both DEA and TFP methods. This large number of studies shows that comparative efficiency analysis has become an important topic.

A general efficiency-improvement projection model including a DFM model is able to calculate either an optimal input reduction value or an output increase value to reach an efficient score of 1.0, even though in reality this may be hard to achieve. For example, it is nearly impossible for one small local airport to be as efficient as one large metropolitan or regional airport (e.g., Tokyo Haneda or Osaka Itami).

We propose here a distance friction minimization (DFM) model in DEA model that is based on a generalized distance friction function and serves to improve the performance of a DMU by identifying the most appropriate movement toward the efficiency frontier surface. This approach may address both an input reduction and an output increase as a strategy of a DMU.

As a complementary approach, Seiford and Zhu (2003) developed a gradual improvement model for an inefficient DMU. This context-dependent (CD) DEA has an important merit, as it aims to reach a stepwise improvement through successive levels toward the efficiency frontier. We also proposed a Stepwise Improvement-DFM model that is an integration of the DFM and the CD model in order to design a stepwise efficiency-improvement projection model for a conventional DEA. However, this model does not take into account a non-controllable or a fixed factor, caused by rigidity in input adjustment.

We introduce now an adjusted DEA model, emerging from a blend of the Stepwise Improvement-DFM model and Fixed-Factor model, in Sect. 5.5 (and see Suzuki and Nijkamp 2014). This model can provide a stepwise efficiency-improvement projection model to reflect realistic circumstances and requirements in an efficiency-improvement projection.

The abovementioned stepwise fixed-factor projection model will be illustrated on the basis of an application to the efficiency analysis of airport operations in Japan.

Table 12.1 A listing of DMUs

No.	DMU	No.	DMU
1	Tokyo Haneda	14	Kochi
2	Osaka Itami	15	Kitakyushu
3	New Chitose (Sapporo)	16	Nagasaki
4	Fukuoka	17	Kumamoto
5	Okinawa	18	Ooita
6	Wakkanai	19	Miyazaki
7	Kushiro	20	Kagoshima
8	Hakodate	21	Okadama
9	Sendai	22	Komatsu
10	Niigata	23	Miho
11	Hiroshima	24	Tokushima
12	Takamatsu	25	Misawa
13	Matsuyama		

12.2 Database and Analysis Framework

DEA has found several applications in airport management studies. For applied airport studies based on DEA, we refer among others to Graham (2005) and Kamp et al. (2007) for a more extensive overview of the literature. These studies show that there is a lot of substantive and policy heterogeneity between such studies. Most studies using DEA to analyze airport efficiency use the number of passengers and the number of aircraft movements; these are usually seen as the "core activities" of the airport. For example, Yoshida and Fujimoto (2004) analyze the efficiency of Japanese airports based on DEA using data sets of passenger loading, cargo handling, and aircraft movement for the output side; for the input side, runway length, terminal size, etc. are used. The factors mentioned above may be seen as "core activities." It is worth noting that in recent years, a data set on management information regarding main airports in Japan has been disclosed. There is a fair chance that these data may be used to directly measure airport management efficiency by simultaneously considering input and output variables.

In our empirical work, we use input and output data for a set of 25 airports in Japan. The various DMUs used in our analysis are listed in Table 12.1.

In the present airport efficiency study, we use the following inputs and outputs:

- Input:

  (I) Nonlabor material costs (except employment costs) (in 2007) (approximated by operating costs)
  (I) Labor input (in 2007) (approximated by employment costs)
  (IF) Total runway length (in 2007)

- Output:

  (O) Operating airport revenues (in 2007)

All data were obtained from the Revenue and Expenditure 2007 database of the Ministry of Land, Infrastructure, Transport, and Tourism in Japan (2010). It should be noted that the DFM model retains the property of the standard DEA approach that the measurement units of the different inputs and outputs used need not to be identical, so that varying input and output measures can be employed. Some inputs or outputs may have a fixed character, implying that they cannot be changed in direct or flexible strategies to improve overall airport efficiency. This inertia is an element that has to be taken into account in the efficiency analysis. In the present context, the total runway length may be interpreted as a fixed factor. This factor cannot easily be changed, at least not in the short run. Clearly, other capacity constraints (such as gate congestion or additional airport facilities) may also be present, but unfortunately, these data sets are still not available in Japan.

In our application, we will first apply the standard CCR model, while next the results are used to determine the CCR and DFM-FF projections. In addition, we will also employ the CD model, and then the results can be used to determine the CD and Stepwise Improvement-DFM-FF projections. Finally, these various results will be mutually compared.

12.3 Performance Evaluation Based on a CCR-I Model

The efficiency evaluation results for the 25 airports based on the CCR model are given in Fig. 12.1. From Fig. 12.1, it can be seen that Tokyo Haneda, Osaka Itami, and Komatsu are efficiently operating airports. On the other hand, Wakkanai, Kushiro, Okadama, and Miho have a low efficiency. It is noteworthy that Wakkanai, Kushiro, and Okadama are located in Hokkaido Prefecture which is the most northern part of Japan.

12.4 Optimum Weights of Input and Output Items

The optimum weights of the input and output variables for the 25 airports based on the CCR model are given in Figs. 12.2 and 12.3, respectively.

It should be noted that (v^*, u^*) is the set of most favorable weights for each DMU, so that we can find the relative importance of each indicator with reference to the value of each $v_m^* x_{mo}$ and $u_s^* y_{so}$ for each DMU. From these results, it can be seen that, for instance, New Chitose (Sapporo) obtains a weight for operating cost equal to 0.886 and for total runway length equal to 0.114 in its inputs, while it obtains for operating revenue a weight of 0.953 in its output. These results offer meaningful insights for policies on efficiency improvement of airport operation.

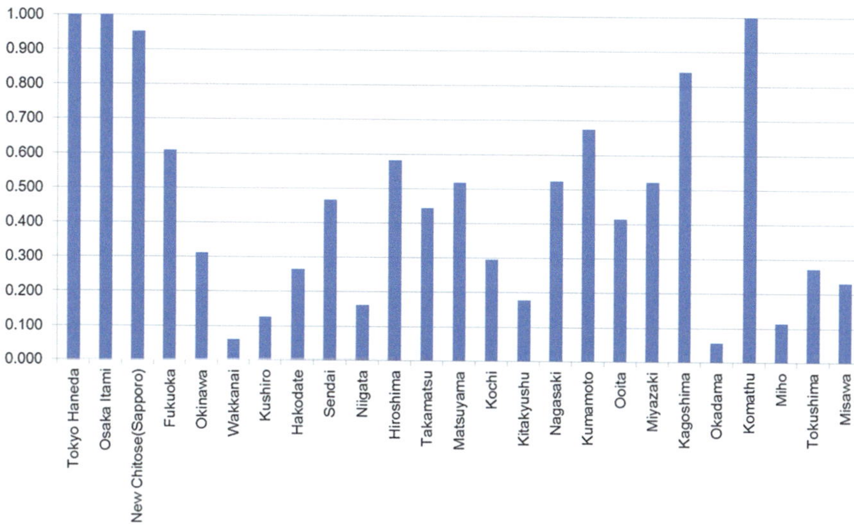

Fig. 12.1 Efficiency score based on the CCR model

12.5 Performance Improvement Projection Based on a CCR and DFM-FF Model

The efficiency-improvement projection results based on the CCR and the DFM-FF model for inefficient airports (only of a non-slack type) are presented in Fig. 12.4.

In Fig. 12.4, it appears that the empirical ratios of change in the DFM projection are smaller than those in the CCR projection, as was expected. In Fig. 12.4, this particularly applies to Okinawa, Kushiro, Hakodate, Niigata, Takamatsu, Kochi, Kitakyushu, Nagasaki, Ooita, and Tokushima, which are apparently non-slack-type (i.e., s-** and s + ** are zero) airports. The DFM-FF projection involves both an input reduction and output increase, and, clearly, the DFM-FF projection does not involve a uniform ratio, because this model looks for the optimal input reduction (i.e., the shortest distance to the frontier or distance friction minimization). For instance, the CCR projection shows that Tokushima should reduce the operating cost (OC) and the employment cost (EC) by 72.7% and the total runway length (TRL) by 91.7% in order to become efficient. On the other hand, the DFM-FF results show that a reduction in the operating costs (OC) of 40.1% and the employment costs (EC) of 66.7% and an increase in the operating revenues (OR) of 57.2% are required to become efficient. This result shows that the DFM-FF projection can indeed be generated as a solution where total runway length is fixed. Apart from the practicality of such a solution, the models show clearly that a different – and perhaps more efficient – solution is available than the standard CCR projection to reach the efficiency frontier.

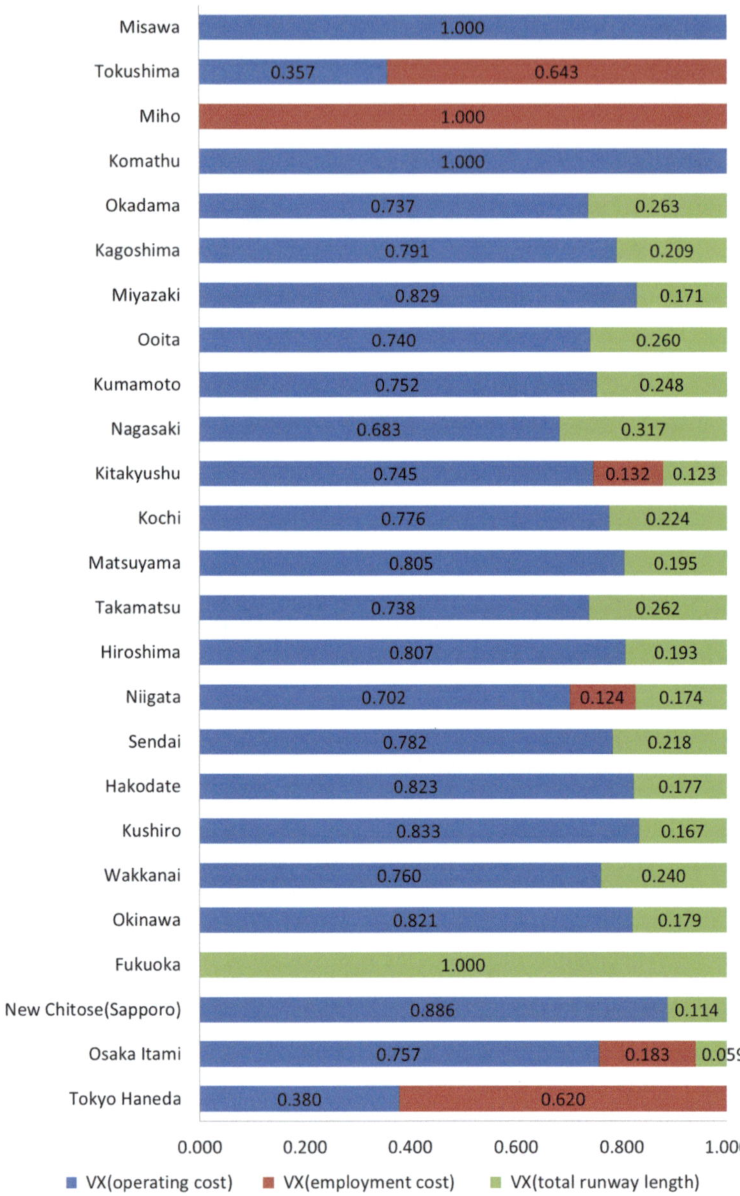

Fig. 12.2 Input optimum weights

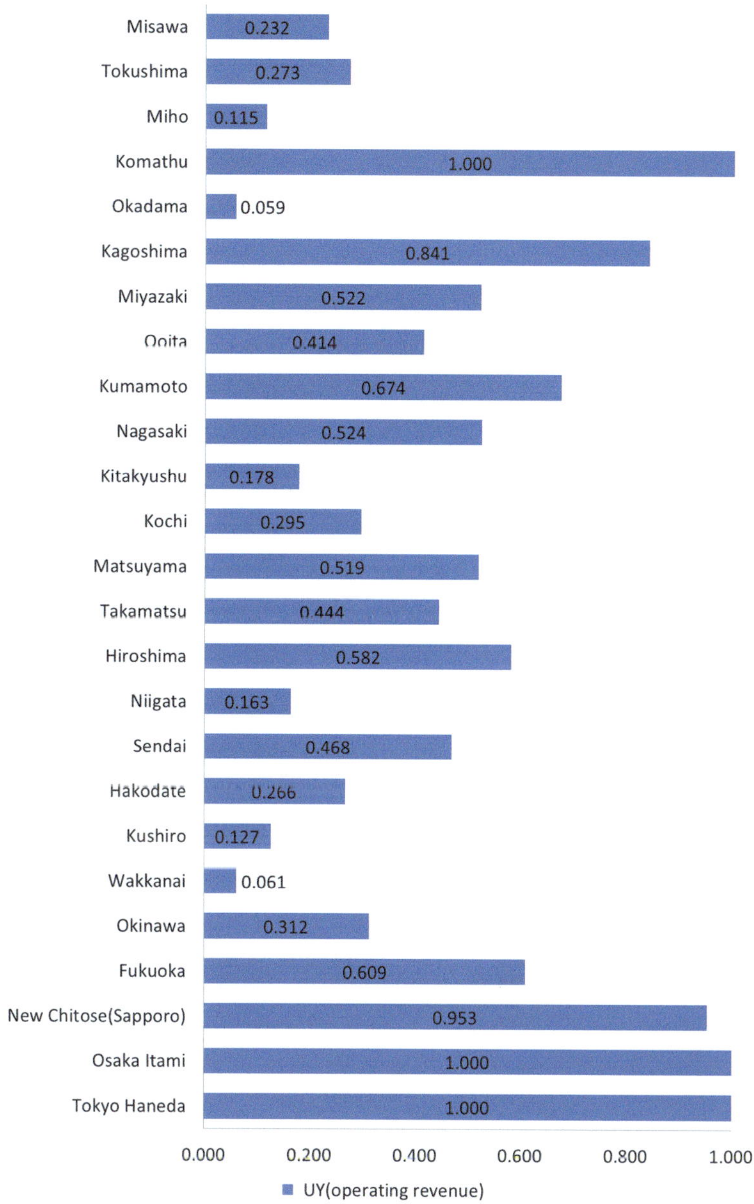

Fig. 12.3 Output optimum weights

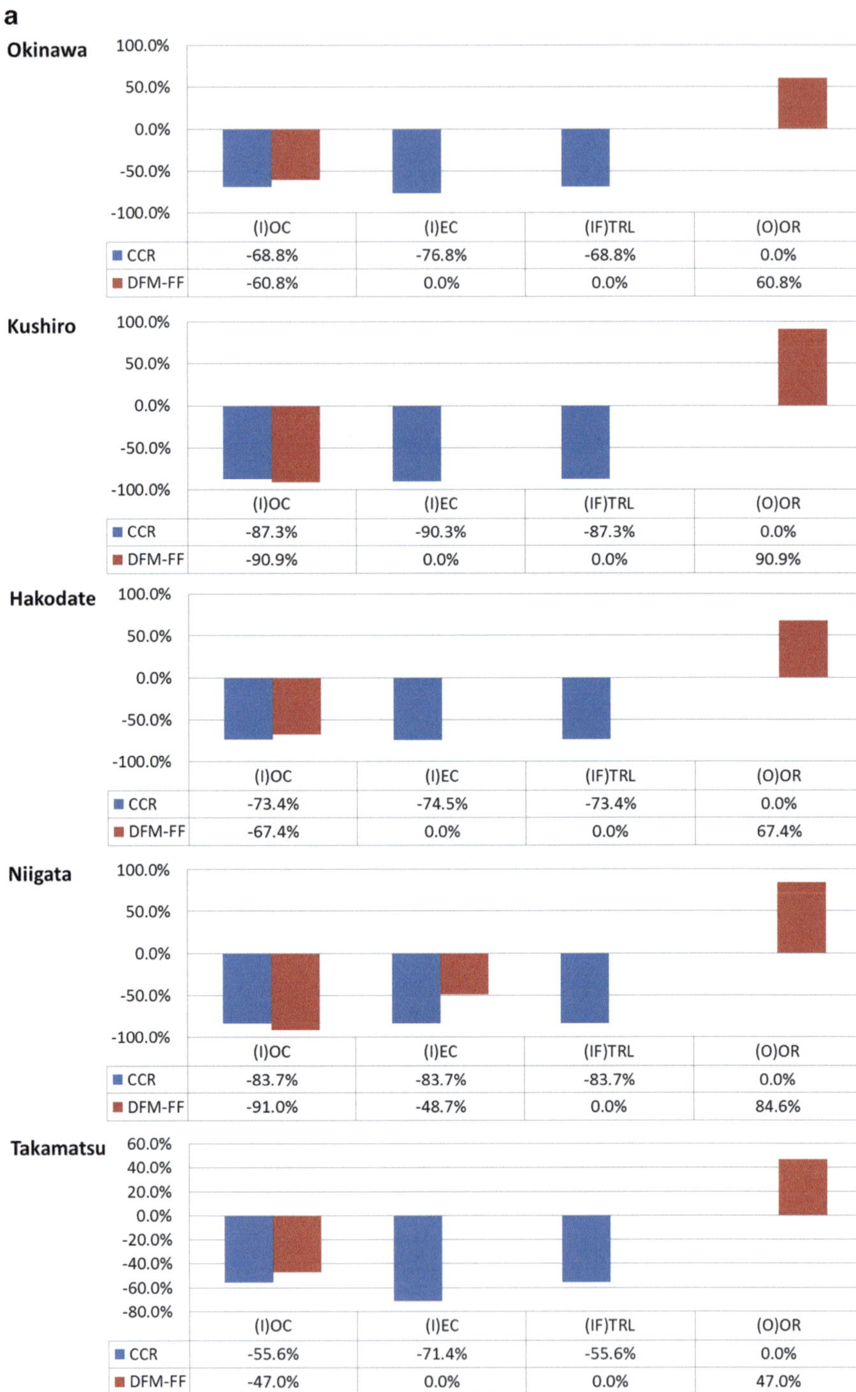

Okinawa

	(I)OC	(I)EC	(IF)TRL	(O)OR
CCR	-68.8%	-76.8%	-68.8%	0.0%
DFM-FF	-60.8%	0.0%	0.0%	60.8%

Kushiro

	(I)OC	(I)EC	(IF)TRL	(O)OR
CCR	-87.3%	-90.3%	-87.3%	0.0%
DFM-FF	-90.9%	0.0%	0.0%	90.9%

Hakodate

	(I)OC	(I)EC	(IF)TRL	(O)OR
CCR	-73.4%	-74.5%	-73.4%	0.0%
DFM-FF	-67.4%	0.0%	0.0%	67.4%

Niigata

	(I)OC	(I)EC	(IF)TRL	(O)OR
CCR	-83.7%	-83.7%	-83.7%	0.0%
DFM-FF	-91.0%	-48.7%	0.0%	84.6%

Takamatsu

	(I)OC	(I)EC	(IF)TRL	(O)OR
CCR	-55.6%	-71.4%	-55.6%	0.0%
DFM-FF	-47.0%	0.0%	0.0%	47.0%

Fig. 12.4 An efficiency-improvement projection results of the CCR and DFM-FF model

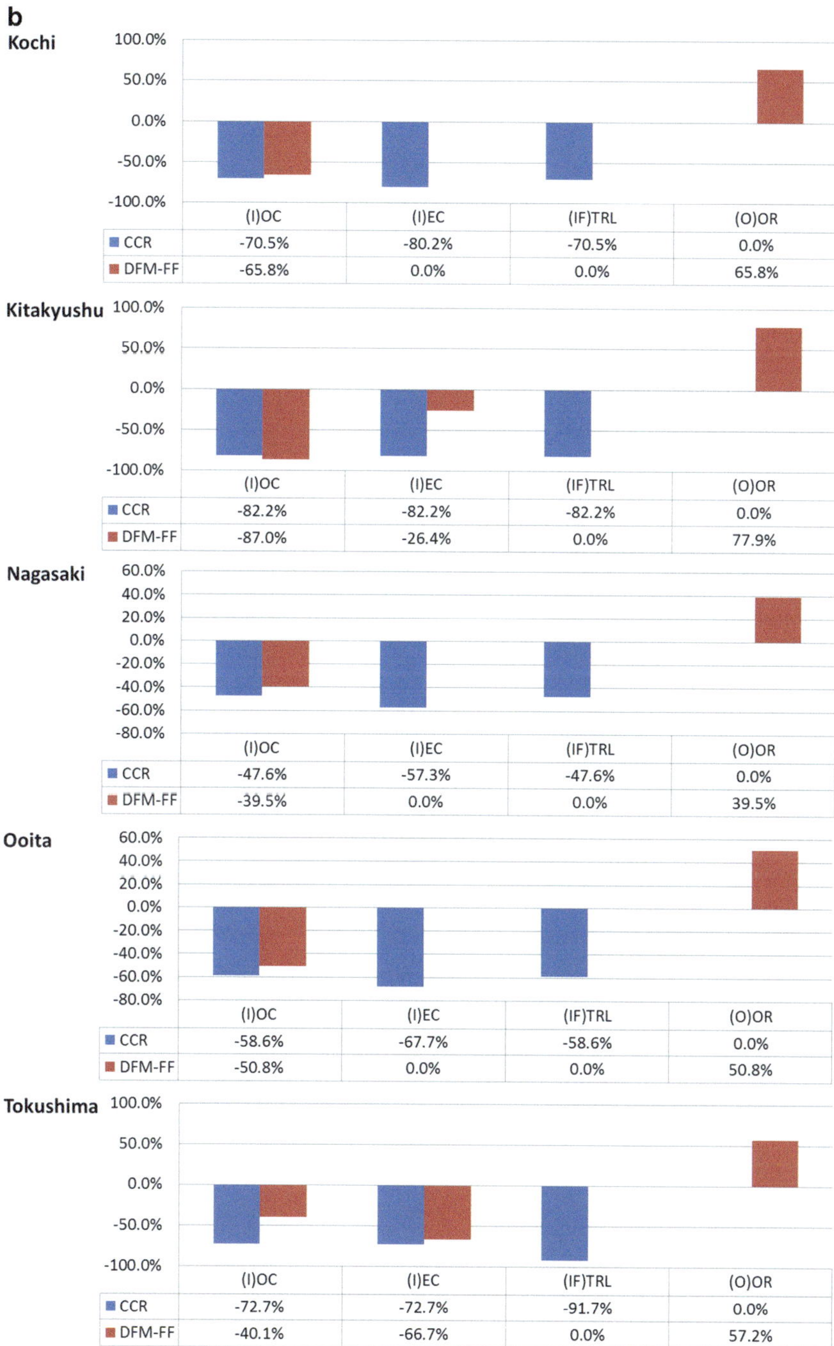

Fig. 12.4 (continued)

12.6 Performance Improvement Projection Based on a Stepwise Improvement-DFM Fixed-Factor Model

The efficiency-improvement projection results for the nearest upper-level efficient frontier based on the CD and Stepwise Improvement-DFM-FF model for inefficient airports (only of a non-slack type) are presented in Fig. 12.5. In Fig. 12.5, it appears that the ratios of change in the Stepwise Improvement-DFM-FF projection are smaller than those in the CD projection, as was expected. As shown in Fig. 12.5, this particularly applies to Kumamoto, Miyazaki, Hiroshima, Matsuyama, Ooita, Hakodate, and Kochi, which are non-slack-type (i.e., $s-**$ and $s+**$ are zero) corporations. Apart from the practicality of such a solution, the models show clearly that a different – and perhaps more efficient – solution is available than the CD projection to reach the efficiency frontier.

The Stepwise Improvement-DFM-FF model is able to present a more realistic efficiency-improvement plan, which we compared with the results of Figs. 12.4 and 12.5. For instance, the DFM-FF results in Fig. 12.4 show that Hakodate should reduce the operating cost by 67.4% and increase the operating revenues by 67.4% in order to become efficient. On the other hand, the Stepwise Improvement-DFM-FF results in Fig. 12.5 show that a reduction in employment costs of 11.1% and an increase in the operating revenues of 11.1% are required to become efficient. Note also that total runway length is interpreted in the application as a fixed factor in both the DFM-FF and Stepwise Improvement-DFM-FF model.

The Stepwise Improvement-DFM-FF model provides the policy-maker with practical and transparent solutions that are available in the DFM-FF projection to reach the nearest upper-level efficiency frontier. These results offer a meaningful contribution to decision support and planning for the efficiency improvement of airport operations.

In conclusion, this Stepwise Improvement-DFM-FF model may become a policy vehicle that may have great added value for the decision making and planning of both public and private actors. The particular merit of this approach is that it is able to include both flexible and rigid input variables.

12.7 Conclusion

In this chapter we have presented a new methodology, the Stepwise Improvement-DFM-FF model, which integrates a DFM-FF and a CD model. The new method minimizes the distance friction for each input and output separately and in a stepwise manner. As a result, the reductions in inputs and increases in outputs necessarily reach an efficiency frontier that is smaller than in the standard CCR model. Furthermore, the new model can incorporate a fixed factor (i.e., runway capacity), and then it could be adapted to reflect realistic conditions in an

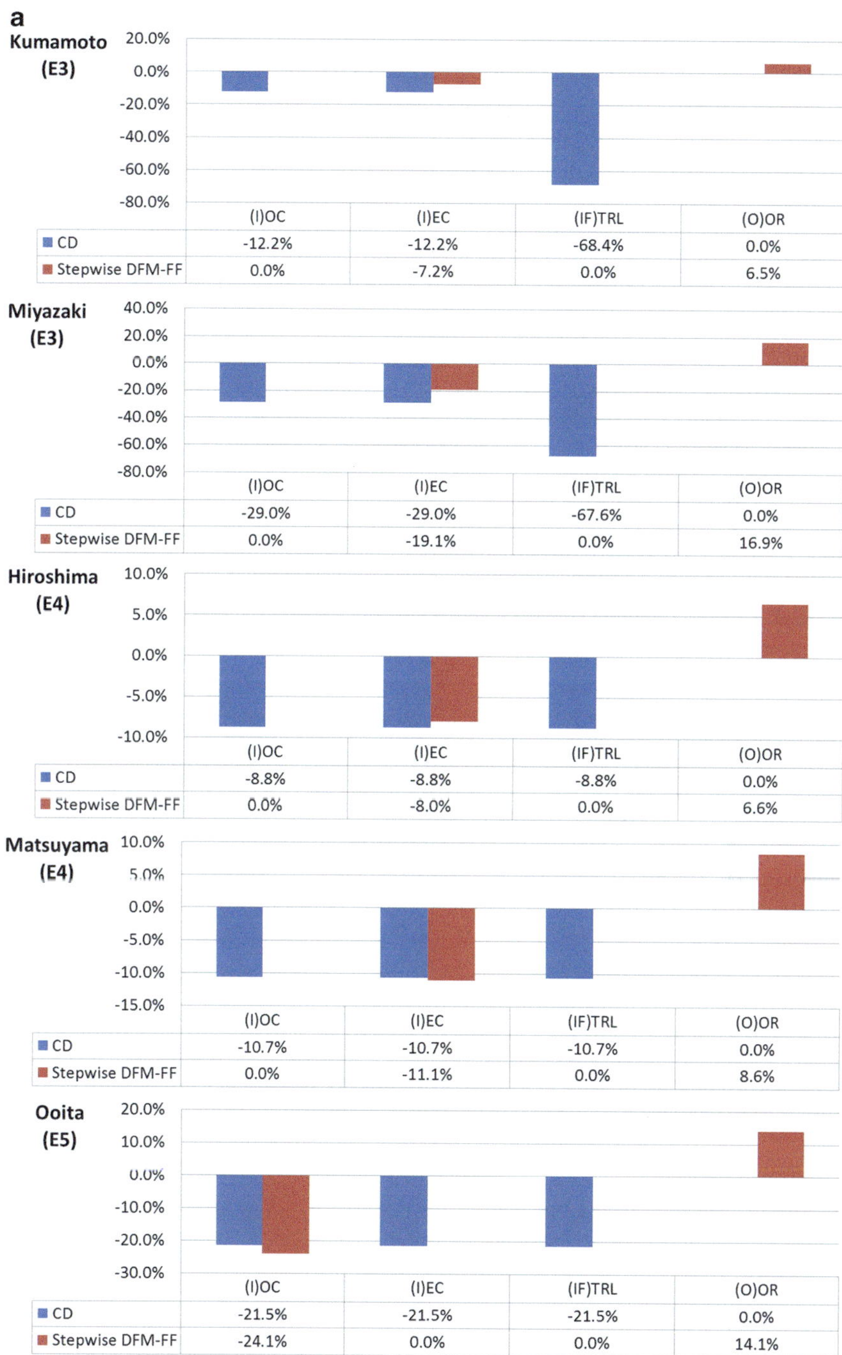

Fig. 12.5 Efficiency-improvement projection results for the nearest upper-level efficient frontier

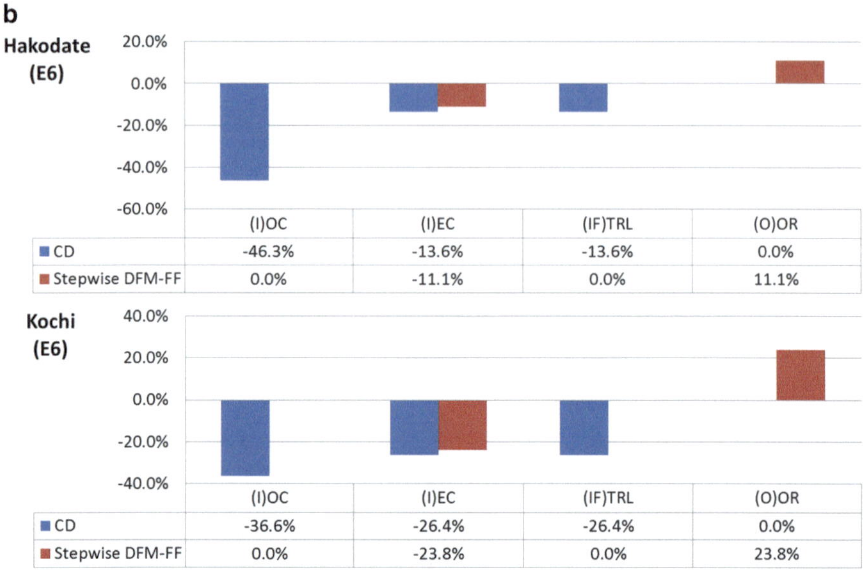

Fig. 12.5 (continued)

efficiency-improvement projection. This would offer more flexibility for the operational management of an airport organization. In addition, the stepwise projection allows DMUs to include various levels of ambition regarding the ultimate performance in their strategic judgment. In conclusion, our Stepwise Improvement-DFM-FF model is able to generate a more realistic efficiency-improvement plan and may thus provide a meaningful contribution to decision making and planning for the efficiency improvement of the relevant agents.

References

Adler, N., & Golany, B. (2001). Evaluation of deregulated airline networks using data envelopment analysis combined with principal component analysis with an application to Western Europe. *European Journal of Operational Research, 132*(2), 260–273.

Bazargan, M., & Vasigh, B. (2003). Size versus efficiency: A case study of US commercial airports. *Journal of Air Transport Management, 9*(3), 187–193.

Charnes, A., Cooper, W. W., & Rhodes, E. (1978). Measuring the efficiency of decision making units. *European Journal of Operational Research, 2*, 429–444.

Fernandes, E., & Pacheco, R. R. (2002). Efficient use of airport capacity. *Transportation Research Part A: Policy and Practice, 36*(3), 225–238.

Graham, A. (2005). Airport benchmarking: A review of the current situation. *Benchmarking: An International Journal, 12*(2), 99–111.

Japanese Ministry of Land, Infrastructure, Transport and Tourism. (2010). Revenue and expenditure 2007.

Kamp, V., Niemeier, H. M., & Müller, J. (2007). What can be learned from benchmarking studies? Examining the apparent poor performance of German airports. *Journal of Airport Management, 1*(3), 294–308.

Martín, J. C., & Román, C. (2001). An application of DEA to measure the efficiency of Spanish airports prior to privatization. *Journal of Air Transport Management, 7*(3), 149–157.

Pels, E., Nijkamp, P., & Rietveld, P. (2003). Inefficiencies and scale economies of European airport operations. *Transportation Research Part E: Logistics and Transportation Review, 39* (5), 341–361.

Seiford, L. M., & Zhu, J. (2003). Context-dependent data envelopment analysis – Measuring attractiveness and progress. *Omega, 31*, 397.

Suzuki, S., & Nijkamp, P. (2014). A stepwise efficiency improvement DEA model for airport management with a fixed runway capacity. *Karlsruhe Papers in Economic Policy Research, 34*, 233–254.

Suzuki, S., Nijkamp, P., Rietveld, P., & Pels, E. (2010). A distance friction minimization approach in data envelopment analysis: A comparative study on airport efficiency. *European Journal of Operational Research, 207*, 1104–1115.

Yoshida, Y., & Fujimoto, H. (2004). Japanese airport benchmarking with the DEA and endogenous weight TFP methods: Testing the criticism of overinvestment in Japanese regional airports. *Transportation Research Part E: Logistics and Transportation Review, 40*(6), 533–546.

Chapter 13
Conclusion

Abstract The aim of this chapter is to summarize this book and to suggest implications for further research in Japan and Asian countries. From the viewpoint of "efficiency," Japan is often regarded as a top athlete in Asia based on many evidence-based results. Nevertheless, it is also clear that there are still many inefficient fields and policy domains in Japan. In this sense, many Asian countries and regions may have to make a more serious effort to improve their performance. Based on the need for a critical assessment of regional and sectoral performance, we argue that DEA – and its related DFM applications – may offer a meaningful contribution to decision making and planning for an operational efficiency improvement in many areas; in particular, the DFM model has proven to be a very appropriate method as a performance improvement model for regions under conditions of a "performance maximization society" and a "regional actualization era." This may also have important benefits for a sustainable future.

Keywords Summary • Implications for Japan and Asia • Looking into the future • Data Envelopment Analysis (DEA) • Distance friction minimization (DFM)

13.1 Lessons and Tasks for Japan and Asia

As we mentioned in Chap. 1, Japan is facing a demographic challenge caused by acceleration of a declining birth rate and an aging population. This represents a new challenge for the country and calls urgently for strategic adjustments through effective policy strategies. In these circumstances, a shift is needed to the new future stage of a "performance maximization society," in which the keyword will be "regional actualization." To reach such ambitious goals of a society in transition, new methodological tools for achieving a balanced sustainable development – from both a socioeconomic and environmental-energy perspective – are needed. This book has made an effort to develop such a new toolbox for policy-makers. From this viewpoint, we may get a more balanced idea on the future space economy of Japan and Asia, based on our analysis results of DEA and its extensions through DFM.

Many cities, regions, local government units, public transport operators, airport authorities, and energy and environmental agencies in Japan are still faced with

S. Suzuki, P. Nijkamp, *Regional Performance Measurement and Improvement*, New Frontiers in Regional Science: Asian Perspectives 9,
DOI 10.1007/978-981-10-0242-7_13

many inefficient operations. To achieve the performance maximization society, we have to recognize the necessity of a serious effort to improve the country's performance. The original DEA model was able to present an improvement projection, but this model focused only on a uniform input reduction or output augmentation, with the consequence that the original model cannot well develop and map out each region's strengths in its improvement strategy. Our DFM model has several merits, mainly since it focuses on the features of each region or decision agency and capitalizes on the region's or actor's strengths; in other words, it develops the region's or actor's strengths in its realistic improvement. Against these backgrounds, DFM applications appear to offer a meaningful contribution to decision making and planning for an operational efficiency improvement in these fields.

From the viewpoint of "efficiency," Japan is sometimes seen as a top athlete in Asia based on empirical productivity and efficiency results. Nevertheless, it is clear that there are still many inefficient fields in Japan. In that sense, many Asian countries and regions or agencies need a serious effort to enhance their performance. For example, on the basis of our DEA analysis results in Chap. 11, it can be seen that the energy-environment-economic performance of EU countries is on average higher than that of the A&A countries. We also noticed that the gap between the performance of EU and A&A countries has widened year by year. Given the above findings, it seems necessary to make a serious effort for a drastic efficiency improvement of the energy-environment-economic efficiency for ASEAN countries. Each country in this part of the world is required not only to favor economic growth but also to develop a solid sustainability strategy. Under such circumstances, our DFM methodology can offer a meaningful contribution to sustainable decision making and planning for an efficiency improvement in the energy-environment-economic sector in these countries.

As confirmed by these results, DFM is an appropriate method as an operational performance improvement model of regions or agencies in case of a "performance maximization society" and a "regional actualization era." This does not only hold for Japan but also for many other countries.

13.2 The Next Steps

In this book, we have introduced a new projection method, called the distance friction minimization (DFM) approach. This new DFM is a suitable approach for a performance improvement strategy of regions or agencies under conditions of a "performance maximization society" and a "regional actualization era." In our book, we have also presented various amended and extended DFM models in which the extension was useful to suit more realistic circumstances, such as the "Target approach (Goals-Achievement model, a Stepwise Improvement model, and a Target-Oriented model)" and "Adjustment approach (e.g., an Adjusted-Improvement model and Fixed-Factor model)."

The existence of these complementary classes of models suggests a great application potential of DFM models, as these models may be expected to have a great relevance for various fields in regional science. Clearly, further adjustments of DFM models may still be expected, leading to a long-lasting improvement. For example, a new approach may be to incorporate a time series concept and a frontier shift effect in a DFM model. Additionally, it may be desirable to consider the dependency between each item and DMUs in improving the projection.

We hope and believe that this book can support an operational actualization of the performance maximization society in Asian countries – and elsewhere – in the future.

Appendix A: Manual for DFM Solver

Introduction to DFM Solver

This is a manual for the DFM Solver. The DFM Solver was developed by Soushi Suzuki. All responsibility is attributed to Soushi Suzuki.

The DFM Solver can be downloaded via the website http://www.lst.hokkai-s-u.ac.jp/~soushi-s/DFM-Solver.html.

S. Suzuki, P. Nijkamp, *Regional Performance Measurement and Improvement*, New Frontiers in Regional Science: Asian Perspectives 9,
DOI 10.1007/978-981-10-0242-7

S. Suzuki and P. Nijkamp

Regional Performance Measurement and Improvement
-New Developments and Applications of Data Envelopment Analysis–

Springer Science+Business Media Singapore 2017

New Frontiers in Regional Science: Asian Perspectives, Vol. 9

Amsterdam Boss, The Netherlands

Download DFM-Soler

Click on its title

DFM-Solver

Then you can get access to the Excel file.

This use is free of charge. However, when you use this software and/or publish papers or articles on this DEA, you should use the following citation:

Suzuki, S., Nijkamp, P., Rietveld, P. and Pels, E. (2010) A distance friction minimization approach in data envelopment analysis: a comparative study on air-port efficiency. European Journal of Operational Research 207: 1104–1115,

as well as:

Suzuki, S., and Nijkamp, P., (2017) Regional performance measurement and improvement –new developments and applications of data envelopment analysis-, New Frontiers in Regional Science: Asian Perspective, Vol. 9. Springer Science+ Business Media Singapore.

	A	B	C	D	E
1	AMS	(I)RN	(I)TS	(I)GN	(I)EN
2	v	3.26E-02	0	8.54E-03	3.44E-05
3	x	5	370000	89	2231
4	d^x	0.000	0.000	0.000	0.000
5	$x-d^x$	5.000	370000.000	89.000	2231.000
6	$v(x-d^x)$	0.163	0.000	0.760	0.077
7	Fr^x	0.027	0.000	0.578	0.006
8	T-value	0.933			
9	$\Sigma v(x-d^x)$	1.000			
10	ΣFrx	0.781			
11	%	0.0%	0.0%	0.0%	0.0%
12					
13					
14		(O)PN	(O)AM		
15	u	2.19E-08	0		
16	y	39960400	392997		
17	d^y	0.000	0.000		
18	$y+d^y$	39960400.000	392997.000		
19	$u(y+d^y)$	0.875	0.000		
20	Fr^y	0.766	0.000		
21	T-value	0.933			
22	Σu(y+dy)	0.875			
23	Σfry	0.875			
24	%	0.0%	0.0%		
25					
26					

DMU	Score		V:RN	V:TS	V:GN	V:EN
AMS	0.875009423	input optimum weight	3.26E-02	0	8.54E-03	3.44E-05

	U:PN	U:AM
output optimum weight	2.19E-08	0

DFM projection	d	Slack	Projection	Difference	
	d^x, d^y	s^{-**}, s^{+**}	$x-d^x$, $y+d^y$	dx,dy	%
(I)RN	0.000	0	5.0	0.000	0.0%
(I)TS	0.000	-234763.5575	370000.0	-234763.558	-63.4%
(I)GN	0.000	0	89.0	0.000	0.0%
(I)EN	0.000	0	2231.0	0.000	0.0%
(O)PN	0.000	0	39960400.0	0.000	0.0%
(O)AM	0.000	168893.6846	392997.0	168893.685	43.0%

i-model	o-model
0.781319	0.875009
4	2
TRUE	FALSE
TRUE	100
TRUE	
TRUE	
FALSE	
100	

Original Data	(I)RN	(I)TS	(I)GN	(I)EN
AMS	5	370,000	89	2,231

(O)PN	(O)AM
39,960,400	392,997

Projection Data	(I)RN	(I)TS	(I)GN	(I)EN
AMS	5.0	370000.0	89.0	2231.0

(O)PN	(O)AM
39960400.0	392997.0

A.1 Platform

The platform for this file is MS-Excel 2010 or later.

A.2 Data Preparation

We recommend using "DEA Solver" (Cooper, W.W., Seiford, L.M., Tone, K., (2007), Data Envelopment Analysis, A Comprehensive Text with Models, Applications References and DEA-Solver Software, Springer Science, Business Media, New York), to compute efficiency scores, optimum weights for input and output items, and slacks.

You need a preparation for all data sets as follows:

1. Input and output data sets for all decision making units (DMUs)
2. Efficiency scores for all DMUs based on the CCR-I model
3. Optimum weights for all input and output items (these data can be found in the "weight" sheet, in the computed results by DEA Solver)

A.3 Starting DFM Solver

1. After completion of all data sets at A.2, open the "DFM Solver."
2. This is an example of Amsterdam Airport Schiphol, a four-input ([Input 1] RN, number of runways; [Input 2] TS, terminal space; [Input 3] GN, number of gates; [Input 4] EN, number of employees; [Output 1] PN, number of passengers; [Output 2] AM, aircraft movements) case.
3. Enter the data as follows:

   - Cell I2: name of one DMU.
   - Cell J2: efficiency score of one DMU.
   - Cell L2 to O2: optimum weight of inputs for one DMU.

     If your case has two inputs, then you should change "Cell L2 to M2." You should adjust a data input cell based on your case.

   - Cell L5 to M5: optimum weight of outputs for one DMU.

     If your case has one output, then you should change "Cell L5." You should adjust a data input cell based on your case.

   - Cell U2 to X2: input datasets for one DMU.

     You should adjust a selection cell based on your case.

   - Cell U5 to V5: output datasets for one DMU.

You should adjust a selection cell based on your case.

- Cell D1 to E11: if your case has two inputs, then you should delete the data in "Cell D1 to E11."

  You should adjust a data input cell based on your case. If you wish to add a number of inputs, then you should copy E1–E11 and paste to F1–F11. Also you need to adjust the selection cell information in Cell B9 and B10.

- Cell C14 to C24: if your case has one output, then you should delete the data in "Cell C14 to C24."

  You should adjust a data input cell based on your case. If you wish to add a number of outputs, then you should copy C14–C24 and paste to D14–D24. Also you need to adjust the selection cell information in Cell B22 and B23.

4. Click "Solver" in Excel toolbar.
5. Click "load model" and select Cell I18 to I25 and load.

   - This program is for a four-input case. If you need to adjust a number of inputs, you should change "By Changing Cells" in the Solver Parameters dialog box. If your case have two inputs, then you should change "B1:$C $4" in "By Changing Cells" in the Solver Parameters dialog box and delete "D5 > =0" and "E5 > =0" in "Subject to the Constraints" in the Solver Parameters dialog box.

6. Click "Solve" and then compute results for Cell B4 to E4. If your case has two inputs, it computes results at Cell B4 to C4.
7. Click "load model" and select Cell J18 to J21 and load.
8. Click "Solve" and then compute results for Cell B17 to C17.

   - This program is for a two-output case. If you need to adjust a number of outputs, you should change "By Changing Cells" in the Solver Parameters dialog box. If your case has one output, then you should change "B17" in "By Changing Cells" in the Solver Parameters dialog box.

9. Cells U8 to V8 are the projected input data sets, and Cells U11 to V11 are the projected output data sets.
10. Using these projected data sets, you should recompute an efficiency score to check a result (efficiency score will be 1.000) and to confirm the existence of a slack (these data can be found in the "Slack" sheet in the computed results by DEA Solver).
11. If a slack exists, you need to add the slack data to cell K9 to K14.
12. Finally you get the DFM projection results in cells I7 to N14.

MIX
Papier aus verantwortungsvollen Quellen
Paper from responsible sources
FSC® C105338

If you have any concerns about our products,
you can contact us on
ProductSafety@springernature.com

In case Publisher is established outside the EU,
the EU authorized representative is:
Springer Nature Customer Service Center GmbH
Europaplatz 3, 69115 Heidelberg, Germany

Printed by Libri Plureos GmbH
in Hamburg, Germany